ILLUSION OF CONSENT

ILLUSION OF CONSENT

ENGAGING WITH CAROLE PATEMAN

Edited by Daniel I. O'Neill, Mary Lyndon Shanley,
and Iris Marion Young

The Pennsylvania State University Press
University Park, Pennsylvania

Library of Congress Cataloging-in-Publication Data

Illusion of consent : engaging with Carole Pateman / edited by Daniel I. O'Neill, Mary Lyndon Shanley, and Iris Marion Young.
　　　　　　p.　　cm.
Includes bibliographical references and index.
Summary: "A collection of essays that discuss the writings of Carole Pateman, with emphasis on her theories of democracy and feminism"—Provided by publisher.
ISBN 978-0-271-03351-8 (cloth : alk. paper)
1. Democracy.
2. Liberalism.
3. Feminist theory.
4. Social contract.
5. Pateman, Carole.
I. O'Neill, Daniel I., 1967- .
II. Shanley, Mary Lyndon, 1944- .
III. Young, Iris Marion, 1949- .

JC423.I43 2008
321.8—dc22
2007050226

Copyright © 2008 The Pennsylvania State University
All rights reserved
Printed in the United States of America
Published by The Pennsylvania State University Press,
University Park, PA 16802-1003

The Pennsylvania State University Press is a member of the
Association of American University Presses.

It is the policy of The Pennsylvania State University Press to
use acid-free paper. This book is printed on Natures Natural,
containing 50% post-consumer waste, and meets the minimum requirements
of American National Standard for Information Sciences—
Permanence of Paper for Printed Library Material, ANSI Z39.48-1992.

Contents

Preface vii
Introduction 1
Daniel I. O'Neill, Mary Lyndon Shanley, and Iris Marion Young

I. LIBERALISM AND CONTRACT

Carole Pateman: Radical Liberal? 17
Jane Mansbridge
Paradoxes of Liberal Politics: Contracts, Rights, and Consent 31
Moira Gatens
The Domination Contract 49
Charles W. Mills
Human Rights and the Epistemology of Social Contract Theory 75
Brooke A. Ackerly

II. AUTONOMY AND CONSENT

Free to Decide for Oneself 99
Anne Phillips
Women's Work: Its Irreplaceability and Exploitability 119
Robert E. Goodin
A Democratic Defense of Universal Basic Income 139
Michael Goodhart

III. DEMOCRACY, POLITICAL PARTICIPATION, AND WELFARE

Participation Revisited: Carole Pateman vs. Joseph Schumpeter 165
Alan Ryan
Participation, Deliberation, and We-thinking 185
Philip Pettit
Deliberative Democracy, Subordination, and the Welfare State 205
John Medearis

Afterword 231
Carole Pateman

List of Contributors 245
Index 250

Preface

Creating this book has carried with it both great satisfaction and great sadness. Great satisfaction because the intellectual vibrancy of these pages is testimony to the ongoing significance of Carole Pateman's work. But also great sadness because one of the editors, Iris Marion Young, died of cancer as the book was nearing completion. It is fitting that Penn State, where Young received her doctoral degree in philosophy, is publishing this volume; its director, Sandy Thatcher, published Iris's first book, *Justice and the Politics of Difference*, when he was an editor at Princeton University Press. In putting together this volume of essays, Young, Shanley, and O'Neill hoped to continue the pursuit of democracy and social justice at the heart of Pateman's work.

Introduction
Daniel I. O'Neill, Mary Lyndon Shanley, and Iris Marion Young

Few scholars have had as great an impact on contemporary political theory as has Carole Pateman. She has written centrally important works about democracy; liberalism and political obligation; feminism and contract theory; and the social, legal, and economic prerequisites for citizenship. Most writers would consider themselves fortunate if they could make a significant contribution to theory on just one of these topics. Carole Pateman has profoundly influenced thinking about all of them.

The title of this book, *Illusion of Consent*, evokes an argument that runs through much of Pateman's work. Pateman has consistently interrogated the central role of consent in her writings, both with respect to classical "social contract" theory and "liberal democracy," and contracts such as employment and marriage contracts. And she has just as consistently warned us against assuming that the "consent" allegedly justifying these myriad contractual arrangements actually guarantees the freedom and equality of those who make them. On the contrary, she argues, some acts of "consent" may actually impede the realization of both these ideals.

Our subtitle, *Engaging with Carole Pateman*, signals that while these diverse essays take up the challenge posed for contemporary political theory by Pateman's claim about the illusory nature of consent, none constitutes a simple commentary on her work. Rather, each author's essay is informed by different themes that animate Pateman's arguments, and each makes its own distinctive contribution to the ongoing discussions she has helped to spur. Those conversations deal with the evaluation of liberalism and theories of an original contract; the meaning of such notions as autonomy, consent, sexual equality, and difference; and the defense of democracy and political participation, basic income, and welfare. In this brief introduction we outline the scope and fundamental commitments of Pateman's work, identify the themes of these essays, and review some debates and questions they generate, questions that remain at the core of contemporary political theory. There is no "last word" on these topics. While Pateman herself responds to the essays in an afterword, the book will undoubtedly provoke further inquiry about the nature of the problems that are at the heart of Pateman's sterling body of work.

The Scope of Pateman's Work

Pateman's engagement with issues of consent and contract appears in her earliest writings. Her first book, *Participation and Democratic Theory* (1970), develops a participatory theory of democracy inspired by the work of Jean-Jacques Rousseau, John Stuart Mill, and G. D. H. Cole. Having observed the odd disjuncture between the increasing demands for political participation in the late 1960s and a contemporary theory of democracy that regarded widespread participation as a source of danger and instability, Pateman challenges the conceptual foundations and empirical evidence supporting the contemporary theory. She contrasts the myth of a "classical" theory of democracy found in the writings of Schumpeter, Dahl, and others with a carefully reconstructed account of the link between participation and political efficacy, and she marshals evidence to support this account. The prevailing view of the time extrapolated from sociological evidence of apathy and feelings of low political efficacy to generate a theory of democracy that discouraged participation and focused on elite competition as a means of preserving stability. In contrast to this view, Pateman shows that participation in industrial democracy, her primary empirical example, amounts to a democratic education for workers that increases their sense of political effectiveness. She makes her case by using the very sociological evidence mishandled by the contemporary theorists of elite democracy. Pateman's emphasis on the beneficial effects of participation, at the levels of both individual psychology and system stability, made a persuasive case for a renewed theoretical interest in participatory democracy and helped to produce a renaissance of democratic theory in the 1970s.

This renewal of democratic theory then led Pateman to evaluate the theoretical underpinnings of what is often simply and uncritically referred to as "liberal democracy." In *The Problem of Political Obligation: A Critique of Liberal Theory* ([1979] 1985), Pateman questions the easy assumption that liberalism and democracy fit neatly together. Liberal theory, especially in its influential contractual variant, rests on the idea that political obligations derive from voluntary acts made by free and equal individuals. However, liberal institutions belie the radical implications of this idea—that self-assumed obligations are the only legitimate source of political commitments—precisely because they do not encourage the kind of participation that would signal real consent. Consequently, in liberal theory an autonomous basis for political obligation rooted in true consent evaporates, leaving behind the reality of mere obedience to elite political representatives, employers, and others. Pateman contends that this problem is wholly insoluble in the absence of thoroughgoing democratization of liberal political and economic institutions.

Given her commitments to and theorizing about participation, self-development, and antisubordination, it is easy to understand why Pateman turned her attention to issues of sexual subordination and the problematic arguments surrounding women's inclusion (and exclusion) from the polity. In a collection of essays, *The Disorder of Women* (1989), she made groundbreaking contributions to feminist theory. For example, in "Women and Consent" (first published in 1980), Pateman argues that both theory and practice in modern liberal societies have constructed women as men's natural subordinates and hence as incapable of the sort of consent that would give them the status of full citizens. Consider, as one example, the gulf between theory and practice in rape law. The legal difference between intercourse and the crime of rape turns on whether the woman did or did not consent. In practice, however, judges and juries routinely assume that women consent to intercourse in most situations. The requirement that a woman's testimony be corroborated by evidence of physical violence renders the distinction between consent and refusal irrelevant. As Pateman shows, however, the problem of consent encapsulated in rape law also inheres in a wide range of issues beyond this specific example. Many citizens—men as well as women—are presumed to consent to actions of government but lack the freedom and equality that are the preconditions for true consent. Many liberal theorists link "consent," "freedom," and "equality" but ignore the impossibility of consent under relationships of domination, subordination, and inequality. Pateman's examination of rape law therefore calls not only for the reconstruction of our sexual lives, but also for a new understanding of the conditions necessary for democratic equality and nonsubordination writ large.

Other essays in *The Disorder of Women* raise another theme that weaves its way through Pateman's work, that is, the issue of women's embodiment and what difference (if any) it should make for political theorizing. In a particularly influential piece, "The Patriarchal Welfare State," Pateman mapped the theoretical contours posed by the issue of bodily difference through the articulation of a highly influential concept she termed "Wollstonecraft's Dilemma." On one horn of the dilemma, women can choose to become like men (for example, by entering the paid labor force) in order to be eligible for benefits like welfare. Equal citizenship in the polity thus seems to require sameness. However, similarity inevitably confronts the fact of differential sexual embodiment, particularly pregnancy and lactation. Similar treatment therefore may not secure for women the supports they need when they become mothers, and is therefore a strategy that can only be pressed so far. On the other horn of the dilemma, women can choose to stress their specific capacities, needs, talents, and concerns *as women* in a way that makes their citizenship different from men's. The problem, however, is that this focus on difference has historically meant women's relegation to second-class citizenship in a liberal world where equality is only understood as synonymous with similarity.

Pateman's landmark feminist book, *The Sexual Contract* (1988), represents a broadening and deepening of the concerns with obligation, consent, participatory democracy, and gender evident in her earlier work. That work had begun to push against the confines of contract theory itself, because Pateman recognized the legacy of problems left by classic contract theorists concerning women's specific incorporation into and obligations within civil society. Her understanding of feminism as a unique mode of critique not linked either to liberal or to socialist frameworks enabled Pateman to provide a particularly challenging reading of some of the classic texts, and to raise fundamental questions about the whole enterprise of what she believes is mistakenly referred to simply as "social contract" theorizing, one of the dominant modes of legitimating political power in the modern tradition of Western political thought.

In *The Sexual Contract,* Pateman argues that for Hobbes, Locke, and others the original contract generates civil society and is both the modern means of ensuring rule by men as a fraternal brotherhood of equals, and of subordinating women. As such, it requires paradoxical assumptions about women's capacity for consent. On the one hand, women are considered lacking in the individual attributes required to consent and therefore denied any part in making the original contract. On the other hand, women are not only deemed capable of consent, they are each presumed to give it to an individual man, a husband, via the sexual contract.

As a dimension of the original contract, the sexual contract does not leave women behind in the state of nature. Instead, it enables them to be incorporated into the brave new world of freedom and equality in a distinctly subordinate fashion via the marriage contract. What many regard today as the foundational texts of liberal theory therefore deny women any place in the public political sphere created by consent, yet simultaneously depict women as saying "yes" all the time in private, and in so doing agreeing to their inferior status in both spheres. The result, as Pateman convincingly demonstrates, is women's second-class status in both public and private institutions. This intellectual breakthrough paved the way for Pateman to engage in an extraordinary reevaluation of a number of contemporary contractual relationships that still rest, as they did for John Locke, on the peculiar myth of an alienable "property in the person."

Pateman defines contracts based on "property in the person" as those that give one individual control over another's use of his or her own body, and which therefore inevitably culminate in civil subordination, whether such contracts are "freely consented to" or not. Examples include patriarchal marriage, employment contracts, prostitution, surrogate motherhood, and perhaps a whole new range of contracts pursuant to markets in human organs and genetic materials.

Pateman's critique of contracts resting on what she regards as the pernicious fiction of alienable property in the person puts her argument directly at odds with those she calls "contractarians," more commonly known as libertarians, for whom contract is the paradigmatic mark of freedom. The distance between the two sides can be seen in the difference between Robert Nozick's argument that a morally and politically just society would allow for voluntary slave contracts, and Pateman's belief that "voluntary" slavery, like other forms of slavery, is wholly unacceptable. Moreover, Pateman's understanding of the structural constraints on real autonomy and meaningful consent under conditions of massive social, economic, and gender inequality enables her to trouble the concepts of autonomy and consent in ways that libertarians like Nozick deny, ignore, or dismiss.

Against this backdrop, it is theoretically consistent that much of Pateman's most recent work concerns contemporary issues of citizens' rights, particularly the question of a guaranteed basic income. Her interest in a basic income continues her insistence that a just society must work to eliminate social institutions and practices that produce relationships of domination and oppression. Basic income, an unconditional social transfer that assures all citizens a subsistence income, is a way to counter the subordination that stems from the capitalist organization of production and the differential access to political power generated by economic inequality. In Pateman's view basic income is a core entitlement of citizenship, because the democratic commitment to making some form of political participation available to all requires it. Conceptions of social justice falter if they do not consider how redistributive schemes affect political participation. Pateman's justification for basic income therefore depends on the opportunities it creates for people to exercise their autonomy, give meaningful consent, and engage in participatory democratic activities.

Themes of these Essays

Liberalism and Contract

Several of the essays in this volume engage with Pateman's trenchant and controversial claims about the nature of liberalism and theories of an original contract. Like modern liberals, Pateman endorses the values of individual autonomy, self-assumed obligation, political equality, and inalienable rights. However, some versions of liberal theory assume that hierarchies in "nonpolitical" spheres, such as the family and workplace, are compatible with political equality; advocate relinquishing the business of self-government to representatives; and defend the alienability of "property in the person." When it allows or espouses such positions, liberalism is, in Pateman's view, either incoherent, hypocritical, or a rationalization of modern forms of domination and subordination, a disease whose antidote is the democratization of public and private life.

But is Pateman's hostility to liberalism inevitable? In her contribution to this volume, Jane Mansbridge takes up this question directly and asks if the wedge between liberalism and democracy is as thick as Pateman seems to suggest. Citing the ideas of Arnold Kaufman, Mansbridge raises the question of whether Pateman's philosophical orientation might not be thought of instead as "radical liberalism." After all, Pateman does in fact endorse some ideals associated with liberalism, such as autonomy, political equality, and individual rights. If this is the case, might it be reasonable to interpret her positions as claiming that the insights of liberalism should be deepened and extended in order to make them logically consistent—hence "radical" liberalism?

While Mansbridge raises this question, however, she ultimately argues that taking such an interpretive tack misses the distinctive core of Pateman's political theorizing. To the extent that liberalism asserts that one of the most important political principles is that individuals should be left alone to act on their preferences, whatever they are, Pateman could never be a liberal even in the most ideal circumstances. The liberal focus on choice turns political reflection away from the more important question; that is, what are the structural background conditions of people's choices, and do they enable the exploitation of some people by others? Democratic values that require individuals to see their own good as connected to the good of the entire community are incompatible with such subordination. In Pateman's thought, the egalitarian and other-regarding values of democracy that reject the social relations of subordination and domination, even when the subordination is the result of apparently voluntary commitments, come from a different framework of justification than that employed by even the most radical liberalism that has consent at its core.

Recognizing that Carole Pateman is not alone among feminist theorists who question central concepts of liberalism, Moira Gatens compares her arguments to the claims of Wendy Brown and Joan W. Scott that ideas such as liberal individualism, freedom, equality, and rights generate paradoxes for feminism. In Gatens's view, both Scott and Brown perform their analyses too exclusively on discourses—of rights, of individualism, of contract—and this explains why they conclude that such paradoxes are irresolvable. Gatens asserts that this focus on discourse effectively hobbles the conceptualization of women's agency. In contrast, Pateman argues that the paradoxes facing feminism are rooted in the structural context of capitalist and male-dominated social relations. On this account, Pateman is not opposed to the idea of contract per se, but rather to the false premise of property in the person that underlies the marriage, surrogacy, and employment contracts. If we join with Pateman in rejecting the fiction of property in the person, and the social, political, and economic relationships that it sustains, Gatens contends, it should become possible to imagine new social relationships and a new social order. In such a world, men and women would create, and agree to uphold, the social conditions that would make autonomy possible for both sexes, dissolving a number of the paradoxes that confront contemporary feminism.

Charles Mills also takes up the question of Pateman's relation to liberalism, and its most famous justificatory schema, the theory of an original contract. In *The Sexual Contract*, Pateman famously concluded that "A free social order cannot be a contractual order" (1988, 232). What should we make of this claim, which if taken literally would seem to indicate Pateman's rejection of contract theory in its entirety? Mills argues that Pateman has been misinterpreted as rejecting the contract tradition *tout court* when in reality she was simply rejecting patriarchy, libertarianism (or "contractarianism"), and the various forms of contract predicated on property in the person. By developing this distinction, Mills seeks to rescue some form of contract theory, if not liberalism as a whole, from Pateman's critique.

Mills identifies two strands in the "social contract" tradition. One uses the language of universalism but in fact applies only to a privileged minority of the population. This "domination contract" justifies current relationships of social and economic inequality and subordination as the result of a primordial bargain. Both Pateman's account of the sexual contract and Mills's own reconstruction of modern liberalism as a racial contract expose the way in which the domination contract legitimates inequality and subordination by ignoring group differences. Despite this failure, which extends from the early days of social contract theory to discussions of contemporary social relations, Mills sees the fundamental moral egalitarianism of contract theory as central to a theory of social justice. He concludes not only that ideals of mutual recognition, equality of status, individual autonomy, and obligation grounded in consent remain appropriate aspirations for contemporary societies, but that rightly understood, the so-called social contact tradition can be a means of achieving them.

Brooke Ackerly's essay takes up the more expansive reading of Pateman's concluding claim in *The Sexual Contract* to argue, *contra* Mills, that even a critically grounded restoration of contract theory is theoretically unconvincing and proves itself incapable of providing a sufficiently robust defense of human rights, Ackerly's primary concern. Moreover, Ackerly argues that this conclusion about the undesirability of social contract models as a means of grounding human rights is in fact a logical extension of Mills's own arguments. In her view, the power inequalities that make consent to the contract illusory include asymmetries of authoritative knowledge, or an exclusionary "epistemological contract" between dominant and subordinate groups. These asymmetries ensure that subordinate groups' understandings of what human rights should be are never even heard. Ackerly calls for an epistemological approach that acknowledges that seemingly universal ways of knowing can render some experiences invisible or treat them as apolitical. For this reason, Ackerly indicates the need for a different, more democratic conceptualization of the basis of human rights that can preserve people's autonomy. Because human rights theory is useful and necessary precisely in circumstances when some people are subordinated and when people disagree about what is just, Ackerly suggests that any adequate human rights theory would need to transcend the mechanism of contract altogether.

Autonomy and Consent

A number of essays in the book consider two related questions: What constitutes real autonomy? And what signals meaningful consent? Pateman sees both of these ideals as essential for the realization of a fully participatory democratic polity. Two chapters in this collection analyze the implications of Pateman's concern that voluntary consent may not be so easy to identify under circumstances of structural inequality, and furthermore that whether a person has consented to an element of her situation may not ultimately be the main issue.

Anne Phillips probes questions concerning the conditions of autonomy and consent by analyzing recent public policy debates in Britain concerning whether the state should regulate conditions for entering marriage. Some parents believe that they have the right to choose marriage partners for their children, or to insist that their children marry persons from specific ethnic or religious communities. Phillips argues that the distinction between "coerced" and "voluntary" marriages that many assume in these policy debates is too coarse. Many of the situations and practices in question do not fall neatly into either category. Honestly recognizing this, moreover, puts some actions of "Western" or "Christian" parents and communities as much into question as some of those of immigrant parents and communities in Britain.

Phillips argues that because Pateman's analysis of contract distinguishes between the conditions under which someone enters into a contract and the possibly exploitative nature of the contractual relationship once it exists, it can be used to shift the terms of the debate about arranged or forced marriages in necessary and productive ways. Formal consent can create structural relations of domination and subordination. If government is justified in scrutinizing such contracts, it is not because young women's consent is meaningless or invalid, but because of the kind of relationship that marriage entails. Pateman's insight that fulfilling the terms of a (freely entered) contract can nevertheless create a relationship of subordination is, for Phillips, crucial for forging public policy and legal responses to arranged and forced marriages that do not rest on the assumption that the young woman did not or could not consent.

Like Phillips, Robert Goodin wants to dig beneath issues of choice versus coercion as the terms for assessing women's subordination. He focuses on the fact that in many contemporary "liberal democratic" societies many women do more unpaid household work than do their male partners. Because such women are not "forced" to do this work, it might appear from the perspective of market liberalism, or "Chicago school" economics, that there is no reason to object to this unequal division of labor. Moreover, when a woman chooses not to hire someone to do all the carework of a household, the Chicago School economist sees this as a legitimate expression of individual preferences understood as a "pure consumption act." Goodin draws on Pateman's and John Roemer's theories of exploitation to argue that even when caregiving work is "chosen" and not coerced, a person who invests significantly in the productive and irreplaceable caring work for particular persons in a family finds herself structurally disadvantaged in carrying her skills and experiences to other settings. Goodin suggests that to understand what might be morally and politically problematic about the continuing gendered division of labor, we need to move away from a strict dichotomy between consent and coercion, an analysis that suggests that we rethink this dichotomy in other contexts as well.

Addressing similar concerns about autonomy and consent raised by Ackerly, Phillips, and Goodin, Michael Goodhart draws on Pateman's critique of liberalism to distinguish between a liberal and a democratic account of human rights. Most accounts of human rights either assume a liberal justification of them, or elide liberalism and democracy in their understanding of human rights. Goodhart argues that a conception of human rights within a liberal framework puts the individual at the center of rights discourse, and conceives human rights as spheres of control or mobility within which each individual resides. Instead, Goodhart puts forward a democratic justification of human rights; human rights include the social bases people need in order not to be subordinate and to be able to exercise their participatory capacities. Goodhart thus understands democracy as a political commitment to universal emancipation that requires securing fundamental human rights, or those basic rights necessary for the enjoyment of all other rights. In his account, these social bases include a Universal Basic Income, which is required to realize democracy's foundational commitment to universal emancipation.

The first two sections of the book also suggest further questions about liberalism, contract, autonomy, and consent beyond those specifically raised by the contributors to this volume. For example, should sexual difference yield a different slate of inalienable rights, including human rights, for women as opposed to men? Likewise, should Universal Basic Income be calibrated differently for men and women based on the empirical sociological fact that women do the overwhelming preponderance of caring work within the household? Or, to put it in her terms, is what Pateman has called "Wollstonecraft's Dilemma" capable of being resolved? Is it possible to theorize and practice both equality and difference simultaneously?

Democracy, Political Participation, and Welfare

Three essays in this collection consider the contemporary question of the relevance of participatory democracy, to which Pateman has been committed from the time of her earliest writings. By extension, these contributions also ruminate upon the appropriate relationship between elite, deliberative, and participatory models of democracy, and their prerequisites for our own time.

Alan Ryan reflects on the extent to which the issues and arguments in Pateman's *Participation and Democratic Theory* retain force in contemporary theory and practice. A central project of Pateman's book was to challenge the then received political science wisdom, inherited at least partly from Schumpeter's theory of democracy, that a "realistic" theory defines democracy in terms of plebiscite. In the modern world, on this account, a democracy is simply a political regime in which an electorate periodically chooses and ousts its rulers. The spirit of Pateman's rejection of such a thin and cynical understanding of democracy is found in many subsequent arguments for participatory democracy. However, Ryan suggests, ideals of participatory democracy have little direct institutional influence. He finds that it is difficult to imagine implementing the direct democracy of the workplace or small community in our complex societies. Nevertheless, Ryan believes that certain of the values expressed by the ideals of participatory democracy remain important. In this vein, he explores some alternative forms of representation in which a distinction between elites and electorate might not be so strong, including rethinking the possibilities of representation by lot.

Philip Pettit also questions the practicality of Pateman's notion of participatory democracy in large-scale modern contexts. Pettit argues that modern mass democracies are participatory enough if they provide means for everyone living under a government to have some say in the process of its decision making. With the theory of deliberative democracy, Pettit also thinks that the say that people ought to have should involve their considered judgments and not merely their pre-given preferences. Nevertheless, Pettit contends, theorizing public opinion in terms of judgment rather than preference does not avoid some of the paradoxes of aggregation. The pooling of different voices and judgments runs the risk of producing incoherence in collective judgment. Pettit believes, however, that when participants adopt the participatory perspective of the collective as Pateman prescribes, or engage in what he calls "we-thinking" in making their own judgments, the problem of aggregating individual judgments can be surmounted.

John Medearis draws on Pateman's work in developing his claim that we can and should distinguish liberal and deliberative from truly democratic justifications of redistributive welfare policies. Like Michael Goodhart, he prefers democratic to liberal grounds for securing welfare rights. In particular, Medearis argues that some deliberative democrats focus on the material security welfare recipients need in order to develop their deliberative capacities. These theorists justify welfare by arguing that recipients have the right to engage in public discourse about welfare policy and other political issues, and to debate the norms that ideally should govern such discourse. Such discussions, Medearis believes, rest on an inadequate understanding of the connection between democracy and welfare. If, like Pateman, we conceive democratic values as primarily about nonsubordination rather than as about deliberation and choice, then we must evaluate justifications for welfare programs by their ability not simply to increase deliberation but also to undermine social structures that produce or reinforce subordination.

Conclusion

In tackling the issues of liberalism, contract, consent, autonomy, and democracy, the essays in this volume address central concerns not only of political philosophy, but also of practical politics at the beginning of the twenty-first century. Together they show the truth of Pateman's contention that freedom in the so-called private sphere of marriage and family life is inseparable from freedom in public life. These essays share, with one another and with Carole Pateman, a commitment to enlarging the scope of freedom in both realms.

The first step in this enterprise is to realize the often illusory nature of consent and to rethink the relationship between contract and freedom. The next is to diminish the social and economic subordination that precludes the kind of participation in which free persons engage. And to do this requires redistributive measures that provide everyone with the material preconditions for political deliberation and activity. The contributors to this volume, despite their many differences, all share a commitment to trying to make political theory contribute to such new possibilities of political participation and social justice. In this way, the essays stand as a testament to the importance and influence of Carole Pateman's work to scholars and activists around the globe, and to the vision of human emancipation that animates every word she writes.

References

Pateman, Carole. 1970. *Participation and Democratic Theory*. Cambridge: Cambridge University Press.

———. [1979] 1985. *The Problem of Political Obligation: A Critique of Liberal Theory.* 2nd ed. Cambridge: Polity; Berkeley and Los Angeles: University of California Press.

———. 1988. *The Sexual Contract.* Cambridge: Polity; Stanford: Stanford University Press.

———. [1980] 1989. "Women and Consent." In *The Disorder of Women: Democracy, Feminism, and Political Theory,* 71–89. Cambridge: Polity; Stanford: Stanford University Press.

———. [1988] 1989. "The Patriarchal Welfare State." In *The Disorder of Women: Democracy, Feminism, and Political Theory,* 210–25. Cambridge: Polity; Stanford: Stanford University Press.

———. 1989. *The Disorder of Women: Democracy, Feminism, and Political Theory.* Cambridge: Polity; Stanford: Stanford University Press.

SECTION I
Liberalism and Contract

Carole Pateman: Radical Liberal?

Jane Mansbridge

Arnold Kaufman, who coined the term "participatory democracy," also coined the term "radical liberal" to describe his own politics.[1] In his terms, a radical liberal is one who takes seriously, at the root, the commitment of liberalism to liberty. His understanding of liberty, being far from libertarian, assumed that full autonomy required society.

The implicit and explicit stress on consent throughout Carole Pateman's work led me for many years to think of her as a radical liberal. Her work on participation and contract in particular seemed to me to insist on decisions made with full autonomy. Pateman herself, however, resisted this label when I suggested it. In rereading her work, I can see why. I use Pateman's resistance to the label briefly to illuminate a tripartite distinction between a thin liberalism based on the most restrictive reading of "liberty," a thicker liberalism based on a rich understanding of autonomy, and an expansive liberalism stretched to cover all the goods and values of liberal democracy. I argue that "liberalism" and "liberal" democracy in all these versions, including the most expansive, still have an understanding of liberty as noninterference indissolubly at their root, and that Pateman's deep opposition to subordination distinguishes her work from this tradition. This essay thus examines Pateman's work as an extended engagement with the concept of consent.

Participation and Democratic Theory

Carole Pateman burst upon the scene in 1970 with the most important book on participatory democracy in political science—a book that helped create the

---

1. For "participatory democracy," see Kaufman [1960] 1969. He entitled his first and only book *The Radical Liberal* (Kaufman 1968).

present field of "democratic theory." Its first words were, "During the last few years of the 1960s the word 'participation' became part of the popular political vocabulary." The irony of the many calls for more participation from students and public officials, Pateman pointed out, was that at that time in the reigning theory of democracy in political science, the "concept of participation" had "only the most minimal role" (Pateman 1970, 1). She recognized that political scientists might be wary of participation because citizens participated at high rates in totalitarian countries and in the Weimar Republic before it collapsed into fascism, because many citizens in Western democracies had little interest in participation, and because nonparticipating citizens from low socioeconomic groups, impatient with the democratic process, often had authoritarian attitudes. Yet, against the then-current "defense of apathy" literature, and against Schumpeter's theory that democracy should be defined only as competition among leaders for the people's vote, Pateman argued that democracy requires the active participation of citizens in the important decisions that affect them, particularly in the workplace.

Rereading this book is always a pleasure. Early on Pateman explodes the idea that there is a "classical theory of democracy" that unrealistically expects each citizen to act with great rationality and "independently of pressure groups and propaganda" (1970, 17, citing Schumpeter). She then establishes the important distinction between two groups of thinkers: Bentham and James Mill, for whom citizen participation had a "purely protective function" (20) and Rousseau, John Stuart Mill, and G. D. H. Cole, "theorists of participatory democracy," for whom participation had an educative function.

This stress on the educative function of participation was a key move for all future democratic theory. Arnold Kaufman had earlier argued that the "main justifying function" of participatory democracy was "the contribution it can make to the development of human powers of thought, feeling and action,"[2] but Pateman was the first to distinguish the educative from the protective function, locate its lineage so forcefully in J. S. Mill, and make it a central argument for workers' control.

Her focus on the educative function of participation is one reason not to consider Pateman a liberal of any sort, even a radical one. If liberalism means valuing individual liberty in such a way that one treats an individual's prefer-

2. Kaufman [1960] 1969, 184; also 188, 190, 198. (An advisor to the authors of the Port Huron Statement, Kaufman's intellectual career in philosophy was cut short by his premature death in a plane crash in 1971. See Mattson 2002 for an analysis of Kaufman's ideas in historical context.) In the case of Rousseau, the transformations expected from democracy may have derived less from any feature of the experience of making decisions with others than from an internal moral commitment to taking responsibility for the whole (Mansbridge 1999).

ences at any moment as sacred, then Pateman cannot be a liberal. J. S. Mill differed from Bentham on exactly this point, adding to utilitarianism the separate, orthogonal, and even contradictory insight that some pleasures were intrinsically better than others. If Socrates dissatisfied is better than a fool satisfied, then educating the fool to become more like Socrates is a worthy aim in itself. Mill's democracy does not take the voter as given, but aims to improve that voter. If having an external goal other than the voter's own preferences and trying to move the voter in the direction of that external goal is not liberal, then Mill himself is not a liberal.

The continuing possibility of education assumes that no individual in the here and now is all that he or she underlyingly wants to be, and that no individual's current preferences can therefore be taken as necessarily expressing what that individual retrospectively would want to have preferred. The women's movement of the late 1960s and early 1970s, taking a point from the Marxists, argued further that members of subordinate groups are even less likely than others to have preferences that reflect what a more knowledgeable and less oppressed self would think was best for them.

Pateman picked up in particular on J. S. Mill's point, which he learned from Tocqueville, that ongoing participation at the local level provides the most involving citizen education. She pointed out, however, that Mill himself did not draw the obvious conclusion from his theory. He should have concluded, she wrote, that "the maximum amount of opportunity should be given to the labouring classes to participate at [the] local level so they would develop the necessary qualities and skills to enable them to assess the activities of representatives and hold them accountable." Yet Mill "says nothing of the sort." Instead, he advocated votes of greater weight for the university educated and was oblivious to this "inconsistency in the various elements of his theory" (Pateman 1970, 32–33).

Pateman also shows that in his later work Mill saw cooperative workplaces as leading, in his own words, to a "moral transformation" of those who worked in them, as each worker's daily experience became a "a school of the social sympathies and the practical intelligence." Indeed, again in Mill's own words, "no soil" could be more conducive to training an individual to feel "the public interest as his own" than an "association of the labourers themselves on terms of equality, collectively owning the capital with which they carry on their operations, and working under managers elected and removable by themselves," an association that he called "communist."[3]

3. Mill [1848–70] 1965, 792, 775 (bk. IV, chap. VII, sect. 6), 205 (bk. II, chap. I, sect. 3), cited in Pateman 1970, 34; Pateman remarks in a footnote that "Mill uses the word 'communist' more loosely than we do today."

Turning to G. D. H. Cole, Pateman endorses his argument that, in her words, to be "self-governing," individuals must "participate in decision-making" on an equal basis in all the important associations of which they are members (1970, 36). Of these associations, the workplace is the most critical. In Cole's view, the democratic principle should be applied "not only or mainly to some special sphere of social action known as 'politics,' but to any and every form of social action, and, in especial, to industrial and economic as much as to political affairs." Without self-government in the workplace, the result, in Cole's words, was "SLAVERY." Moreover, Cole thought that participation in the workplace, "in the conduct of those parts of the structure of Society with which he is directly concerned, and which he has therefore the best chance of understanding," would allow "the expression of the human personality." It would also be educative, allowing workers to "learn democracy."[4]

Further chapters incorporate the social science literature showing a strong association between political participation and political efficacy, expose the manipulative quality of many past efforts to facilitate worker participation without in any way making the worker a political equal in those decisions, and present evidence on the relatively successful attempts at genuine worker democracy in what was then Yugoslavia. The final chapter argues for a more participatory society, in which families, universities, housing projects, and other areas of importance to the lives of citizens became more democratic and more participatory, so that experience in each realm produces learning that can be applied to the others. It concludes not by arguing, as chapters earlier in the book did, that participation produces goods for the individual, in self-expression, largeness of view, and political efficacy, but rather by stressing the good effects on society as a whole of the more participative individual.

Pateman's first book had a great impact on an entire generation of theorists and practitioners in many fields of the social sciences. Academics in particular may have found resonance with the central points—that participation has an educative function and that democratic learning might best take place in the workplace—because many of us have experienced these truths in our own lives. In the real world, however, enthusiasm for participation faded as what social movement theorists call the "political opportunity structure" changed. The window of hope that we now call "the sixties" passed without major structural changes in the participatory structure. New laws in the United States and later globalization weakened unions rather than strengthening them.

---

4. Cole 1920a, 12; 1919, 34; 1920b, 114; 1920a, 25; 1919, 157. All cited in Pateman 1970, 37–38.

Moreover, as Michael Walzer once pointed out, most workers failed to agitate for this promised improvement in their lives. The ideal of worker ownership with worker control nevertheless remains alive, and many "alternative" organizations still conduct themselves as deeply egalitarian participatory democracies.

In political theory, the stress on the educative function of participation also slipped away, in part, I believe, because it is hard to show in practice that something as diffuse in its effects as political participation does indeed have causal effects, as opposed to correlations. It took, after all, forty years and finally a meta-analysis of all previous studies to demonstrate persuasively that psychotherapy, a practice specifically aimed at changing one's psyche, had any measurable effect. With no empirical demonstration until very recently of any important effects of political participation on the participants (the recent work of Gastil et al. 2002 and Luskin et al. 2002 does show some effects), the dynamic of "practice-thought-practice" proved hard to maintain (Mansbridge 1999).

Yet the theory of participation took root in other soil, as G. D. H. Cole suggested when he wrote that work without self-government was "slavery." Pateman's work and the work of other participatory theorists (e.g., Barber 1984) sensitized at least the profession of political science to the idea that what had previously been thought adequate consent through participation was no more than a shadow of the real thing.

The Problem of Political Obligation

It is no surprise, then, that Pateman's next book focused explicitly on consent, arguing that the only polity to which we owe obedience is the fully participatory polity, in which each citizen either wills each law or actively consents to a majority that wills the law. Such political obligation is "self-assumed." Accordingly, Pateman states bluntly on her first page that "political obligation cannot be given expression within the context of [current] democratic institutions. The problem of political obligation can be solved only through the development of the theory and practice of participatory or self-managing democracy" (Pateman 1979, 1).

This is the work that made me begin to think of Pateman as a radical liberal. Early in the book, it is true, she explicitly denigrates liberalism, arguing, "Liberal democratic societies are in origin, and remain today in institutional form and ideology, essentially *liberal* societies. Their one democratic element was introduced when universal suffrage was granted" (Pateman 1979, 5). The subtitle of the book is *A Critical Analysis of Liberal Theory*. Her primary model, Rousseau, she makes clear was "*not* a liberal" (143, quoting Fetscher 1962). She locates "liberal democracy" firmly in the existing institutions of the liberal democratic state, buoyed by theories of hypothetical voluntarism and anchored in possessive individualism. In its essence, she wrote, the liberal social contract requires that "substantive political freedom and equality, necessary if citizens are to create their own political obligations, are given up or exchanged for the protection of the liberal state" (169–70).[5]

Yet Pateman also indicates early on that she intends what might be considered precisely a radicalization of the liberal project. Her book rests upon this premise: "Free and equal individuals can justifiably have obligations if and only if they have taken them upon themselves. The concept of self-assumed obligation is a necessary corollary of the liberal ideal of individual freedom and equality" (1979, 13). Thus, she concludes, "My own argument agrees with the liberal theorists." It just has "implications" that "liberal theorists cannot pursue" (13).[6]

Those implications are indeed strong. In Pateman's view, neither hypothetical consent nor tacit consent can produce obligation, because consent has no meaning when "people do not know that to perform a certain act is to consent" (1979, 73). Thus, no one incurs an obligation through voting whenever a government significantly manipulates public opinion or the policy consequences of voting are difficult to decipher. Pateman suggests at times (e.g., with the word "direct" on page 18 and her discussion of representation on pages 19–20 and 152) that referenda are her preferred (perhaps only) vehicle for expressing consent.

Moreover, for Pateman political obligation is horizontal rather than vertical, based on understanding "that to vote is simultaneously to commit oneself, to commit one's fellow citizens, and also to commit oneself to them in a mutual undertaking" (1979, 161). In addition, although accepting obligation to

---

5. Pateman continues, presaging her next book: "The liberal social contract is, in this respect, exactly like other contracts in which obedience is exchanged for protection; it is like the traditional marriage contract, the employment contract, and even like a contract of slavery, for the master must protect his slaves if he is to obtain satisfactory service. The liberal social contract is exactly what the words imply—a contract, not a promise. It is a contract that embodies an exchange of security for obedience, but the contract is then presented as a promise, and the hypothesis of political obligation in the liberal democratic state begins its long history" (1979, 170).

6. This conscious and clearly articulated theme frames the first and last chapters of the book. Pateman states explicitly throughout that liberal theory has a "conception of self-assumed obligation" at its heart (e.g., 1979, 6, 163, 167).

others necessarily involves accepting restrictions on one's actions, such an acceptance is never once and for all; it must be constantly regenerated.

In one sense, then, Pateman seems the perfect radical liberal. She explicitly derives her theory from what she herself calls the "liberal ideal of individual freedom and equality." She simply returns to the root of liberalism, insisting on following out its implications rather than discarding them. This is surely the textbook definition of a radical approach.

It seems unwise, however, to cast aside so easily Pateman's own distinction throughout this book between the object of her criticism, which she calls "liberal theory," and the theory she elaborates, which she calls "democratic theory." Again and again she contrasts the "liberal" approach, which deploys the language of liberty and equality to mask the bondage and hierarchy that liberalism makes possible, to the "democratic" approach, which generates the vision of a participatory society. Pateman's "democracy" poses a contrast not only with "liberalism" as instantiated in current liberal democratic institutions but also with a liberal theory that undermines the substantive equality necessary for genuinely free choice.

Whether Carole Pateman is or is not a radical liberal depends on what understanding of "liberty" lies at liberalism's root. If the liberty at the root of liberalism remains, in essence, the Hobbesian absence of impediments to motion, radical liberalism will always find itself drawing sustenance from that root. By contrast, Kaufman's interpretation of radical liberalism as promoting the autonomy of a being who "wants to live authentically" (Kaufman 1968, 3) and "develop his potentialities as fully as possible" (4), Pettit's understanding of liberty as nondomination (Pettit 2000), and Sen's understanding of "substantial" freedom as involving full agency through capability (Sen 2002) all move in different ways away from liberalism's original base in liberty as noninterference. Pateman's participatory democracy does the same. Pateman's difference with liberal theory insists on a robust equality as the base of democracy.

The importance of equality in Pateman's project emerged first in *Participation and Democratic Theory*, in her discussion of Cole's hatred of "subservience" and his desire to eliminate any system that separated "managers" and "men" (Pateman 1970, 38–39). More than any other participatory democrat of the time, Pateman stressed that in participatory theory "participation" refers to "(equal) participation in the making of decisions" and that "'political equality' refers to equality of power in determining the outcome of decisions" (43). No system could count as fully participatory if it could not guarantee "equal power." This was not what Kaufman, for example, had had in mind.

In *The Problem of Political Obligation,* the bitterest fruit of the liberal deception appears when "the poor now also believe that social inequality results from 'fortune,' not the logic of the development of civil society" (Pateman 1979, 149). Thus "the liberal contract is freely entered into, but the agreement is procured by deception. It is a contract that gives 'all to one side' [in Rousseau's words] and is based on inequality; its function is to maintain and foster that inequality by legitimizing political regulation by the liberal state" (149–50). The liberal vision not only ignores the centrality of equal power, it facilitates the obfuscation of inequality.

Pateman herself makes central to her rejection of liberalism her particular interpretation of Rousseau's general good. In *Participation* she had interpreted Rousseau, unconventionally, as saying that "the only policy that will be acceptable to all is the one where any benefits and burdens are equally shared" (Pateman 1970, 23; also 1979, 153–56). In *Obligation* she goes further to conceive the general good (and indeed the social contract rightly understood) as a "principle of political morality" that has the characteristic of (and perhaps consists only of) benefiting and burdening all citizens equally (Pateman 1979, 153, 156). This is her major antiliberal move. Through its central characteristic of benefiting and burdening all equally, she writes, "the general will excludes the social and political inequality of civil society, and thus constitutes a rejection of the central liberal claim that these inequalities are compatible with political obligation" (155).

At this moment, Pateman's commitment to equality interweaves inextricably with consent. In her vision, the minority who vote against a winning proposal are obliged by the ensuing law only if they judge individually either that in voting the majority followed the principle of equal benefit and burden (and perhaps other principles of political morality) or that the majority at least acted in good faith, thinking it was following this egalitarian principle. Yet even the very principle of benefiting and burdening all citizens equally must "be created by and agreed to by the citizens themselves" (Pateman 1979, 154) and, while "made only once," is always up for continual reassessment (154). What might have been an independent common good or principle of morality based on equality depends itself on consent. The "self-assumed obligation" and "the vision of social life as a voluntary scheme" that the penultimate sentence of the book describes as "invaluable democratic kernels that deserve to be extracted from the shell of liberal hypothetical volunteerism," must themselves be radically equal. To stress only self-choice and voluntarism would miss the determined streak of social egalitarianism that runs through the very center of Pateman's work. Consent and equality intertwine at every point, procedurally and substantively.

The Sexual Contract

The Sexual Contract begins where the last book left off. It too rejects social contract entirely. And it too rests normatively on the "revolutionary claim . . . that individuals are naturally free and equal to each other" (Pateman 1988, 38). Here, however, Pateman's hatred of subordination is revealed in its true strength.

Throughout *The Sexual Contract* Pateman argues against contract as a subterfuge for subordination. She uses the language of consent when she argues that her aim is always a form of political relations in which "free women and men . . . willingly agree to uphold the social conditions of their autonomy. That is to say, they must agree to uphold limits" (Pateman 1988, 232). But in her view, whenever contracts bind the "person," they always obscure relations of subordination. The fiction that individuals have property in their persons allows men and women to sell their persons into wage slavery, prostitution, or other forms of subordination in which the buyer acquires the "right of command" over that person.

The book focuses on the unequal sexual contract that produces modern patriarchy, which is coextensive with the social contract, entered into—even in the modern Rawlsian version—implicitly or explicitly by men. Much of the book consists of detailing the ways that sexual subordination is either smuggled into the ostensibly equal contract or is quite overtly built into it. Yet the fundamental thrust of the book is against contract itself when contract involves "property in the person."

The Sexual Contract may seem radically liberal in its refusal to recognize even contract as truly voluntary. Pateman insists that "a free social order cannot be a contractual order." Rather, when "free women and men . . . willingly agree to uphold the social conditions of their autonomy," that is, to "uphold limits," they must do so only through the ever-ongoing agreements, open constantly to refusal, sketched briefly in *The Problem of Political Obligation.*

But Pateman's own emphasis is less on the denial of liberty in any contract than on the inherent subordination in a certain form of contract. Thus in an employment relation within a firm, when an employer creates a single contract for all kinds of work in place of a series of contracts for each specific kind of work, it becomes "the employer's prerogative to direct the worker in his work" (Pateman 1988, 59). That single contract "creates a relation of subordination" (59). It is the "attachment of labour power to the person" (150) that makes this kind of contracting "unfree" (151), for in order to put that labor power to use, the worker must labor in the way that "the new owner requires.... The employment contract must, therefore, create a relationship of command and obedience between employer and worker" (151).

One might argue that contracts increase freedom as capacity-to-do-what-one-wants, because (imagining two equal bargainers) in many circumstances A can create a forward-looking interdependent interaction (such as delivering two tons of concrete in April in return for the wherewithal to purchase the ingredients of the concrete in March) only by promising to perform the future act for B in conditions that will punish A if she or he does not deliver to B. But contracts between equals for specific tasks are not the object of Pateman's interest. Her objections to contract all center on the problem of subordination, which she locates specifically in "contracts about property in the person." At the very outset of her argument, she states that "contracts about property in the person place right of command in the hands of one party to the contract" (Pateman 1988, 8):

> Capitalists can exploit workers and husbands can exploit wives because workers and wives are constituted as subordinates through the employment contract and the marriage contract. The genius of contract theorists has been to present both the original contract and actual contracts as exemplifying and securing individual freedom. On the contrary, in contract theory universal freedom is always an hypothesis, a story, a political fiction. Contract [regarding property in the person] always generates political right in the form of relations of domination and subordination (8).[7]

In Pateman's view, contracts regarding property in the person always create a relation of subordination because "if one party is in an inferior position (the worker or the woman), then he or she has no choice but to agree to disadvantageous terms offered by the other party" (58). If one interprets this argument solely as an argument about "choice," it might seem radically liberal. In its full thrust, however, it is an argument against subordination.

---

7. Pateman follows these lines with a reprise of G. D. H. Cole's description of the capitalist organization of production as "slavery."

A Radical Liberal?

Carole Pateman's resolute rejection of the terms "liberal" and "liberalism" to describe her work, even when each of her major books seems explicitly and deeply founded on the rock of radical choice, alerts us to the central problem of liberalism. A thin liberalism based on the most restricted and individualist reading of "liberty" to mean absence of impediments to motion risks degenerating into libertarianism, the refusal to subordinate any part of the self to the constraints required for common action. Accordingly, Arnold Kaufman, who coined the phrase "radical liberal," espoused a thick liberalism based on a deep understanding of autonomy. Autonomy in this view sheds the thin and restrictive meaning of liberty as absence of impediments to motion, replacing it with a concept derived from Rousseau, Kant, and Marx that lifting the shackles in the process of emancipation reveals a positive potentiality for giving laws to oneself and for expanding one's capacities as a human being. But we may question, as we skip down the road toward autonomy, whether we are not in fact leaving "liberalism" behind. That word has historical connotations that keep revolving in practice back to the root concept of noninterference, resisting implicitly the efforts of well-meaning philosophers to make more central its connotations of expanding capacity and resisting domination. Similarly, an expansive liberalism that encompasses all the goods and values traditionally associated with the phrase "liberal democracy" is not a coherent logical construct, although for practical reasons several of its associated parts usually hang together in real democratic polities.

Pateman continually shows us, in each of her books, how the classic liberal emphasis on liberty as (in my terms, borrowed from Hobbes) absence of impediments to motion easily—all too easily—masks actual subordination. Whether the mechanism is pseudoparticipation, as in *Participation and Democratic Theory*, manipulation and obfuscation, as in *The Problem of Political Obligation*, or contract in the person, as in *The Sexual Contract*, in a world of actual unfreedom the liberal emphasis on free individuals makes the theory itself the bearer of subordination. Pateman's vision, by contrast, is of a human being fully engaged without subordination in her interaction with others—in the workplace, in a partnership at home, and in the larger polity. Although this vision of engagement is one that many liberals have shared, it does not seem either linguistically or traditionally demanded by the term "liberal."

To make Pateman into a radical liberal, we would need to scrap in the liberal tradition the elements of a fictitious or real social contract as well as two features not discussed here, a division between public and private, and a "special" relationship with capitalism. Even then, for Pateman to be a radical liberal, one further adaptation would be necessary. The element of equality would have to carry far more weight in the traditional formula of "free and equal" beings at the base of a liberal polity. Whether Pateman writes of the worker who must bow to the orders of the employer or of the woman whose "no" Rousseau says a man may interpret as "yes,"[8] all that is in her springs to the defense of the subordinated being. This strong egalitarian commitment runs deep in all her writing. Although one can incorporate equality in liberalism by the two mechanisms of moving away from making "liberty" the core of liberalism and moving away from interpreting "liberty" as noninterference,[9] the narrower interpretation and the more restrictive definition are not likely ever to lose all of their magnetic pull in that theory.

In short, if we are to make Pateman a radical liberal, against her will, we must do more than tweak the liberal tradition. We must divest it not only of its current democratic institutions but also of its grounding in a social contract, its separation of private and political, and its failure to value fully the equal in the formula of "free and equal." It is certainly questionable whether a liberalism so divested of many elements that some consider integral can continue to bear the name. The temptation to think of Pateman as a radical liberal always beckons, because she is so deeply committed to liberty. But it is truer to her deepest convictions to take her at her word. We must then consider her proudly and simply a democrat.

References

Barber, Benjamin R. 1984. *Strong Democracy: Participatory Politics for a New Age.* Berkeley and Los Angeles: University of California Press.
Cole, G. D. H. 1919. *Self-government in Industry.* London: G. Bell and Sons.
———. 1920a. *Guild Socialism Restated.* London: Leonard Parsons.
———. 1920b. *Social Theory.* London: Methuen.
Fetscher, I. 1962. "Rousseau's Concepts of Freedom in the Light of his Philosophy of History." In *Liberty* (Nomos IV), edited by Carl J. Friedrich, 29–56. New York: Atherton Press.
Gastil, John, E. P. Deesse, and P. Weiser. 2002. "Civic Awakening in the Jury Room: A Test of the Connection between Jury Deliberation and Political Participation." *Journal of Politics* 64:585–95.

---

8. Rousseau [1762] 1911 and [1758] 1968, cited in Pateman [1980] 1989, 76.
9. See, e.g., the writers analyzed in Gutmann 1980.

Gutmann, Amy. 1980. *Liberal Equality*. Cambridge: Cambridge University Press.

Kaufman, Arnold. [1960] 1969. "Human Nature and Participatory Democracy." In *The Bias of Pluralism*, edited by William E. Connolly, 178–200. New York: Atherton Press.

Kaufman, Arnold. 1968. *The Radical Liberal*. New York: Atherton Press.

Luskin, Robert C., James S. Fishkin, and Roger Jowell. 2002. "Considered Opinions: Deliberative Polling in Britain." *British Journal of Political Science* 32:455–87.

Mansbridge, Jane. 1999. "On the Idea that Participation Makes Better Citizens." In *Citizen Competence and Democratic Institutions*, edited by Stephen L. Elkin and Karol E. Soltan, 291–325. University Park: Pennsylvania State University Press.

Mill, John Stuart. [1848–70] 1965. *Principles of Political Economy*. In *Collected Works*, edited by J. M. Robson. Toronto: University of Toronto Press.

Pateman, Carole. 1970. *Participation and Democratic Theory*. Cambridge: Cambridge University Press.

———. 1979. *The Problem of Political Obligation: A Critical Analysis of Liberal Theory*. New York: John Wiley and Sons.

———. [1980] 1989. "Women and Consent." In *The Disorder of Women: Democracy, Feminism, and Political Theory*, 71–89. Stanford: Stanford University Press.

———. 1988. *The Sexual Contract*. Stanford: Stanford University Press.

Pettit, Philip. 2000. *Republicanism: A Theory of Freedom and Government*. Oxford: Oxford University Press.

Rousseau, Jean-Jacques. [1762] 1911. *Emile*. Trans. B. Foxley. London: Dent/Everyman.

———. [1758] 1968. *Politics and the Arts*. Trans. Alan Bloom. Cornell University Press.

Sen, Amartya K. 2000. *Development as Freedom*. New York: Anchor Books.

Paradoxes of Liberal Politics: Contracts, Rights, and Consent
Moira Gatens

Sir Henry Maine's 1861 text, *Ancient Law*, is often cited as the locus classicus that articulated the shift from premodern "status" societies to modern "contractual" societies. He there describes the shift from social relations that are determined by one's familial status to those arising from the choices and interests of individuals. This movement tracks, he says, "the gradual dissolution of family dependency and the growth of individual obligation in its place. The Individual is steadily substituted for the Family, as the unit of which civil laws take account." "Nor," Maine continues,

> is it difficult to see what is the tie between man and man which replaces by degrees those forms of reciprocity in rights and duties which have their origin in the Family. *It is contract.* Starting, as from one terminus of history, from a condition of society in which all the relations of Persons are summed up in the relations of Family, we seem to have steadily moved towards a phase of social order in which *all these relations arise from the free agreement of Individuals.* (Maine 1920, 172–73; emphasis added)

Thus, in Maine's view, "the movement of the progressive societies has hitherto been a movement from status to contract." It would be hard to overestimate the importance of the roles of consent and contract in modern conceptions of legitimate social, economic, and political relations. The "free agreement" of "the individual" in modernity is expressed through contracting with others in ways that he judges will further his own interests. These are the bare elements out of which social contract theory is constructed: the individual, free agreement, and equal right. However, many contemporary political theorists have argued that the social contract story generates puzzles and paradoxes about the category of "the individual" and the concepts of "freedom," "equality" and "right." Is every human being, qua human, an "individual" in the relevant sense? Does freedom allow the "free agreement" to enslave oneself? Does the "equality" of all hold firm across sexual and racial differences? Do rights prevent or facilitate domination? This chapter considers these questions by focusing on three prominent critics of liberal political theory who have drawn attention to its paradoxical nature: Carole Pateman, Joan W. Scott, and Wendy Brown. The first section concentrates on Pateman's critique; the second on those of Scott and Brown. The third and final section argues that Pateman's analysis of the paradoxes of liberalism is preferable to the others because it provides the means to move beyond, if not definitively resolve, those paradoxes.

Contractarianism and the "Illusion of Choice"

A uniting theme of Pateman's work is her abiding concern with all forms of subordination in modern societies—whether these are of a political, economic, social, or conjugal sort—and the problems that these pose for the constitution of a genuinely democratic polity. Indeed, on her account, these very different kinds of subordination are historically, conceptually, and substantially interconnected. The common thread that connects them all is the political fiction of "property in the person" that allows certain kinds of contracts to appear legitimate. Modern contractual societies, far from freeing us from hierarchy, have merely transformed the ways in which social relationships are constructed as relations of domination and subordination. Contract "is the specifically modern means of creating relationships of subordination" (Pateman 1988, 118) and it does so through the promulgation of the political fiction that the individual stands in a relation of ownership to his property in the person.

The clearest articulation of the idea of property in the person is to be found in John Locke's *Second Treatise*. His notion of property includes "life, liberty and estate," but these diverse forms of property all have their origin in the property *every* man enjoys in his own person, and this "nobody has any right to but himself." After all, it is this latter form of property that determines which parts of the world—initially held in common—may be transformed into legitimate private property. By mixing one's own person with previously unowned nature, one thereby "excludes the common right of other men" (Locke 2003, 112). Locke's influential theory of property and its role in underwriting the equality of individuals in civil society is well known. Pateman, however, challenges this theory at its root. The "individual," she argues, is not a sex- or race-neutral category. Rather, the individual in modern contractual societies is a certain kind of man: namely, one who stands in relation to other men as the bearer of the right to proprietorship over his "person." And only a certain kind of human being was recognized as a "person" at law in the modern period. The social contract theorists' critique of premodern understandings of the natural inequality between men did not extend to the "natural" subordination of women. The doctrine of "coverture," for example, denied married women the legal status of persons. They were considered "civilly dead." The "individual"—when understood as the proprietor of his property in the person—is not a synonym for "human being." Some kinds of human beings were seen to lack the crucial capacity to hold a right to their property in the person. Understood in terms of natural kinds (women, "blacks," "natives"), these human beings were understood to be under the *natural* authority of others and so incapable of creating or maintaining *political* right (Pateman 1988, 96).

An adequate critique of modern contractarianism, or libertarianism,[1] needs to show how different forms of subjection interconnect. Pateman's understanding of modernity considers that its key institutions—employment, marriage, and citizenship—developed together, are mutually reinforcing, and are constitutively contractual. Furthermore, each institution crucially depends on the political fiction of property in the person. In her analysis, it is this fiction that generates the interlocking paradoxes of liberal societies. If these paradoxes are to be resolved, the fiction must be exposed and its function in each institution must be replaced by a viable, genuinely democratic, alternative.

The employment contract in modern societies creates the paradox of the rights-bearing individual who, possessing nothing other than the property in his person, "freely" chooses to subordinate himself to an employer in exchange for a wage. Locke, along with other early contract theorists, attempted to distinguish a wage laborer (and a servant) from a slave in terms of the duration and content of the contract: the master or employer enjoys only "a temporary power" over the use of particular, contractually specified, capacities of the

---

1. Some interpretations of *The Sexual Contract* fail to note that, for Pateman, contractarianism and libertarianism are essentially equivalent. See Pateman 1988, 14.

worker (Locke 2003, 136). But workers cannot be separated from their capacities in this manner. As Pateman states:

> Capitalist employment, and the argument that the worker is the exemplar of a free labourer, who paradoxically, can exemplify his freedom by entering into a civil slave contract, depends on the claim that the worker is not a commodity; labour power is the commodity that can be subject to contract. The idea of the individual as owner is thus central to an understanding of the employment contract. That the idea of ownership of property in the person *is a political fiction* is equally central to an understanding of the employment contract. [. . .] In short, the contract in which the worker sells his labour power is a contract in which, since he cannot be separated from his capacities, he sells command over the use of his body and himself. To obtain the right to the use of another is to be a (civil) master. To sell command over the use of oneself for a specified period is not the same as selling oneself for life as another's property—but it is to be an unfree labourer. The characteristics of this condition are captured in the term *wage slave*. (Pateman 1988, 151; emphasis in original)

The inevitable result of "voluntary entry into the employment contract is civil subordination" (Pateman 2002, 38; see also 1988, 153), and wage laborers cannot be subordinated in the economy and still maintain their status as free and equal self-governing citizens in a democratic polity. "Employment thus provides [a] version of the paradox of (modern) slavery," namely, "that slaves have no standing at all, they are mere property" (Pateman 2002, 47). In the absence of a viable alternative to wage labor, the free agreement of the worker and the supposed mutuality of the exchange between the civilly "equal" contracting parties are illusory.

If the "choice" available to those who own nothing but their property in the person is highly constrained (that is, wage labor), the "choices" open to those deemed nonpersons (women and slaves) are sham. The wage laborer may be little different from a wage slave in the sphere of employment, but in the private sphere he may be master of his wife. Men who qualify for membership in the civil fraternity are, at least in this sense, equal: they each enjoy the power to command the labor and body of a wife. On Pateman's account, "the subordination of wives was presupposed by the institution of employment" (Pateman 2002, 34; 1988, 135f.). Far from putting an end to patriarchalism, Pateman argues that social contract theory inaugurated a new form of patriarchy in which men, comprising a modern civil fraternity, forcefully excluded women from the rights prerequisite to the enjoyment of civil and political equality. According to Pateman, Mary Wollstonecraft "was the first political theorist systematically to highlight and criticize the interrelationship between sexuality, marriage, the sexual division of labor, and citizenship" (Pateman 2003, 284). Unraveling these interrelated forms of subjection is the task of *The Sexual Contract*. Amplifying the claims of Wollstonecraft, Pateman insists that the rights of the modern individual are two-dimensional. Modern contractualism comprises not only the dimension of the civil and political rights of the individual but also *sex-right*, that is, the political construction of men's right to govern women. Thus, free and equal brothers in the fraternal polity become "masters" of their wives and families in the "natural" private sphere. Political right, and the social contract itself, presuppose sex-right, and the sexual contract.[2]

Civil society is defined in social contract theory by way of contrast with the "private" sphere of marriage and the family, which are understood to provide the *natural* basis for political life. But the telling of the sexual contract story creates fissures in the social contract story. How can contract and consent be the hallmarks of free modernity if all women are naturally subjected? The sexual contract exposes the paradoxical nature of women's social and political status. Did (indeed, do) women enjoy proprietorship over their property in the person? If not, can women be considered to be free individuals? And if they are not free individuals, how may they enter the marriage, employment or citizenship (social) contracts?

Pateman's response to these puzzles is to emphasize the paradox of women and consent. Modern contractarianism must "displace" the sexual contract onto the marriage contract: "[i]f the promise of universal freedom heralded by the story of an original contract is not to appear fraudulent from the start, women must take part in contract in the new civil order" (Pateman 1988, 181). Unlike contracts between free individuals, marriage is a contract between an individual (man) and a woman, constructed as a "natural subordinate" (55). As a "natural subordinate" the wife receives protection from her husband in exchange for obedience, much like a slave contract. The marriage contract

---

2. In *The Sexual Contract* Pateman explains that she knowingly exaggerates when she takes sex-right to be *half* of the missing story of the social contract, and she notes an important *third* dimension: "The men who (are said to) make the original contract are *white* men, and their fraternal pact has three aspects: the social contract, the sexual contract and the slave contract that legitimises the rule of white over black" (1988, 221, emphasis in original). In *The Racial Contract*, Charles Mills offers an account of this third dimension. See also his chapter in this volume.

ensures that a woman's property in the person is under the jurisdiction of her husband. But why would any woman freely agree to this state of affairs? Pateman argues that the issue of consent arises as a meaningful question only for those who are constituted as "free and equal individuals." Women's consent, therefore, is only apparent. In fact, when women marry, the vow to accept their husband's authority "is only a formal recognition of their "natural" subordination" (Pateman 1989, 74). Marriage, and a life in the private sphere, was the only way that women could gain any kind of civil status. However, even this vicarious status generates further paradoxes:

> the private sphere *both is and is not* part of civil society—and women *both are and are not* part of the civil order. Women are not incorporated [into civil society] as "individuals" but *as women*, which, in the story of the original contract, means as natural subordinates (slaves are property). The original contract can be upheld, and men can receive acknowledgment of their patriarchal right, only if women's subjection is secured in civil society. (Pateman 1988, 181; emphasis added)

Hence, women's participation in civil life, in employment, and in politics, is always *as women*, never as the full rights-bearing "individual" of modern contractual society.

Although women in liberal democracies today enjoy many more rights and a far more secure civil status than they did in the past, Pateman is adamant that the difficulties that women continue to experience in securing their democratic rights in the home (e.g., freedom from violence, sexual autonomy), in the workplace (e.g., equal pay, freedom from sexual harassment), in the public sphere (e.g., freedom from fear of assault), and in the political arena (e.g., right to representation, freedom from ridicule and humiliation) cannot be overcome until attention is directed toward the repressed half of the social contract: the sexual contract. The marriage contract, no less than the employment contract, generates paradoxes of freedom, of consent, of political and civil status, and of right.

Historically, the struggles of women, and others who were politically constituted as lacking a proprietorial right to property in their persons, have focused on gaining control over their own bodies and capacities. The fight for equal rights necessarily has meant fighting for ownership over one's property in the person. Women's fragile entitlement to their property in the person is not, however, the crucial issue. To endeavor to make *this* entitlement more robust—as some feminists have advocated in relation to the legalization of prostitution or surrogacy—misses the point (see Pateman 1988, 189–218). It is true that women, along with "blacks" and colonized peoples, only relatively recently have enjoyed the privileges that come with proprietorship over one's person, but this "privilege" is double-edged. Pateman has two important points to make in this context, points that will be elaborated upon in the final section of this chapter. The first is that contracts for the hire of property in the person inevitably involve the whole embodied being, which cannot be separated from the capacities of that being. As such, contracts and rights are always necessarily sexed: they are contracts between embodied persons who are either male or female. Neither the prostitution nor the surrogacy contract, for example, can be performed without engaging the entire being of the person promising the "service." The subordination of women through such contracts merely validates the original sex-right of men, namely, the *right* to have access to a woman's sexual and procreative being, and serves to confirm the power and privilege of modern fraternal patriarchy. The second point is that *all* contracts that are based on the fiction of property in the person are destructive of egalitarian relationships, whether these are conjugal, economic, or political. If the major institutions of a society facilitate the creation of relationships of domination and subordination then such institutions cannot together compose a democratic polity.

The sham character of consent and contract—in employment, in marriage, and in citizenship—provides sufficient reason to argue for the reconstruction of the liberal state along genuinely democratic lines. Such reconstruction necessarily will include "a simultaneous reconstruction of our sexual lives" because at present "these two dimensions [political right and sex-right] are inseparable" for both sexes (Pateman 1989, 84). In sum, a "free social order cannot be a contractual order" and "the sexual contract and the social contract, the 'individual' and the state, stand and fall together" (Pateman 1988, 232). On Pateman's analysis, the paradoxes generated by women, consent, and contract, along with the paradox of the "free" wage slave, will defy resolution as long as the political fiction of property in the person holds sway.

Irresolvable Paradoxes? Scott and Brown on the "Individual" and Rights

Other contemporary theorists also have turned their attention to the paradoxes of liberalism but have reached different conclusions. To highlight the specificity of Pateman's critical contribution to democratic theory, this section of the chapter briefly will consider the approach of two other prominent critics of liberal individualism and liberal rights: Joan W. Scott and Wendy Brown, respectively.

Despite their diverse summations, Scott and Pateman share many points of agreement. Like Pateman, Scott understands the category of "the individual" to be a political construction whose precise meaning varies according to its historical context. What does not vary, however, is that the status of "individual" was reserved for men only. The fundamentally paradoxical nature of the notion of the individual is that while it is "articulated as the foundation of a system of universal inclusion (against the hierarchies and privileges of monarchical and aristocratic regimes), it could also be used as a standard of exclusion by defining as nonindividuals, or less than individuals, those who were different from the singular figure of the human" (Scott 1996, 7). A woman could not count as an individual "both because she was nonidentical with the human prototype and because she was the other who confirmed the (male) individual's individuality" (8). Scott makes the same connections as Pateman had done earlier among "property in the person," "individuality," wage labor, masculinity, and citizenship, arguing that:

> [P]roperty "in the person of the worker" could be a form of property or a means of acquiring it. The ambiguity of the association between labor and property rights opened the space for conceiving political equality among men. [. . .] Property was an expression of self; labor in this sense was a form of property. What men had in common was not only this property, but its objectification in the family, in the wife and child who carried a husband's and father's name and served as the instruments of the transmission of his property—the tangible emblem of his person. (Scott 1996, 63; see also 153)

In addition, both Pateman and Scott are skeptical about the "free consent" of women to their social positioning as "property" and as nonpersons. More significant than these similarities, however, is their mutual identification of the position of women within liberalism as riven by paradox. Indeed, Scott's impressive study of French feminist struggles from the late eighteenth to the mid-twentieth centuries takes as its title a phrase from Olympe De Gouges's writing: *Only Paradoxes to Offer*. Even though these points of agreement between the two theorists should not be downplayed, there are important differences between them that are more important for present purposes.

Scott's historical study leaves little doubt that women offered fierce resistance to their social and political placement and provides ample evidence that they strove to challenge and redraw the parameters of "the political" and "the social" whenever possible. The potency of her study lies, in part, in its definitive demonstration of the great historical variation in the meaning of womanhood (and manhood), along with a detailed analysis of the particular social and political institutions and structures that helped to construct those meanings (see also Pateman 1988, 126–28, for a similar claim). However, insofar as Scott reduces women's agency to the (on her account, *irresolvable*) paradoxes of liberalism, she forgoes the possibility that feminist ingenuity may provide the means for their resolution. In describing the themes of *Only Paradoxes to Offer*, she writes:

> One argument of this book is *that feminist agency is paradoxical in its expression*. It is *constituted* by universalist discourses of individualism (with their theories of rights and citizenship) that evoke "sexual difference" to naturalize the exclusion of women. A second argument is that feminist agency has a history; it is neither a fixed set of behaviors nor an essential attribute of women; rather it is an *effect* of ambiguities, inconsistencies, contradictions within particular *epistemologies*. (Scott 1996, 16; emphasis added)

To understand resistance—political agency—as "effect" *only* is to render it a reactive, even docile, force in history. Feminist agency is thereby reduced to little more than the reiteration, across time, of the various paradoxes generated by women's claims to equality (with men) alongside the unavoidable embodiment of their difference (from men). Feminism is here condensed into the "equality-versus-difference" dilemma; and that dilemma itself is conceived as intractable.[3]

Scott, rightly in my view, wishes to eschew those philosophical accounts of humanity that assume an ahistorical, transcendent, faculty of the will along with the naïve partner position that voluntarism provides the motor for "progress" in history. Revisiting the background knowledge and discursive conditions that served to shape particular historical meanings of "men" and "women" helps to explain how invidious distributions of social and political entitlements and burdens were able to appear justified. Moreover, this historical and contextualist approach allows greater understanding of the nature of

---

3. See Scott 1988 for a full account of her understanding of the sexual equality versus sexual difference debate.

particular rights claims made by women in history by relating these claims to the discourses, norms, and institutions through which social and political actions were rendered coherent (or, indeed, incoherent or "deviant"). However, Scott's approach does not simply argue for the historicity and specificity of *expressions* of agency (that is, the entirely plausible view that actions are always conditioned by circumstances) but further, that specific historical conditions of knowledge invariably *constitute* feminist agency as caught in the grip of paradox. This is not then a compatibilist account of freedom but a strictly determinist one. Add to this account her understanding of paradox as *in principle irresolvable*, and it becomes difficult to see how political paralysis is not the inevitable outcome of her stance. This outcome appears to be confirmed by the observations that close Scott's study: "A reading of the history of *feminism cannot resolve its paradoxes; it is in the nature of paradox to be unresolvable*" (Scott 1996, 174; emphasis added). Before turning to address the feasibility of this view of feminist agency, and indeed, this definition of paradox, I first will consider the views of Wendy Brown on rights and paradox.

Apart from her insistence on paradox, Brown's analysis of contemporary liberalism has little in common with Pateman's approach in *The Sexual Contract*. The brief discussion of that work, proffered in *States of Injury*, makes clear that she regards the sexual contract as obsolete. Pateman's identification of contract as "the mechanism" of modern sexual and civil subordination, Brown says, amounts to "criticizing a fetish." Contract has little relevance to contemporary liberal orders (Brown 1995, 137). The language of contract, according to Brown, has been superseded by "the 'self-evident' superiority of rights discourse and constitutional government." "Rerouting" Pateman's history of contract "in the direction of genealogy" Brown aims to "deliteralize and dematerialize contract in order to examine the operations of a *discourse* premised on a sexual contract even while its perpetuation as a gendered discourse does not depend on that contract nor the naturalized sexual division of labor on which such a contract was premised" (138–39; emphasis in original).[4] But, arguably, Brown has misunderstood Pateman's argument in *The Sexual Contract* and elsewhere. Pateman's target is not so much contract per se as it is contractarianism, or libertarianism—that is, contracts that deal in *property in the person*. Itself a kind of "fetish," the idea of ownership of property in the person is the true focus of Pateman's criticisms. Moreover, this fetish is one

---

4. Although I am in agreement with Brown concerning the untapped role that genealogy could play in retelling the history of contract, I doubt that a genealogy that examined "the operations of discourse" only would be an effective one. For my own effort to apply genealogy to sex and contract, see Gatens 1996.

from which Marx—the source of Brown's phrase "criticizing a fetish"—himself suffered (see Pateman 1988, 13-14, 149-50). Insofar as Brown misses the importance of Pateman's analysis of the notion of property in the person, she also fails to notice the critical path opened by Pateman's argument that contemporary rights discourses depend upon just this notion. Rights—and their alienability—depend upon the fiction of property in the person, without which constitutional government could not exist (see Pateman 1988, chap. 4; Pateman 2002, 31).

Brown's preferred strategy is to concentrate on the paradoxical quality of liberal rights, leaving to one side the argument over whether one is "for" or "against" rights. In *States of Injury,* and elsewhere, Brown uncovers what she calls a "nest of paradoxes" surrounding liberal rights and contemporary identity politics, which include those of women, people of color, homosexuals, and generally "difference" struggles for rights (Brown 1995, 100). This "nest" is home to, at least, the following paradoxes: (i) rights are at once "universal," general, ahistorical, *and* locally circumscribed, historically and socially specific in their content and effects; (ii) rights may be a force for the emancipation of specific peoples at one time *and* a force for their regulation and political control at another; and (iii) rights struggled for by a politicized group, when conferred, are distributed to "depoliticized" individuals. In short, the universal-local paradox of rights gives rise to the following question: "If contemporary rights claims are deployed to protect historically and contextually contingent identities, might the relationship of the universal idiom of rights to the contingency of the protected identities be such that the former operates inadvertently to resubordinate by renaturalizing that which it was intended to emancipate by articulating?" (99). Rights are paradoxical because they operate "both to emancipate *and* dominate, both to protect *and* regulate" (100). While claiming not to be "condemning" rights but rather to be recommending the adoption of a vigilant and interrogative stance in relation to their role in emancipatory politics, Brown nevertheless argues, in a later work, that rights are regressive because "for the systematically subordinated" they tend to "rewrite injuries and inequalities, and [are] impediments to freedom" at the same time that they fail to address the conditions that produce such injuries, inequalities, and lack of freedom (Brown 2000, 239).

Following Scott, Brown distinguishes paradox from tension or contradiction by designating it as *irresolvable* (Brown 2000, 238).[5] In the realm of

---

5. However, in *States of Injury* she had suggested instead that 'paradox designates a condition in which resolution is the most uninteresting aim' (1995, 100).

politics, she claims, "paradox appears endlessly self-cancelling, as a political condition of achievements perpetually undercut, a predicament of discourse in which every truth is crossed by a counter-truth, and hence a state in which political strategizing itself is paralyzed" (239). Of course, such claims need to be tested with reference to actual rights claims made at particular times and in particular places. *States of Injury* endeavors to do just that with reference to late twentieth-century "difference" rights claims in North America (see Brown 1995, 96–134).

However, do such studies add up to a demonstration of her *general* claim about the "regressive" nature of rights? Rights claims that aim to emancipate their claimants from relations of domination and subordination unavoidably do serve to reinscribe human beings in culture. This is because such claims aim, precisely, to challenge and redefine what it means to be an embodied human being—male or female; "black" or "white"; heterosexual, homosexual, or "queer"—and what, if any, are the moral, social, and political implications of these diverse forms of human embodiment. Nevertheless, this feature of rights claims, on its own, cannot count as a criticism of rights struggles since every assertion of freedom inevitably will be a (re)interpretation of what it means to be human. The complaint then must be about the mode or the manner of the redefinition or "reinscription" of social and political identities, namely, the tendency for such redefinitions to merely "rewrite injuries and inequalities." In particular, the central claim appears to be that liberal rights discourses fail to challenge the underlying structures of domination and subordination; essentially, a restatement of Marx's views in *On the Jewish Question* about the inadequacy of the bourgeois "rights of man" (on which, see Brown 1995, 100–115).

Brown's treatment of rights as paradoxes separates rights from those aspects of subordination in contractarian societies that Pateman had highlighted in *The Sexual Contract*. This is consistent with Brown's assessment of that book as relying on a superseded conception of liberal societies. The isolation of rights from contractarianism, as was suggested above, thwarts the potential for forging a path out of the paradoxes they together generate. Brown's move, ironically, cuts off the possibility of linking a critical analysis of rights to the conditions that produce injuries, inequalities, and unfreedom in contemporary contractarian societies. Annabelle Lever is right to suggest that Brown's treatment of rights as paradoxes "risks mystifying and reifying them" (Lever 2000, 244). Furthermore, the corollary of conceiving of rights as paradox—where paradox itself is figured as irresolvable—is to hobble political agency, which in turn results in political paralysis.

In the following section I challenge the characterization of paradox favored by Scott and Brown. Contrary to their stance, there is nothing intrinsic to the nature of paradox that would rule out, in principle, its resolution. Finally, I propose that the promising paths opened up by Pateman's analysis of the paradoxes of liberal society have yet to be fully appreciated and explored by contemporary political theorists.

"The Barber Is a Woman!": Toward Resolving Liberal Paradoxes

Even today most Anglo-American undergraduate philosophy students are likely to be introduced to the topic of paradox by the legendary "Barber's Paradox." There is, so the story goes, an Oxford barber who shaves all and only those Oxford men who do not shave themselves. This generates the paradox that the Oxford barber *both does and does not* shave himself. Resolutions of the paradox might include: the Oxford barber has a beard; or, a person who satisfies the description of "the Oxford barber" does not exist; or, finally—a solution that may not readily suggest itself to the men of Oxford—the Oxford barber is a woman![6] In any case, the common understanding of paradox does not define it as, in principle, unresolvable. On the contrary, a paradox is "a seemingly sound piece of reasoning based on seemingly true assumptions that leads to a contradiction (or other obviously false conclusion). A paradox reveals that either the principles of reasoning or the assumptions on which it is based are faulty. It is said to be solved when the mistaken principles or assumptions are clearly identified and rejected" (Audi 1999, 643).

When powerful political interests are at stake, paradoxes generated by false assumptions and suspect forms of reasoning that aim to justify unwarranted exclusions will be common. Slave-owning societies, for example, generally hold slaves to be objects, that is, mere property, even while—as the autobiography of Frederick Douglass makes clear—the practices of slaveholders confirm their recognition that slaves are human (Douglass 1960; see also Mills 1997). The surprising toleration for inconsistency in belief sets, which then generate paradox, is often the hallmark of worldviews that attempt to justify oppressive social, economic, and political relations. The history of political theory might be read, at least in part, as a record of the endeavor to expose and refute the erroneous assumptions and inconsistencies in reasoning that political privilege and dominance promote. At its best, such theory will make

6. Of course, a woman too might have a beard, but so long as she remains bearded, she will not spoil this resolution.

explicit what it is in traditional ways of thinking that generates paradox. The resolution of a theory characterized by systemically nested paradoxes is likely to require a radical, rather than a piecemeal, reformulation. Such a reformulation may even provoke a "paradigm shift," such as the shift from status to contract societies, for which the social contract theorists argued.

Restoring the systemic links between rights, contractarianism, and modern forms of economic, sexual, and political subordination opens one promising path for the reformulation of democratic political theory. Although Pateman is dismissive of the ability of men (as wage-laborers) and women (as wives and as wage-laborers) to consent genuinely to the contracts that constitute modern liberal societies, she is not, for all that, skeptical about their capacity for freedom and political agency. The "illusion of consent," or the "paradox of agency," in other words, is intrinsic to the social structures produced by the major institutions of contractual societies, not to the human condition as such. There are, Pateman says, "other forms of free agreement through which women and men can constitute political relations."[7] However,

> [i]f political relations are to lose all resemblance to slavery, free women and men must willingly agree to uphold *the social conditions* of their autonomy. That is to say, they must agree to uphold limits. Freedom requires order and order requires limits. In modern civil society individual freedom is unconstrained—and order is maintained through mastery and obedience. If men's mastery is to be replaced by the mutual autonomy of women and men, *individual freedom must be limited by the structure of social relations in which freedom inheres.* (Pateman 1988, 232; emphasis added)

Two important questions arise here. First, what does Pateman mean by "freedom" and "autonomy"? Second, what are these "limits" on the structure of social relationships that must be maintained if citizens are to enjoy free and autonomous relations? Concerning the first question, one thing is certain: freedom and autonomy are *not* to be gained through the achievement of self-ownership or the right to proprietorship over one's property in the person. In Pateman's view, contemporary theories about self-ownership have been usurped by moral philosophy with the result that the *political* problem posed by contemporary marital and economic relations, namely, that they are mar-

---

7. For a recent exploration of what free agreement between women and men in the context of marriage might mean, see Shanley, and her respondents, 2004.

kets in the property in persons, is obscured (Pateman 2002, 33f.). These markets, which deal in the "renting" of persons, are incompatible with an inclusive democratic polity constituted by free and equal citizens. The fiction of property in the person, which *allows* the idea of the alienability of certain rights (including the right to self-government), is what constitutes the liberal social order as composed of relations of domination and subordination. The liberal "illusion of consent," in other words, forecloses the possibility for the development of an "ethic of mutual aid" in which autonomy could flourish (45). This is why, for Pateman, it is so important to attend to the historical vicissitudes, and to current manifestations, of the notion of property in the person. It is also why contractarian society is incompatible with democratic citizenship.

Concerning the second question, it is significant that in more recent work Pateman has drawn even more tightly together the threads that link rights, contractarianism, and modern forms of subordination. In her discussion of James Tully's critique of C. B. Macpherson's thesis about the "possessive individualism" of modern contract theory, Pateman explores how self-ownership is figured in relation to the alienability, or inalienability, of rights. If *all* rights are seen as alienable then the result will be absolute monarchy or radical libertarianism: the rights of the individual may be surrendered to an absolute power (the Leviathan) or to the absolute power of the market (libertarianism). Alternatively, some rights might be seen as alienable and others not: the rights to self-defense and to participate in government, for example, might be seen as inalienable whereas the right to one's property in the person might be seen as alienable. It is this "mixed" view of rights that, according to Pateman, is characteristic of constitutional government. Insofar as government requires the consent of the governed, sovereign power is limited. Although this view presents the image of a democratic polity it is nevertheless marked by relations of subordination in the economy and in the "private" sphere of the family that undermine democracy. However, there is another view of rights to which political theorists rarely refer, namely, that "all rights can be seen as inalienable" (Pateman 2002, 31). It is this latter view that appears to attract Pateman. If *all* contracts in property in the person inevitably serve to create relationships of domination and subordination then such contracts can have no legitimate place in a genuinely democratic polity. Thus, a genuinely democratic polity would limit—presumably meaning *prohibit*—all contracts in property in the person.

If I read Pateman correctly, this is the end result of her arguments and the reason she draws so tight the threads between contract, rights, and subordination. If citizens are to be genuinely self-governing then "the ideas of property in the person and self-ownership have to be relinquished" (Pateman 2002, 50). The right to self-government should not be—even in part—alienable. If this were to be the case then the wage contract, the marriage contract, and constitutional government would be ruled out. It would also rule out prostitution, surrogacy (womb renting), the sale of organs, and the market in patents for genetic materials. In short, markets in the selling, hiring, and buying of bits of persons, that is to say, *persons,* would be prohibited. These are the "limits" that must be drawn, and maintained, if egalitarian relations are to be enjoyed across the entire social body—in the workplace and in the home—as well as in the polity. Certainly, this depiction of what is required for the elimination of subordination and the creation of a self-governing democratic polity—if viable—constitutes a dramatic paradigm shift in political thought.

A few final words on paradox are in order. On Pateman's view, the paradoxes generated by liberal contractarianism may be traced to the political fiction of property in the person. The resolution of these paradoxes lies in the exposure of the notion of property in the person *as a fiction*—a false premise upon which modern contractual society was erected. Property in the person cannot, she argues, be contracted out without the involvement of the whole person. The resolution of paradox lies too in exposing the inegalitarian relationships that result from conceiving of self-ownership, or property in the person, in terms of alienable rights.

When Pateman wrote *The Sexual Contract,* back in the late 1980s, she made the claim that "sperm is the only example of property in the person that is not a political fiction. Unlike labor power, sexual parts, the uterus, or any other property that is contracted out for use by another, sperm *can* be separated from the body (Pateman 1988, 217). Although the claim was contestable then (for example, breast milk and blood also can be separated from the body), it is unsupportable now. Today, ova and genetic materials can be separated from the person without injury. Even some organs (e.g., a kidney) and bone marrow now may be "transferred" to another, generally without lasting injury or harm to the person whose kidney or marrow it was. What was fiction, as so often has been the case in human history, is now fact. How, if at all, does this affect Pateman's thesis?

At best, it obstructs her desire to liberate political theory from the grip of moral philosophy (see Pateman 2002, 33-44). If the commodification of "bits of persons" (i.e., property in the person) is not *always* based in the *fiction* that these "bits" are separable from the person, on what other grounds might one be entitled to criticize it? More pertinently, on what grounds may one argue for placing limits on contracts, at least in relation to these *nonfictive* kinds of property in the person? Ultimately, it seems that prohibiting all contracts in property in the person would require the attribution of *status* to the *literal* integrity of human beings. This status might be ontological, metaphysical, juridical, moral, or, as seems more likely, some combination of these. What is unlikely is that such attribution could amount to a "clean," purely political decision. Rather, it appears to rely upon the moral claim that there are certain things to which a human being should never be subjected, including being sold, bought, or hired either "in part"—as wage labor, organ donor, sex worker, surrogate mother—or "in whole"—as a slave, or a baby.

At worst, Pateman's stance on the limits that must be upheld if democracy is to be achieved might generate again Rousseau's paradox of the citizen who must be forced to be free. However, if these limits were self-imposed—the outcome of the deliberative practices of a genuinely self-governing body—then the result would be no more paradoxical than Ulysses' cries to be unbound from the ship's mast. In other words, it would not be an authentic paradox at all. These concluding remarks manage to gesture toward just two of the many promising paths that the challenging work of Carole Pateman has opened for contemporary political theory.

References

Audi, R., ed. 1999. *The Cambridge Dictionary of Philosophy.* 2nd ed., Cambridge: Cambridge University Press.
Brown, W. 1995. *States of Injury.* Princeton: Princeton University Press.
———. 2000. "Suffering Rights as Paradoxes." *Constellations* 7, no. 2:230–41.
Douglass, F. [1845]. 1960. *Narrative of the Life of Frederick Douglass, An American Slave, written by Himself,* edited by B. Quarles. Cambridge, Mass.: Belknap Press.
Gatens, M. 1996. "Sex, Contract, Genealogy." *Journal of Political Philosophy* 4, no. 1:29–44.
Lever, A. 2000. "The Politics of Paradox: A Response to Wendy Brown." *Constellations* 7, no. 2:242–54.
Locke, J. [1689]. 2003. *Two Treatises of Government and A Letter Concerning Toleration,* ed. I. Shapiro. New Haven: Yale University Press.
Maine, H. S. 1920. *Ancient Law,* ed. F. Pollock. London: John Murray.
Mills, C. 1997. *The Racial Contract.* Ithaca: Cornell University Press.
Pateman, C. 1988. *The Sexual Contract.* Cambridge: Polity.
———. 1989. *The Disorder of Women.* Cambridge: Polity.

———. 2002. "Self-ownership and Property in the Person: Democratization and a Tale of Two Concepts." *Journal of Political Philosophy* 10, no. 1:20–53.

———. 2003. "Mary Wollstonecraft." In *Political Thinkers from Socrates to the Present*, edited by D. Boucher and P. Kelly, 270–87. Oxford: Oxford University Press.

Scott, J. W. 1988. "Deconstructing Equality-versus-Difference: Or the Uses of Poststructuralist Theory for Feminism." *Feminist Studies* 14, no. 1 (Spring): 33–50.

———. 1996. *Only Paradoxes to Offer*. Cambridge, Mass.: Harvard University Press.

Shanley, M. L. 2004. *Just Marriage*. Oxford: Oxford University Press.

The Domination Contract
Charles W. Mills

Carole Pateman's *The Sexual Contract* (1988) has become a classic text of second-wave feminist theory, and it is widely and deservedly seen as constituting one of the most important challenges of the last twenty years to the frameworks and assumptions of "malestream" political theory. Moreover, its influence is not restricted to gender issues, since it was the inspiration for my own book, *The Racial Contract* (1997), in the field of critical race theory. The impact of both books, of course, originates in part from their refusal respectively of "pink" and "black" theoretical ghettoization for a frontal conceptual engagement with a (male, white) intellectual apparatus, social contract theory, that has historically been central to the modern Western political tradition, and which has been spectacularly revived in the past three decades as a result of John Rawls's *A Theory of Justice* ([1971] 1999). Pateman and I assert that the history of gender and racial subordination requires a rethinking of how we do political theory, that it cannot be a matter of some minor, largely cosmetic changes—a few "she's" sprinkled in where there were previously only "he's," a pro forma deploring of the racism of Enlightenment theorists—before continuing basically as before. Rather, contract theory must take as its starting point not the presumed state of nature populated by individuals with no social or political ties, but rather actual societies populated by individuals who are members of socially constructed groups (e.g., of class, race, and sex) already in relationships of domination and subordination. How does this new perspective challenge contract theory in general, and Rawlsian normative theory in particular? Without at all presuming that we are in complete agreement on these issues, I want to offer a possible reconstruction, elaboration, and extrapolation of Pateman's "sexual contract" argument that makes explicit the theoretical innovation involved, and clarifies what the implications are for the theorizing of gender and racial justice.[1]

The "Contract" as Protean

Let me begin—in the "underlaborer" tradition of analytic philosophy—with some preliminary clarifying distinctions. The diverse and contradictory interpretations of Pateman's book arise from three ambiguities in Pateman's revisionist contractarianism: one endemic to the literature in general, even just the mainstream variety; one arising distinctively from her radical and unfamiliar nonmainstream use of the idea of contract; and one generated by her own choice of terminology.

The general problem is the astonishing range of the ways in which the idea of the "contract" has historically been employed, ironically—or then again, not ironically at all—coupled with the fact that in most cases it is actually doing no work, and is, in effect, otiose, a disposable part of the argument. (With only slight exaggeration, one could quip that in the long history of social contract theory, very few actual social contract theorists can be found!) To begin with, there is the notion of the contract as in some sense, whether stronger or weaker, descriptive or factual: the contract as ur-sociology or anthropology, providing us with a literal account of what actually happened. Or, more weakly, the contract as a plausible hypothetical reconstruction of what might have happened. Or, weaker still, the contract as a useful way of thinking about what happened—the contract "as if"—though we know perfectly well it did *not* happen that way. Then within this "descriptive" sense, whether robustly or thinly conceived, there are additional differences (cross-cutting the above) of, so to speak, the object of the contract. Is it a contract to create society, the state, or both? And, to introduce further complications within these categories, is society envisaged as an aggregate of individuals or a transformed collective community, and are rights alienated to the state or merely delegated to it? Then there is the contract as normative. For example, the contract as the outcome of a collective bargaining agreement that brings morality into existence as a conventionalist set of principles. Or the contract as a way of elucidating and codifying preexisting and objective moral principles, whether grounded in natural law or human interests. Or the contract as a thought-experiment, a device for generating moral intuitions about justice through the

---

1. Pateman and I have now written a book together (Pateman and Mills 2007).

strategy of combining prudential motivation with ignorance of crucial features of the self and the social order.

So the concept has been used in radically different ways—the contract as literal, metaphorical, historical, hypothetical, descriptive, prescriptive, prudential, moral, constitutional, civil, regulative ideal, device of representation. It is no wonder then, that, as David Boucher and Paul Kelly (1994b, 2) conclude in an introductory overview of social contract theory, "The idea of the social contract when examined carefully is seen to have very few implications, and is used for all sorts of reasons, and generates quite contrary conclusions." Will Kymlicka (1991, 196) concurs in an encyclopedia essay, "In a sense, there is no contract tradition in ethics, only a contract *device* which many different traditions have used for many different reasons."

Moreover, as if this bewildering array of distinctions were not enough, Pateman's peculiar use of the contract idea revives a strand of the contract tradition that has been so marginalized and ignored that it does not even have a name in the secondary literature: what I have called elsewhere the "domination contract" (Mills 2000). Though Pateman herself does not explicitly make the connection in her own book, and though I have never seen them linked in discussions of her work, a case can be made that the sexual contract develops an idea whose nucleus is actually originally to be found in Rousseau's "class contract" of his 1755 *Discourse on the Origin and Foundations of Inequality among Men*, commonly known as *Discourse on Inequality* ([1755] 1997). Seven years before publishing the *Social Contract* ([1762] 1968), Rousseau condemned and set out to explain the *nonnatural* "political" inequalities of class society, which are the result of "a sort of convention," and that consist in "the different Privileges which some enjoy to the prejudice of the others, such as to be more wealthy, more honored, more Powerful than they" ([1755] 1997, 131). He offered a "hypothetical and conditional" (132) history of technological progress in the state of nature, which eventually led to the development of nascent society, private property, growing divisions between rich and poor, and a state of war. In Rousseau's reconstruction, the wealthy, alarmed by this threat to their property and security, promised to the poor new social institutions that pretended to offer justice, peace, and impartial social rules for the mutual benefit of all. But in actuality these institutions "irreversibly destroyed natural freedom, forever fixed the Law of property and inequality, transformed a skillful usurpation into an irrevocable right, and for the profit of a few ambitious men henceforth subjugated the whole of Mankind to labor, servitude and misery" (173).

Rousseau's contract is therefore a bogus contract, contract as scam, which in its uncompromising demystification of the consensual illusions of mainstream contractarianism anticipates by a century Marx's later critique of supposedly egalitarian liberalism as a mask for the differential power of a capitalist ruling class. In the later 1762 *Social Contract* (1968), of course, Rousseau would go on to outline an ideal contract that prescribed how society *should* be founded and what kinds of institutions would, through the "general will," be necessary to achieve genuine political egalitarianism. But in *Discourse on Inequality*, he is describing, if only in a "hypothetical and conditional" sense analogous to a "Physicist" "reasoning" about "the formation of the World" ([1755] 1997, 132) what might *actually* have happened.

The point is, then, that a clear precedent exists in the Western contract tradition for the idea of an exclusionary manipulative contract deployed by the powerful to subordinate others in society under the pretext of including them as equals. Yet whether because of the unacceptable radicalism of the idea; its polar incongruity with a mainstream conception for which, underneath all the variations listed above, a legitimizing consensuality is the crucial common factor; or the brevity of his treatment, Rousseau's first contract is hardly discussed in the secondary literature, whether on contractarianism in general or on Rousseau in particular. It is mentioned, for example, neither in David Boucher and Paul Kelly's (1994a) anthology on social contract theory, nor Christopher Morris's (1999a) anthology, nor Stephen Darwall's (2003) anthology, nor in three encyclopedia essays on the subject (Laslett 1967; Kymlicka 1991; Hampton 1993). Even *The Cambridge Companion to Rousseau* (Riley 2001) devotes only a few paragraphs to it—not an entire essay, nor even a subsection of an essay.

So given this absence of any developed analysis in the literature, it is perhaps less surprising that the distinctive features of Pateman's "contract" should not have been recognized as homologous to Rousseau's, though centered on gender rather than class. I want to suggest that we remedy this deficiency and formally recognize this use of social contract theory as a strategy for theorizing domination within a contractarian framework, since, as I will argue below, it provides a conceptual entry point for importing the concerns and aims of radical democratic political theory into a mainstream apparatus. And since the formal act of naming an entity helps to make it more real for us, incorporating it into our discursive universe, I move that we call it the "domination contract" (Mills 2000).

Finally, the third factor accounting for misinterpretations of Pateman's position is terminological. "Contractarianism" is usually taken in political theory to be coextensive with social contract theory in general, and as such to be a very broad umbrella covering many different variants. In particular, as both Will Kymlicka (1991) and Jean Hampton (1993; 2001) point out, the Hobbesian variety of contract theory, which derives morality from prudence as a conventionalist set of rules for coordinating the constrained advancing of our interests in a social framework, is radically different in its crucial assumptions from the Kantian variety, for which the contract is merely a regulative ideal, and morality inheres in the objective categorical imperative to respect others' personhood. The former kind leads to David Gauthier's *Morals by Agreement* (1986), the latter to John Rawls's *A Theory of Justice* ([1971] 1999), two books obviously quite different in their prescriptions for social justice despite their common contractarian identity. For this reason, some ethicists and political philosophers, such as T. M. Scanlon and Stephen Darwall, think the distinction is so crucial that it needs to be made explicit in our terminology, and they differentiate accordingly between *contractarianism* (the Hobbesian use of the contract idea) and *contractualism* (the Kantian use of the contract idea) (Darwall 2003). In this vocabulary, Rawls would then be a contractualist rather than a contractarian.

Now Pateman (1988) speaks generally about "contract theory" in her opening pages. But it turns out that she is using the term in a restricted sense, for she specifies that "property" is crucial to her argument, though this is not "property in the sense in which 'property' commonly enters into discussions of contract theory," as including material goods and civil freedom. Rather, "The subject of all the contracts with which I am concerned is a very special kind of property, the property that individuals are held to own in their persons" (5). And she goes on to say:

> I shall refer to the [most radical form of contract doctrine], which has its classical expression in Hobbes' theory, as *contractarian* theory or *contractarianism* (in the United States it is usually called libertarianism . . .). . . . For contemporary contractarians . . . social life and relationships not only originate from a social contract but, properly, are seen as an endless series of discrete contracts. . . . From the standpoint of contract, in social life there are contracts all the way down. (14–15)

When Pateman uses the term *contractarianism*, then, it is really this restricted version of contract she has in mind (Hobbesian/libertarian), involving contracts "all the way down," not social contract theory in general.[2] And obviously this would not be an accurate characterization of Kantian contract theory, for which the will is to be determined not by subjective inclination "all the way down" but objective universal moral law, which—the respecting of others as ends in themselves—is supposed to be the normative bedrock of societal interaction. So when she writes that in contract theory "universal freedom" is always "a political fiction," since "contract always generates political right in the form of relations of domination and subordination" (8), one has to remember that this is not supposed to be, as it might seem, a *general* indictment of social contract theory, but only contract in the specific term-of-art sense she has previously stipulated. But for careless readers (among whom, embarrassingly, I include myself [Mills 1997, 136–37n9]) who are interpreting "contract" in the all-inclusive sense, it will seem as if Pateman is issuing a principled rejection of contractarianism *simpliciter.* Moreover, this mistaken interpretation is unfortunately reinforced by the jacket copy on the paperback edition of *The Sexual Contract:* "One of the main targets of the book is those who try to turn contractarian theory to progressive use, and a major thesis of the book is that this is not possible." The portrayal of Pateman in the secondary literature as one of the feminist theorists most resolutely opposed to any attempt to modify social contract theory to advance a feminist agenda, then, arises from this multiply determined misreading of her theoretical claims.

Hampton, Pateman, Okin: Toward a Theoretical Synthesis

What I now want to do is to argue for a version of the sexual contract that does not preclude using "contractarianism" (henceforth in the standard all-inclusive general sense) to address issues of gender justice, and that can be seen as a particular instantiation of the domination contract. So if Pateman (1999) has been insistent—as for example, she was in a 1999 American Political Science Association panel we were on together—that the widespread view of her as anticontractarian in principle is mistaken, then perhaps she will accept this as a possible development of the sexual contract idea for positive normative ends. Since two of the most prominent feminist advocates of social contract theory were the late Jean Hampton and the late Susan Moller Okin, I will try to show that, suitably modified, Pateman's sexual contract is not at all in necessary theoretical opposition to their views, as is conventionally

---

2. This hybrid formulation raises further complications, since property in the person is, of course, famously associated with Locke, not Hobbes, and it is Locke who is centrally invoked by libertarian theorists in the United States. But I will not pursue this issue.

supposed, but can in fact be thought of as *complementing* them, and should indeed be synthesized with them to produce a distinctively feminist contractarianism that is all the more powerful *precisely for* its recognition of the historic (and ongoing) patriarchal restriction of the terms of the contract.

Consider first Jean Hampton. In her essays on contractarianism, Hampton (1990; 1993; 2001) makes a crucial point that will be useful for us in developing the idea of the domination contract. She reminds us that unlike the contemporary Rawlsian contract, which is merely a normative thought-experiment, at least some of the classic contractarians (though not Kant) "intended simultaneously to describe the nature of political societies, and to prescribe a new and more defensible form for such societies" (Hampton 1993, 382). So for them the contract was both descriptive and prescriptive. Moreover, Hampton believes that—suitably attenuated—this descriptive side of the contract should be revived, since once we realize that contract is basically a matter of "imagery," a "picture," we should recognize that it is not vulnerable to standard objections (e.g., that no promises are explicitly exchanged to support governmental structures), as it is essentially just expressing the insight that "authoritative political societies are human creations," "conventionally generated" (379, 382–83).

So the first great virtue of contract theory for Hampton is its capturing of the crucial factual/descriptive truth that society and the polity are human-made—not organic "natural" growths or the product of divine creation. And this insight is, of course, distinctively modern, demarcating the conceptual universe of the modern period from that of antiquity and medievalism, as manifested in Hobbes's ([1651] 1996, 9) famous anti-Aristotelian characterization of the commonwealth as "an Artificiall Man; though of greater stature and strength than the Naturall." Similarly, contemporary commentators such as Michael Walzer (1995, 164) suggest that: "Perhaps the most significant claim of social contract theory is that political society is a human construct . . . and not an organic growth." Banal as it may seem to us now, this insight was revolutionary in its own time, and I will argue below that indeed its full revolutionary significance has yet to be fully appreciated and exploited, since once we understand how far the "construction" extends, we will recognize that it can be shown to apply to gender and race also.

The second important truth is, of course, the one that the contemporary contract *does* focus on: the moral equality of the contracting parties and its normative implications for sociopolitical structures. Here Hobbes is not the appropriate representative figure since, as noted above (Kymlicka 1991; Hampton 1993, 2001; Darwall 2003), commentators standardly point out that the Hobbesian contract, rooted in the rough physical and mental (rather than moral) equality of the contractors in the state of nature, leads to rational prudence rather than the altruistic regard for others for their own sake, as beings of intrinsic moral worth, that we associate with Kant. Thus, in the most famous contemporary version of the moral contract, John Rawls's ([1971] 1999, 10) thought-experiment to determine what "the principles that free and rational persons concerned to further their own interests would accept in an initial position of equality as defining the fundamental terms of their association," this scenario is not set up to be a process of *bargaining*, but rather, through the veil of ignorance, the modeling of an impartial other-regardingness.

Now it should be obvious that in this weak and minimal sense—contract as committed to society's being a human construct created by morally equal contractors whose interests should be given equal weight in the sociopolitical institutions thereby established—there is nothing that anybody, including those wishing to theorize gender and racial subordination, should find objectionable about contractarianism. Certainly it is not the case that feminists and critical race theorists want to argue, on the contrary, that sociopolitical institutions *are* natural rather than humanly created or that some humans *are* morally superior to others. At this highly abstract level of characterization, social contract theory is unexceptionable.

The problem really inheres, I suggest, in the assumptions that begin to be incorporated, the conceptual infrastructure that begins to be installed, at a *lower* level of abstraction, and the ways in which, whether explicitly or tacitly, they both vitiate the accuracy of the descriptive mapping, obfuscate crucial social realities, embed a certain conceptual partitioning (e.g., the private/public distinction), and thereby undercut the transformative normative egalitarian potential of the apparatus. So my claim is that our critical attention should really be directed at these "thicker" auxiliary shaping assumptions rather than the "thin" idea of the contract itself (in the minimal sense sketched above).

To begin with, on the factual/descriptive side, while it is true that society and the state are human creations, it is obviously false, as mainstream contractarianism classically implies, that all (adult) humans are equal contractors, have equal causal input into this process of creation, and freely give informed consent to the structures and institutions thereby established. The repudiation of this picture was, of course, the whole point of Rousseau's critique in his depiction of what could be termed the "class contract." The wealthy have differential power, and they manipulate the rest of the population into accepting sociopolitical arrangements to which they would not actually consent were they aware of their real consequences. So the human equality of the state of nature becomes the unnatural "political" inequality of a class society ruled by the rich. But this plutocratic polity is not to be thought of as the outcome of free and informed choice among symmetrically positioned individuals, but rather as the outcome of the collusion amongst themselves of *a social group* with far greater influence who have their own self-seeking agenda. The real "contractors" (in the sense of those who are controlling things and know what is going on) are the rich. Similarly, in Pateman's sexual contract and my racial contract, men and whites, through a mixture of force and ideology, subordinate women and people of color under the banner of a supposedly consensual contract. So the latter are the victims, the objects, of the resulting "contract" rather than subjects, freely contracting parties, and are oppressed by the resulting sociopolitical institutions.

But note that there is not the least inconsistency between pointing out these usually unacknowledged facts of class, gender, and racial subordination and continuing to affirm the "weak" (arguably defining) contractarian assertion of a humanly created society and polity. Contractarianism in *this* minimal sense is not refuted by the actual history of social oppression and political exclusion since it is still true that it is humans who have been responsible for this history. The problem is that the *actual* "contracts" and their agents have been quite different from how they have been represented in the mainstream literature. But far from the subordinated being motivated as a result to want to *deny* the role of human agency in creating the resulting polity, surely this is all the more reason for them to want to affirm, indeed insist upon it! Class society, patriarchy, and white supremacy come into being not "naturally" but as the result of collective human causality—in which, however, some humans have a far greater causal role than others, and subsequently benefit far more from the sociopolitical and economic institutions thereby established. The social contract in its guise as the domination contract captures these crucial "descriptive" realities while simultaneously, by emphasizing their "artificial" genesis, bringing them across the conceptual border from the realm of the natural into the realm of the political. Class society, patriarchy, and white supremacy are themselves "unnatural," and are just as "political" and oppressive as the (formally and overtly political) white male absolutist rule, predicated on white male hierarchy and moral inequality, that is the exclusive target of mainstream contractarians, and which the contract apparatus prescribes abolishing.

Similarly, on the normative/prescriptive side, the problem is obviously not that moral egalitarianism among humans is an unattractive moral ideal, but rather that in these actual contracts moral egalitarianism was never realized. Pateman (1988) and numerous other feminist theorists over the past three decades (Clark and Lange 1979; Okin 1992; Pateman and Gross 1997) have documented the ways in which women have been seen as unequal by virtually all the male theorists of the classic canon, including (with the qualified and ambiguous exception of Hobbes) the very contractarians who, as paradigmatic theorists of modernity, so loudly proclaimed human equality as their foundational assumption. Moreover, this inequality has been manifest in their drawing of the public/private distinction, their conceptions of marriage, and their view of the appropriate place of women in the sociopolitical institutions supposedly "contractually" established. Though the literature on race is less extensive, a comparable body of work is now emerging (Goldberg 1993; Outlaw 1996; Mills 1997; Mehta 1999; Valls 2005). It argues similarly that people of color have generally been excluded from equal status in liberal thought, and have been seen (in my phrase) as "sub-persons" rather than full persons, thereby justifying their subordination in the various racialized sociopolitical structures—Native American and Australian expropriation, African slavery, Third World colonization—imposed on non-Europeans by Europe in the modern epoch.

But obviously neither feminists nor critical race theorists are seeking to reject moral egalitarianism as such. Rather, their complaint is that this egalitarianism has been *denied* to women and nonwhites both in theory and in practice, and that—at least for those of us still sympathetic to contractarianism—a genuinely inclusive "contract" would need to recognize this legacy and prescribe appropriate corrective and transformational measures in the light of its historic injustice.

The real source of the problem should now have emerged clearly. The mainstream story of the contract builds on top of, or conflates with, the eminently reasonable *minimal* assumptions of human sociopolitical agency and human egalitarianism an *additional* set of assumptions that are quite false, radically untrue to the historical record. Only some humans had effective causal input; only some humans had their moral equality recognized. In this fashion, it completely mystifies the creation (in the ongoing rather than *ab initio* sense) of society, denying or obfuscating the various structures of domination that are either transformed (class, gender), or that come into existence (race), in the modern period. Thus when Christopher Morris (1999b, x), in his introduction to his social contract anthology, writes: "There may, however, be some explanatory import to the idea of states of nature and social contracts that should not be overlooked. . . . our political institutions and arrangements are, in some sense, our creations," the obvious and classic retort is: Just who are "we"? ("What do you mean *we,* white man?") Did women create patriarchy? Did nonwhites create white supremacy? Obviously not—these "political institutions and arrangements" were created by *some* humans, not all. By its undifferentiated individualism, by its failure to advert to the existence of, and need to eliminate, "political institutions and arrangements" of group domination, the mainstream version of the contract sabotages the radical potential of the apparatus.

And it is here, I would suggest, that Hampton's contract theory becomes deficient and needs supplementation. Normatively, Hampton (2001) endorses a feminist Kantian contractarianism based on the intrinsic worth of all persons (as part, though not all, of a comprehensive ethic). Moreover, as noted at the start, she also argues for the revival of the descriptive dimension of contract theory. This proposal is in keeping with her emphasis elsewhere, for example in her book on political philosophy (Hampton 1997, xiii–xv), that the subject should not be thought of as purely normative, but as extending to factual issues as well. The political philosopher, Hampton argues, should seek to understand the "political and social 'deep structure' which generates not only forms of interaction that make certain kinds of distributions [of resources] inevitable but also moral theories that justify those distributions." But she never brings these insights together, in the sense of asking how the revived descriptive contractarianism she advocates would need to be rethought in the light of sexist exclusions, or how the descriptive and the normative sides of the contract would now need to be related given patriarchy as a "deep structure" with such a fundamental shaping influence on society (including, reflexively, the very contractarian moral theories generated about its founding). Instead, like Morris, she speaks of "political societies as conventionally-generated human creations" (Hampton 1993, 383) and, without asking who these "humans" and these "people" are, glosses the contractarian claim as equivalent to the assertion that "Certain institutions, practices and rules become conventionally entrenched (in a variety of ways) in a social system, and in so far as the people continue to support them, these conventions continue to prevail, and thus comprise the political and legal system in the country" (382).

Despite her feminism, then, Hampton does not press the further question of how we should think of this supposedly contract-equivalent "support" once the gender subordination of half the population is taken into account. Pateman's *sexual* contract fills this theoretical gap, making clear that a "contract" of gender domination would more accurately illuminate than the mainstream version not merely the "deep structure" of a society based on patriarchy, but also its justificatory moral theories and how they become "conventionally entrenched." We would then be better positioned theoretically not merely to apply, in a gender-inclusive way, the Kantian contractarianism Hampton endorses, but to understand, on the metatheoretical level, why its previous (male) application has been so systematically and structurally, not just contingently, exclusionary. For we would then be in a position to recognize gender *itself* as a political system established by the contract, and prescribing accordingly its own ground rules about the cartography of the social and the appropriate distribution of rights, privileges, and freedoms in the polity.[3]

The relation between the normative contract and the descriptive aspects of the contract is thus necessarily more complicated in this revisionist contract theory than it is in mainstream contractarianism. In the mainstream contract, a (supposedly) consensual founding establishes an egalitarian moral code. But once this contract is unmasked as really a contract of domination, this code itself needs to become an object of scrutiny for us. Under cover of egalitarianism, the domination contract generates norms, and stipulations about how to apply these norms, that will themselves reinforce domination, and so which need to be interrogated by those seeking to end their subordination by the contract. A greater degree of reflexivity, of self-conscious metatheoretical distancing from and questioning of concepts and values, is therefore required, insofar as the new normative contract has to take account of realities ignored or misdescribed by the terms of the old normative contract—certainly in its original form, but also later, even when nominally updated and purged of its original sexism and racism.

For even when the contemporary contract seems to drop the descriptive dimension, as in Rawls's thought-experiment, it continues tacitly to manifest itself, if only by default, in an underlying factual picture, a version of history, and a set of assumptions about society that continue to reproduce the inequi-

---

3. By contrast, Hampton's (2001, 352) apparent naivety about Kant is well illustrated when she writes at one point: "Kant also has opponents who, while agreeing that our value is noninstrumental and objective, reject the idea that all humans are of equal value—for example, those who think human beings of a certain gender or race or caste are higher in value (and so deserving of better treatment) than those of a different gender, race, or caste." But of course *Kant himself* was a notorious sexist and racist, for whom women could only be "passive citizens," while blacks and Native Americans were "natural slaves." (See Eze 1995; Schröder 1997; Bernasconi 2001; 2002.) The concepts of the sexual and racial contracts enable us to understand how these seemingly contradictory commitments are reconcilable, not merely in Kant but in most other thinkers of the period, through the workings of white male moral psychologies and moral boundaries created by the exclusionary "particularistic universalism" of the domination contract.

ties and obfuscations of the historic contract, and, correspondingly, an apparatus that retains many of its deficiencies. The famous early feminist critique of Rawls was, of course, that knowledge of gender was not one of the things listed as being stripped from us behind the veil. Nor was there any awareness, in the "general" social and historical facts we take with us there, of the historic subordination of half the human race—surely "general" enough to have made the cut! By assuming heads of households as the representative contractors, by taking the family as ideal, by not challenging the role of the public/private distinction, Rawls naturalized the family in the same way the classic contractarians did.

Consider now the reclamatory work of Susan Moller Okin (1989). Okin's insight was to recognize that Rawls's moral contractarian apparatus had the potential to go beyond Rawls's own conclusions, once we admit a "veiled" knowledge of crucial nonideal facts on gender:

> There is strikingly little indication, throughout most of *A Theory of Justice*, that the modern liberal society to which the principles of justice are to be applied is deeply and pervasively gender-structured. Thus an ambiguity runs throughout the work. . . . On the one hand, as I shall argue, a consistent and wholehearted application of Rawls's liberal principles of justice can lead us to challenge fundamentally the gender system of our society. On the other hand, in his own account of his theory, this challenge is barely hinted at, much less developed. . . . [This] potential critique of gender-structured social institutions . . . can be developed by taking seriously the fact that those formulating the principles of justice do not know their sex [behind the veil]. (89, 105)

Okin thus seeks to appropriate the contract for feminism, and in the closing chapter of her book shows how such a critique of a gender-structured social order can be developed from behind the veil. Correspondingly, in her review essay (1990) on *The Sexual Contract*, she criticizes Pateman for rejecting in principle (as Okin sees it) the attempt "to employ contractual thinking in the service of feminism" (659). But we can now appreciate that there need be no principled opposition at all between their two approaches once we recognize that they are engaged in different tasks, with Pateman's view of the contract as intrinsically subordinating paradigmatically meant as a specific characterization of the Hobbesian/proprietarian contract in particular. Okin's skepticism about the sexual contract idea—"it is not clear to me what we gain in understanding by tracing [the forms of patriarchal power] to a supposed contract made by men" (660)—misses the value of a theoretical innovation that can provide the very knowledge behind the veil that Rawls's idealized contractarianism avoids. The gender-structured social institutions Okin cites are precisely what are summarized in Pateman's nonideal contract: the sexual contract. So we can bring them together under a division of conceptual labor in a *common* enterprise: Pateman doing the actual nonideal contract, Okin doing the normative contract. As emphasized, the relation between the descriptive and normative sides of the contract becomes radically different once the descriptive contract is acknowledged to be a domination contract. For as a "contractor" in the original position, one is now making a prudential choice informed by the possibility of ending up female in a society structured by the sexual contract. Gender subordination in its manifold dimensions and institutions can thus become the object of normative critique, since these "general facts" are not ignored as in the mainstream contract. The full ramifications of patriarchy not just for the family but society in general (the state, the legal system, the differential status of men and women), as well as typical male moral psychology and dominant androcentric ideology, can all now legitimately be considered within a "contractual" framework.

In this fashion, I claim, we could bring together the crucial insights of Hampton, Pateman, and Okin to produce a feminist contractarianism stronger than any of them individually: Hampton's *moral* Kantian contractarianism, informed behind the veil by Pateman's *factual* Rousseauean contract, synthesized so as to generate an expanded variant of Okin's *nonideal* version of Rawlsian contractarianism, all deployed to achieve gender justice. From Hampton, the idea of contract as a descriptive metaphor capturing the key insight of society as a human creation, and the normative endorsement of Kantian contractarianism. From Pateman, the idea that the actual (factual) contract is an exclusionary sexual contract, not a gender-inclusive one, that incorporates assumptions of female inequality and inferiority, thereby shaping both society and, reflexively, our ideas about society. From Okin, the idea that a feminist agenda on justice can nonetheless still be promoted in a contractarian framework by imagining oneself behind Rawls's veil with knowledge of these nonideal gender realities. So if in the mainstream contract the circumstances of the creation of the sociopolitical imply the moral endorsement of the institutions thereby created, in the radical use of the domination contract, this is inverted. The characterization of the descriptive contract here serves to alert us to the structures of institutional oppression, which need to be dismantled.

The Domination Contract

Let me now turn to a more detailed account of the contrast between these two contracts, and the ways I think progressives can use the domination contract to address issues of gender justice, and social justice more generally. Consider the following table, which summarizes what I see as the crucial differences:

MAINSTREAM CONTRACT	DOMINATION CONTRACT
Ethical Framework	
Ideal theory	Nonideal theory
Starting Point	
Ground zero (state of nature, original position)	Unjust stage of society
Role in History	
None presupposed	Historical account presupposed
Basic Agents	
People as pre-social atomic individuals	People as members of social groups in relations of domination and subordination
Status Norm in Society	
Equality (ostensibly)	Inequality (explicitly)
Economic Transactions	
Typically mutually beneficial	Typically exploitative
Juridico-Political Sphere	
Egalitarian	Biased toward dominant groups
Human Divisions	
Class, race, and gender as natural	Class, race, and gender as artificial
Human Psychology	
Basically imported from nature	Fundamentally transformed by society (*amour de soi* → *amour propre*)
Obstacles to Accurate Social Cognition	
Individual bias, "passions," "inclination," short-term self-interest	Dominant-group interests, dominant-group ideation

Locus of Problems

Human nature   Corrupting social institutions

Goal of Contract

To create a just society (laws,   To reinforce and codify unjust
government, etc.)   institutions

Heuristic Purpose for Us

Readers' endorsement of the contract as   Readers' condemnation of the contract,
creating an ideally just society   and corresponding awakening to
                                           systematic social injustice and the need
                                           for appropriate corrective measures to
                                           realize a just society

The key points are as follows:

(i) The overarching framework is nonideal theory. In the historic version of the mainstream contract, conceived of (though falsely) as consensual and inclusive, the circumstances of the polity's founding are supposed to confer on it a positive normative status. As such, the mainstream contract assumes ideal circumstances: society and government are brought into existence in a way that is fair, respecting the rights of those involved. By contrast, we know perfectly well from history that oppression of one kind or another has been the social norm since humanity left the hunting-and-gathering stage. The domination contract begins from this simple reality. Though the contemporary Rawlsian contract drops any historical claims, it nonetheless inherits this orientation in that Rawls sets out to ask what principles people *would* choose in ideally just circumstances. Thus he makes clear throughout the book that his contract is an exercise in ideal theory, intended to work out "the principles of justice . . . defining a perfectly just society, given favorable conditions," and presuming "strict compliance" ([1971] 1999, 308–9). However, he claims that this starting-point is ultimately intended to illuminate the nonideal: "If ideal theory is worthy of study, it must be because, as I have conjectured, it is the fundamental part of the theory of justice and essential for the nonideal part as well" (343).

But a case can be made that, however well-intentioned, such a starting-point handicaps his enterprise, and certainly the manifest failure in his own work, and in the thousands of articles it has inspired over the last thirty-plus years, to apply his theory to the "nonideal" realities of gender and race does not encourage confidence in it. By definition, problems arise in nonideal theory that do not arise in ideal theory, and one will need mapping concepts and data sets that are not readily extrapolatable from those of ideal theory. So it raises the question of how useful, let alone "essential," it actually is. The mainstream contract—unsurprisingly given its conceptual ancestry—tends to abstract away from issues of social subordination, since historically it is really predicated on the experience of the bourgeois white male subject, that subsection of the population emancipated by modernity. By contrast, the revisionist contract, through utilizing the device of the domination contract, makes such issues its primary focus, since (following Rousseau) it starts not from the state of nature but from an *already-existing* unjust society, and then asks what measures of justice would be necessary to correct for them.

At the very least, then, Rawlsian ideal theory needs to be informed by the nonideal. As just pointed out, to the extent that Rawls's method has been found useful in theorizing gender justice, most notably in Okin's (1989) work, it has been precisely through the *repudiation* of the key Rawlsian assumption of the ideal nature of the family, as a supposed paradigm of human interaction to be sharply contrasted with the interaction of strangers, and thus not requiring justice to regulate it. The disadvantaging of female children and women is only able to appear on the conceptual radar screen through the rethinking of the public/private boundary, and the unsentimental scrutiny of the actual, real-life family. In the case of racial justice, the nonideal looms even more definitively, since measures of compensatory justice (affirmative action, reparations) presume by definition the need to correct for a history of *injustice* that Rawls's ideal-theory focus avoids (Pateman and Mills 2007, chap. 4). In other words, ideally, behind the veil, one would not choose a white-supremacist society, since one would not know whether one was white or not. But this does not help us in determining—given the historic fact of white supremacy—what compensatory measures justice demands of us now. It is noteworthy that while in *The Cambridge Companion to Rawls* (Freeman 2003) there is at least a chapter by Martha Nussbaum (2003) called "Rawls and Feminism," there is no comparable chapter—indeed no section in *any* chapter—on race. And apart from the fact that the whiteness of the profession is even more overwhelming than its maleness, apart from the fact that most white political theorists, whether political scientists or political philosophers, take for granted what Rogers Smith (1997) describes as the misleading "anomaly" view of American racism, the role of the ideal-theory framework itself must surely be a major contributory factor to this pattern of systematic omission and evasion. What has supposedly been intended to facilitate discussion of the remediation of injustice has served instead to obstruct it.

(ii) Relatedly, the domination contract is necessarily *historical*. Though contemporary poststructuralism is something of an exception, radical political theory, whether of class, gender, or race, traditionally emphasizes the importance of investigating the real history that has brought us to this point, and that explains who the political players are and what are their agendas. Thus it seeks to contest both mystified histories and ahistorical naturalized accounts that deny *any* history, which simply sever the present from the past. Marx (to cite a very unfashionable figure) was famous for excoriating liberals and those he dubbed the "vulgar" economists for their timeless and decontextualized portrayal of the "free exchange" between capitalist and worker, without attention to the sequence of events (for example, the enclosures in Britain) that had reduced people who had previously been able to make a living from the land to workers with only their labor-power to sell. In the radical use of contract he pioneers, Rousseau establishes the precedent by giving an alternative narrative—naïve by our standards, but expressing underlying truths nonetheless—of the origins of class inequality. Similarly, Pateman offers a conjectural account of the origins of patriarchy, while I—comparatively advantaged by the fact that European expansionism takes place in the modern period, accompanied by massive documentation—was able to draw on actual events in describing how global white supremacy was established. But in all three cases, the crucial point is that the nonideal structure of domination in question, whether of class, gender, or race, is not "natural," not the outcome of the state of nature, but a sociohistorical product. The greater realism of radical contractarianism as against mainstream contractarianism is manifested in its recognition that the "contract" is really (à la Hampton) a way of talking about the human creation of sociopolitical institutions as the result of previous sociohistorical processes, not ex nihilo from the state of nature.

(iii) And this history is, of course, one of group domination and subordination rather than the classically individualist social ontology, and of transactions among equal individuals, of the mainstream contract. The general facts of history and society that people take behind Rawls's veil apparently do not include the subordination of women or the subordination of nonwhites. (There is, of course, some sensitivity to class issues.) But we are certainly not bound by Rawls's ignorance. What makes radical contractarianism better suited to make use of the device of the veil is its demystified, nonidealized view of recent human history as largely a history of social oppression, so that groups in interlocking patterns of domination constitute the real social ontology. The class, sexual, and racial contracts each capture particular aspects of social domination (while missing others), so that, whether singly or (ideally) in combination, they register the obvious fact that society is shaped by the powerful acting together, not individuals acting singly.

As such, the domination contract, which makes groups the key players, is obviously truer to the actual history of the world. If, as argued at the start, contractarianism in the minimal sense does not specify who the crucial human actors are that create the sociopolitical, then a group-based contractarianism is not a contradiction in terms, and we should embrace it as a more useful philosophical concept for political theory. While it may be an interesting intellectual exercise to work out just how Hobbesian individuals would be able to self-interestedly come together to create Leviathan, this conundrum sheds so little light on the actual history of humanity that it is an exercise largely without point outside of very restricted circumstances, and so—if not to be abandoned altogether—is surely not deserving of the huge amount of attention it has received in the secondary literature. The descriptive side of the contract is more accurately represented in the domination contract, and is certainly vastly more illuminating as a conceptual framework for orienting the normative contract, since it points us toward the really important moral issues, namely, how do we dismantle these structures so as to achieve genuine egalitarianism? With such knowledge behind the veil, Rawlsian contractors would not be able to ignore gender and racial subordination as they currently do.

As a corollary, in understanding human motivation, one needs to take account of people's group membership, and how, whether as privileged or subordinated, it shapes their psychology and their cognition. Rousseau's famous critique of his contractarian predecessors was that they attributed to natural man what was really the psychology of civil man. A healthy *amour de soi* had been corrupted into an unhealthy *amour propre*, which contractarians like Hobbes, not recognizing its social genesis, then took to be part of the human condition as such. Similarly, in Marx's critique of a specifically bourgeois vision of *homo economicus*, in feminist theorists' work on the production of "male" and "female" traits by gendered parental upbringing, in critical race theorists' analyses of "whiteness" and its influence on its possessors, the conceptual door is opened to a much richer set of resources for theorizing actual human motivation and its social shaping than in the impoverished psychological framework of mainstream contractarianism.

(iv) The relation between equality as a value and the contract also needs to be rethought. The mainstream contract is, of course, famous for its nominal egalitarianism, its emphasis that in the state of nature all men are equal, whether in physical and mental abilities, as in Hobbes, or in moral status, as in Locke and Kant. And this equality is then supposed to translate itself (in the societies created by these equal men) into a juridico-political equality, equality before the law and equality of citizenship, and in economic (and other) transactions that are nonexploitative in nature.

But however attractive this may be as an ideal, it obviously bears no correspondence with real life for the majority of the population, even in the modern period. Rousseau's concern is that the artificial class inequalities of society undermine this moral equality, and in Marx's more sophisticated treatment, this is elaborated into the point that formal equality at the level of the relations of exchange is substantively undercut by economic compulsion at the level of the relations of production. But for gender and race, the situation is even worse. As feminists have long documented, in the case of gender the "equality" was originally not even nominal, let alone substantive, since with the qualified exception of Hobbes, all the classic contractarians saw women as inferior to men, and so as appropriately to be regulated by male authority. Moreover, this theoretical inferiority was, of course, also manifest practically, in real life, in legal and political institutions. So the value that is perhaps most intimately associated with the social contract tradition—equality—was not at all meant to be extended to half the human race. Likewise, as various theorists of race and imperialism have pointed out, once one examines the representations ("savages," "barbarians") and the experiences of people of color in the modern period—expropriated and exterminated Native Americans and Australians, enslaved and later Jim-Crowed blacks, colonized Third Worlders—it becomes clear that both in theory and in practice, only white men were equal. Not merely as a matter of fact, but as a matter of proclaimed moral and legal norms, nonwhites had a schedule of rights that was inferior to nonexistent— and were thus non- or at best second-class citizens. How, then, can it make sense to conceptualize society as if, in the modern period, equality becomes the generally accepted norm, when in fact such a small section of the population was actually seen as equal?

In the domination contract, by contrast, this reality is frankly faced: *inequality* is the actual social norm obtaining for the majority. The evasive conceptual assimilation of the status of white women and nonwhites to the status of white men that is embedded in the mainstream contract, thereby burying the distinctive problems the former groups face, is thus precluded. Correspondingly, the radical contract recognizes that the crucial juridico-political institutions are not egalitarian in their functioning either, but biased in various ways by class, gender, and racial privilege. The huge body of literature standardly ignored by contractarians—the original left analyses of the workings of the state in capitalist society, the more recent work on the gendered and racial state (MacKinnon 1989; Marx 1998; Goldberg 2002), as well as all the biases in the legal system—can then legitimately enter here, rather than being conceptually blocked by the otherworldly and completely fanciful pictures of a neutral juridico-political realm assumed by mainstream contractarianism. And far from fair and reciprocal advantage being the norm—Rawls suggests, absurdly, that we think of society as *actually* "a cooperative venture for mutual advantage" ([1971] 1999, 4)—exploitation of various kinds—of class, gender, and race—is the norm (Sample 2003). Accordingly, one of the main aims of the normative contract will be the elimination of these structures of exploitation—unequal chances for the poor and working class, sexual exploitation, differential white advantage and corresponding wealth (Barry 1984; Oliver and Shapiro 1995; Shipler 2004)—that the individualist perspective of mainstream contractarianism tends to obfuscate.[4] In addition, the group interests of the privileged, and their resulting desire to maintain their privilege, will become both a material obstacle to progressive change and an ideational obstacle to achieving social transparency, which will need to be taken into account in theorizing the dynamics of social cognition and the possibilities for social transformation. So again, one will be equipped with a far more sophisticated and realistic view of the workings of the polity and its dominant illusory self-conceptions than in the mainstream contract.

(v) Finally, apart from (I would claim) all of these obvious merits, the domination contract has the great and overwhelming virtue of conceptualizing class, gender, and race *as themselves artificial*, not natural as in the mainstream contract. So it is not merely that society is seen as a complex of groups in dominance and subordination, but that the formation of the groups *themselves* is a product of the contract(s). The familiar claim of recent radical democratic theory that gender and race are "constructed"—not just the systems (patriarchy, white supremacy) organized around them, but what we take to be gender and race themselves—is thus perfectly accommodated.

Rousseau deserves the credit for this too, though, as noted, the lack of discussion in the secondary literature of his class contract, and his own notorious sexism, means that he has not been fully recognized for it. As emphasized at the start, the social contract as it comes into its own in the modern period emphasizes the "artificiality" of society and the polity. These are human-made, not organic growths as in the discourse of antiquity, and the descriptive side of the contract expresses that insight. But Rousseau goes a startlingly radical step further: he suggests that in a sense humans themselves are artificial,

---

4. Rawls's left-liberal, social democratic contract is, of course, good on class—that is its main strength, from a radical point of view—though even here some on the political left argue that it did not go far enough and was unrealistic or evasive about the implications for political power and people's social status of the economic inequalities it left intact. See, for example, Peffer (1990).

human-created products. What to his predecessors were "natural" divisions of class he sees as a result of domination and convention. Extended to gender and race, this gives us the sexual and racial contracts, which in a dialectical relationship both consolidate in an oppositional relationship with one another the entities of men and women, whites and nonwhites, and create these groups themselves. So the (bad) contractual transformation of the nonideal descriptive domination contract is far more thoroughgoing than in the mainstream descriptive contract: it is social institutions that form and corrupt us. And the implications for the (good) contractual transformation envisaged in the ideal prescriptive contract are, correspondingly, far more sweeping than in the mainstream version, since radical contractarianism then points us toward the necessity not merely of dismantling these structures of domination, but *the contractors themselves* as intrinsically gendered and raced beings. As Marx envisaged a classless society, so the sexual and racial contracts, emphasizing the constructed nature of gender and race, open up for us the possibility and desirability of a genderless and raceless society.

Appropriating the Contract

My recommendation, then, is that we—egalitarians, feminists, critical race theorists, and all progressives in political theory concerned about real social justice issues—work toward a paradigm shift in contractarian theory, not conceding the contract to mainstream theorists, but seeking to appropriate it and turn it to emancipatory ends. Recall Kymlicka's observation (1991, 196) that contract is really just a "*device* which many different traditions have used for many different reasons." Rawls ([1971] 1999, 19), similarly, sometimes refers to his updating of the contract (the veil, the original position) as an "expository device." So given this essentially instrumental identity of the contract, there is no principled barrier to developing it in a radical way: the domination contract as an "expository device" for nonideal theory. Once one recognizes how protean the contract has historically been, and how politically pivotal is its insight of the human creation of society and of ourselves *as* social beings, one should be able to appreciate that its conservative deployment is a result not of its intrinsic features, but of its use by a privileged white male group hegemonic in political theory who have had no motivation to extrapolate its logic. Far from being a necessarily bourgeois or necessarily sexist or necessarily racist apparatus, contractarianism has a radical potential barely tapped, and can serve as a vehicle for translating into conventional discourse most, if not all, of the crucial claims of radical democratic political theory.

The key conceptual move is to strip away the assumptions and corresponding conceptual infrastructure of an individualism once restricted to bourgeois white males and still shaping the contract's features today, and replace it with an ontology of groups (Young 1990). Rousseau's class contract, Pateman's sexual contract, my racial contract (ideally, at some future stage, combined, of course—see for example Pauline Schloesser's [2002] work on "racial patriarchy"), can all then be conceptualized as still being within the contractarian tradition in the minimal defining sense outlined above, viz, the assertion of, indeed insistence upon, the historic role of human causality in shaping the polity and the commitment to the substantive realization of moral egalitarianism in its necessary transformation. By contrast, the assumptions of the mainstream contract in its contemporary form, presuming universal inclusion and general input, handicap the apparatus in tackling the necessary task of corrective justice by, in a sense, assuming the very thing that needs to be substantively achieved. Once one adds women of all races, and male people of color (to say nothing of the white male working class), one is actually talking about the *majority* of the population's being excluded in one way or another from the historical contract, and its present descendant! A theoretical device whose classic pretensions are to represent universal sociopolitical inclusion actually captures the experience of just a minority of the population. Inequality is not the *exception* but the *norm* in modern societies.

Far from the "domination contract" representing "minority" concerns, it actually provides an accurate depiction of the situation for the majority. And far from being anti-Enlightenment, it has a much better claim to be carrying on the Enlightenment legacy. Getting the facts right is supposed to be an essential part of the Enlightenment mission, and in its mystified picture of the origins and workings of modern polities, mainstream contractarianism certainly does not do that. And if the Enlightenment is supposed to be committed to moral egalitarianism and a transformation of society to realize this imperative, then ignoring the ways in which class, gender, and race void nominal egalitarianism of real substance is hardly the way to achieve such equality. Through the more accurate mapping of the domination version of the descriptive contract, the emancipatory reach of the egalitarianism of the prescriptive contract can then gain its full leveling scope rather than being, as at present, effectively confined to achieving the freedom and equality of a few.

In sum, a case can be made that radical contractarianism, which deploys the domination contract as its descriptive mapping device, is, far from being a theoretical usurper, the *true heir* to the social contract tradition at its best, and it is mainstream contractarianism that has betrayed its promise. If war is too important to be left to the generals, one could say that social contract theory is too important to be left to the contractarians. We should reclaim it.

References

Barry, Kathleen. 1984. *Female Sexual Slavery.* New York: New York University Press.

Bernasconi, Robert. 2001. "Who Invented the Concept of Race? Kant's Role in the Enlightenment Construction of Race." In *Race,* edited by Robert Bernasconi, 11–36. Malden, Mass.: Blackwell.

———. 2002. "Kant as an Unfamiliar Source of Racism." In *Philosophers on Race: Critical Essays,* edited by Julie K. Ward and Tommy L. Lott, 145–66. Malden, Mass.: Blackwell.

Boucher, David, and Paul Kelly, eds. 1994a. *The Social Contract from Hobbes to Rawls.* New York: Routledge.

———. 1994b. "The Social Contract and Its Critics: An Overview." In *The Social Contract from Hobbes to Rawls,* edited by David Boucher and Paul Kelly, 1–34. New York: Routledge.

Clark, Lorenne M. G., and Lynda Lange, eds. 1979. *The Sexism of Social and Political Theory: Women and Reproduction from Plato to Nietzsche.* Toronto: University of Toronto Press.

Darwall, Stephen, ed. 2003. *Contractarianism/Contractualism.* Malden, Mass.: Blackwell.

Eze, Emmanuel Chukwudi. 1995. "The Color of Reason: The Idea of 'Race' in Kant's Anthropology." In *Postcolonial African Philosophy: A Critical Reader,* edited by Emmanuel Chukwudi Eze, 103–40. Cambridge, Mass: Blackwell.

Freeman, Samuel, ed. 2003. *The Cambridge Companion to Rawls.* New York: Cambridge University Press.

Gauthier, David P. 1986. *Morals by Agreement.* Oxford: Clarendon Press.

Goldberg, David Theo. 1993. *Racist Culture: Philosophy and the Politics of Meaning.* Cambridge, Mass.: Blackwell.

———. 2002. *The Racial State.* Malden, Mass.: Blackwell.

Hampton, Jean. 1990. "The Contractarian Explanation of the State." In *Midwest Studies in Philosophy: The Philosophy of the Human Sciences,* edited by Peter A. French, Theodore E. Uehling, Jr., and Howard K. Wettstein, 344–71. Notre Dame, Ind.: University of Notre Dame Press.

———. 1993. "Contract and Consent." In *A Companion to Contemporary Polit-*

ical Philosophy, edited by Robert E. Goodin and Philip Pettit, 379–93. Cambridge, Mass.: Blackwell.

———. 1997. *Political Philosophy*. Boulder, Colo.: Westview Press.

———. 2001. "Feminist Contractarianism." In *A Mind of One's Own: Feminist Essays on Reason and Objectivity*, edited by Louise M. Antony and Charlotte E. Witt, 337–68. 1993; rev. 2nd ed. Boulder, Colo.: Westview Press.

Hobbes, Thomas. [1651] 1996. *Leviathan*. Ed. Richard Tuck. 1991; rev. student ed. New York: Cambridge University Press.

Kymlicka, Will. 1991. "The Social Contract Tradition." In *A Companion to Ethics*, edited by Peter Singer, 186–96. Cambridge, Mass.: Blackwell Reference.

Laslett, Peter. 1967. "Social Contract." In *The Encyclopedia of Philosophy*, edited by Paul Edwards, 7:465–67. New York: Macmillan Publishing Co. and The Free Press.

MacKinnon, Catharine A. 1989. *Toward a Feminist Theory of the State*. Cambridge, Mass.: Harvard University Press.

Marx, Anthony W. 1998. *Making Race and Nation: A Comparison of the United States, South Africa, and Brazil*. New York: Cambridge University Press.

Mehta, Uday Singh. 1999. *Liberalism and Empire: A Study in Nineteenth-Century British Liberal Thought*. Chicago: University of Chicago Press.

Mills, Charles W. 1997. *The Racial Contract*. Ithaca: Cornell University Press.

———. 2000. "Race and the Social Contract Tradition." *Social Identities* 6:441–62.

Morris, Christopher, ed. 1999a. *The Social Contract Theorists: Critical Essays on Hobbes, Locke, and Rousseau*. Lanham, Md.: Rowman and Littlefield.

———. 1999b. Introduction to *The Social Contract Theorists: Critical Essays on Hobbes, Locke, and Rousseau*, edited by Christopher Morris, ix–xi. Lanham, Md.: Rowman and Littlefield.

Nussbaum, Martha. 2003. "Rawls and Feminism." In *The Cambridge Companion to Rawls*, edited by Samuel Freeman, 488–520. New York: Cambridge University Press.

Okin, Susan Moller. 1989. *Justice, Gender, and the Family*. New York: Basic Books.

———. 1990. "Feminism, the Individual, and Contract Theory." *Ethics* 100:658–69.

———. 1992. *Women in Western Political Thought*. 1979; Princeton: Princeton University Press.

Oliver, Melvin L., and Thomas M. Shapiro. 1995. *Black Wealth/White Wealth: A New Perspective on Racial Inequality*. New York: Routledge.

Outlaw, Lucius, Jr. 1996. *On Race and Philosophy*. New York: Routledge.

Pateman, Carole. 1988. *The Sexual Contract*. Stanford: Stanford University Press.

———. 1999. "The Sexual and Racial Contracts at the End of the Twentieth Century." Presented at the panel "The Reality of Gender, Race, and Class in Political Theory" at the American Political Science Association Annual Meeting, September 2–5, 1999 (Atlanta).

Pateman, Carole, and Elizabeth Gross, eds. [1987] 1997. *Feminist Challenges: Social and Political Theory*. Boston: Northeastern University Press.

Pateman, Carole, and Charles Mills. 2007. *Contract and Domination*. Malden, Mass.: Polity.

Peffer, R. G. 1990. *Marxism, Morality, and Social Justice*. Princeton: Princeton University Press.

Rawls, John. [1971] 1999. *A Theory of Justice*. Rev. ed. Cambridge, Mass.: Harvard University Press.

Riley, Patrick, ed. 2001. *The Cambridge Companion to Rousseau*. New York: Oxford University Press.

Rousseau, Jean-Jacques. [1762] 1968. *The Social Contract*. Trans. Maurice Cranston. London: Penguin.

———. [1755] 1997. *Discourse on the Origin and Foundations of Inequality among Men*, or *Second Discourse*. In *The Discourses and Other Early Political Writings*, edited and translated by Victor Gourevitch, 111–222. New York: Cambridge University Press.

Sample, Ruth J. 2003. *Exploitation: What It Is and Why It's Wrong*. Lanham, Md.: Rowman and Littlefield.

Schloesser, Pauline. 2002. *The Fair Sex: White Women and Racial Patriarchy in the Early American Republic*. New York: New York University Press.

Schröder, Hannelore. 1997. "Kant's Patriarchal Order." Translated by Rita Gircour. In *Feminist Interpretations of Immanuel Kant*, edited by Robin May Schott, 275–96. University Park: Pennsylvania State University Press.

Shipler, David K. 2004. *The Working Poor: Invisible in America*. New York: Alfred A. Knopf.

Smith, Rogers M. 1997. *Civic Ideals: Conflicting Visions of Citizenship in U.S. History*. New Haven: Yale University Press.

Valls, Andrew, ed. 2005. *Race and Racism in Modern Philosophy*. Ithaca: Cornell University Press.

Walzer, Michael. 1995. "Contract, Social." In *The Oxford Companion to Philosophy*, edited by Ted Honderich, 163–64. New York: Oxford University Press.

Young, Iris Marion. 1990. *Justice and the Politics of Difference*. Princeton: Princeton University Press.

Human Rights and the Epistemology of Social Contract Theory

Brooke A. Ackerly

Carole Pateman's critique of social contract theory and contracts in general is important not only for revealing the myth of individual liberty and autonomy within contract-based accounts of democracy and economics but also for identifying the epistemological deception of social contract theories. This deception—that social unity is a function of shared ontology and values rather than a function of the exercise of power—is the more pernicious aspect of social contract theories. I will argue that, like social contract arguments, much (not all) human rights theorizing depends on certain epistemological assumptions that disguise power and represent subordination as freedom. This is true most obviously of overlapping consensus arguments about human rights, but it is true of nondiscrimination arguments and entitlement arguments as well. In each of these three cases, I expose the underlying exercise of epistemological power—that is, whose knowledge counts—and show that socially dominant epistemology undermines human rights claims by (or on behalf of) those marginalized through social conditions. In the process, I affirm and expand Pateman's argument in *The Sexual Contract* that social contract theory recasts inequality as freedom and equality, giving a false appearance of legitimacy to the injustice of the social, economic, and private conditions of inequality and unfreedom that characterize the basic structure of society (Pateman 1988,

---

Special thanks to Iris Young, Dan O'Neill, Molly Shanley, and Michael Goodhart for invaluable criticism. This project was influenced by a joint lecture by Carole Pateman and Charles Mills organized by the Robert Penn Warren Center for the Humanities at Vanderbilt University.

1992). I locate the political problem with social contract theories not in "contract" per se but rather in the unchallenged epistemology that limits the experiences of injustice that fall within these theories' purview.

We might parse the field of human rights political theory loosely into those who support a minimal list of "urgent" or "basic" human rights and those who understand the list of human rights to be more broad. Or, as Neil Stammers encourages, we might notice the link between certain forms of power and the kinds of rights—political, economic, social—that certain nations prioritize (Stammers 1993). For the purposes of this chapter, however, the interesting thing to note is that even theorists who appreciate the complex interweavings of human rights and social conditions legitimate a conservative scope of "human rights" and human rights claimants when they define "human rights" with epistemological boundaries that preclude the reexamination of those boundaries. However, if we attend to the conditions necessary to develop and exercise important human capabilities, we see the need for continual reexamination and modification of those boundaries that tell us whose knowledge counts in judging social practices and institutions.

To make the argument, I extend my critique of the epistemological basis of overlapping consensus-based arguments by drawing on Charles Mills's account of the domination contract as an epistemological "contract"—a contract whose knowledge system will be used to determine the basis of justice. Mills uses this argument as a basis for a critical restoration of social contract theory. Pateman argues that such a restoration is not possible. My argument provides further evidence for that view.

According to Mills, the basis for the social contract is an epistemological contract about who is a full free and equal person and who has subordinate standing.

> The Racial Contract is that set of formal or informal agreements or meta-agreements (higher-level contracts *about* contracts, which set the limits of the contracts' validity) between the members of one subset of humans, henceforth designated by (shifting) "racial" (phenotypical/genealogical/cultural) criteria C1, C2, C3 . . . as "white," and coextensive (making due allowance for gender differentiation) with the class of full persons, to categorize the remaining subset of humans as "nonwhite" and of a different and inferior moral status, subpersons, so that they have a subordinate civil standing. (1997, 11)

The racial contract is an actual contract that excludes some people as "subpersons" based on race.[1]

An epistemological contract is an agreement among some people about what constitutes knowing and knowledge. An epistemological contract is a social contract *among some people with certain power* about which people or categories of people are "persons" in the sense of being cognitive equals (Mills 1997, 59) and about the meaning of the basic terms used to describe their experiences (125). By controlling the categories of persons *and* the characterization of their experiences, the epistemological contract ossifies a "set of power relations" (127). When discussing race, we may see that "set of power relations" as determined by color (127) and when discussing gender, we may see that "set of power relations" as determined by sex. But in fact, the epistemological move is in the use of an existing political power to reify that power through our knowledge systems. Recognizing this, we can see that the Pateman-Mills critique applies not only to social contract theories, but also to any theory that treats as apolitical existing knowledge systems.

In this chapter, I argue that certain human rights theories share an epistemological flaw with social contract theories. Those that do are predisposed to a narrow view of which human rights are politically legitimate. The argument generalizes Pateman's epistemological insight in *The Sexual Contract*. Just as social contract theory mischaracterizes an experience of being dominated as an exercise of freedom and autonomy, so too many approaches to human rights provide mechanisms for concealing the exercise of oppressive power. While a full account of an alternative basis for human rights theory is beyond the scope of this chapter, the key features of such a theory are consistent with Pateman's proposal to found political community in the terrain of political and social relationships that can sustain people's autonomy.

Throughout her scholarship, Pateman theorizes as if politics is experienced in the full range of human contexts—political, economic, social, familial, interpersonal, cultural, and geographic. Attempts to treat these interrelated contexts as separable, natural, or apolitical are themselves political moves. As Pateman notes, we *can* be attentive to the exercise of power through contract by noticing when people resist this characterization (1988, 15–16, and throughout the whole book). A theory of human rights must be attentive to the ways in which certain "shared" epistemologies legitimate domination and

---

1. In her contribution to the racial contract, Pateman offers extensive empirical evidence from Australian colonization that such contracts were not conceptual, but rather legal.

deprive those who would object of the epistemological ground from which to criticize its abuse.

Why Is Social Contract Theory a Problem for Human Rights Practice?

Human rights practice—that is, the practice of claiming injustice based on "human rights" violations—exhibits two claims:

I. It is politically legitimate for this person to make a human rights claim (even if his or her government, family, employer, or other person with whom he or she has relationships thinks otherwise) and
II. This claim is a "human rights" claim.

Though ostensibly a claim that references shared understandings about what human rights are, in practice, many use "human rights" to challenge local, national, and international norms. Their rights claims challenge the legitimacy of political agreements that treat some people as subhuman or some rights as not politically legitimate. The legitimacy of rights claims by certain marginalized people and claims associated with politics, civil society, economics, cultural practices, gender norms, and heteronormativity have all taken their turn as the subject of political debate.

Given the politics of the right to make *a* claim and the right to make *this* claim, human rights theory is usefully articulated as nonideal theory.[2] In nonideal theorizing, we recognize that the conditions necessary to bring about our theoretical objectives are lacking. In fact, they are so lacking that we lack the ability to see clearly all that the theory should entail once fully articulated.

Theorizing about human rights as ideal theory, as if the conditions for bringing about the theory were able to be envisioned *and are even in reach*, is more than empirically unsupportable (that alone shouldn't stop us; there is a role for utopian theorizing). Ideal theorizing about human rights is problematic because it is premised on epistemological infallibility. The legitimacy of each claim depends on a shared epistemology. The requirement of shared epistemology is problematic in human rights theories for the same reasons that it is problematic in social contract theories: it treats a *political* agreement among some people about other people as if it were an *epistemological* agree-

---

2. The reference is explicitly to Rawls's distinction between ideal and nonideal theory (Rawls [1971] 1999).

ment among all people reflecting knowledge they all share, and it obfuscates the reality that the epistemological "agreement" is not the result of a full, free, and equal participatory process.

In such human rights theories, only those rights claims that assert that certain practices or acts are inconsistent with *accepted* human rights are viewed as legitimate rights claims. There is no reason for rights claims that challenge the premise of the authority that sets out those rights. Rights claims that challenge the boundaries of who gets to make a rights claim and what rights they may claim are not theoretically supported by these approaches to human rights. To treat such questions as morally settled prior to political engagement constrains the critical scope of human rights to Aristotelian refractory justice which focuses on the justice of an act, not on the justice of the context of all action. Any form of human rights theorizing that—like social contract theorizing—conceals the exercise of power behind the mask of shared epistemology creates boundaries that should *themselves* be subject to criticism in a human rights theory.

There are three ways in which the epistemological problems of social contract theories are perpetuated in human rights theories:

I. In those that justify human rights based on an "overlapping consensus,"
II. In those that deploy the nondiscrimination paradigm, and
III. In those that conceptualize rights exclusively as entitlements.

In each case, human rights criticism is constrained by a prior norm that leaves the epistemology of the norm uninterrogated and that renders the account inherently conservative.

Overlapping Consensus Arguments about Human Rights

We can see the inherent conservatism of the social contract approach in the overlapping consensus approaches to human rights of Steven Lukes and Charles Taylor. Both treat the social conditions that create political subordination as if they are politically unimportant.

According to Lukes, human rights are limited *because* a broader list could not secure broad support: "the list of human rights should be kept both reasonably short and reasonably abstract. It should include the basic civil and political rights, the rule of law, freedom of expression and association, equality of opportunity, and the right to some basic level of material well-being, but probably no more. *For only these have a prospect of securing agreement across the broad spectrum of contemporary political life"* (1993, 38; emphasis added).

Human rights activism shows us that Lukes draws the wrong conclusion from observing contemporary political life. He recognizes that social and economic structures are important and powerful in constraining the recognition of human rights.

> To defend human rights is to protect individuals from utilitarian sacrifices, communitarian impositions, and from injury, degradation, and arbitrariness, but doing so cannot be viewed independently of economic, legal, political and cultural conditions and may well involve the protection and even fostering of collective goods, such as the Kurdish language and culture. For to defend human rights is not merely to protect individuals. It is also to protect the activities and relations that make their lives more valuable, activities and relations that cannot be conceived reductively as merely individual goods. (Lukes 1993, 30)

Despite recognition of the constraints that potentially threaten individuals, in his concluding account of universal human rights, Lukes gives those same constraints normative force by arguing that they are the reason that we cannot recognize more rights than these (1993, 38). Lukes constrains the critical ambition of human rights with an assumed epistemological agreement about the limits of the scope of human rights. In the Lukes model, human rights obligations include identifying and correcting violations of human rights already agreed to, but human rights do not have the critical force to identify the ways in which social and economic relationships and norms support what activists (and other human rights theorists) treat as violations of rights.

Charles Taylor's account of a transcultural overlapping consensus on human rights is likewise based on assumed epistemological agreement that limits the critical possibilities of human rights. Globalizing the concept of "overlapping consensus" that Rawls develops in *Political Liberalism* (1993), Taylor argues that there may be an overlapping consensus on a narrow set of rights at the nexus of differing schemes of community value. Despite incompatible metaphysical views, these cultures may have a common ground from which to deepen and expand a shared notion of universal human rights. Further, while he reifies the boundaries of community and culture, the list of human rights on which communities and cultures may agree, he argues, is not *forever* defined by the present agreement. This is an interesting innovation.

Parenthetically, although Rawls coined the term "overlapping consensus" and developed its use as a tool for thinking about normative issues globally, Rawls himself did not use the concept to develop an account of universal human rights (1993, 1999). In the *Law of Peoples,* human rights are not the result of an overlapping consensus between liberal and decent societies; rather, they are the source of the definition of a decent society (1999).[3] Thus, Rawls's own account of human rights does not make methodological use of the concept of an overlapping consensus to justify universal human rights.

Taylor does, by contrast, see theoretical and political potential in the methodological innovation of the overlapping consensus as an objective of international discourse (Taylor 1999). However, Taylor sees its political legitimacy as contingent on a methodological openness to epistemological differences. Though acknowledging the "overlapping consensus" as Rawls's innovation, the model of an overlapping consensus that Taylor proposes is not Rawls's as developed in *Political Liberalism, The Law of Peoples,* or "The Idea of Public Reason Revisited." For Taylor, political legitimacy comes from mutual respect, not from the justificatory scheme. Because there are multiple justificatory schemes in the world, universal human rights must be a political agreement.

Taylor's view is reflected by one of the authors of the United Nations' Universal Declaration of Human Rights, Jacques Maritain: "I am quite certain that my way of justifying belief in the rights of man and the ideal of liberty, equality, fraternity is the only way with a firm foundation in truth. This does not prevent me from being in agreement on these practical convictions with people who are certain that their way of justifying them, entirely different from mine or opposed to mine, . . . is equally the only way founded upon truth" (Maritain 1949, 10–11; cf. Ramadan 2004). For Maritain, the Universal Declaration is a political agreement, not a metaphysical one. Likewise for Taylor, such an agreement is a *political* agreement, not a theoretical one.

> Different groups, countries, religious communities, and civilizations, although holding incompatible fundamental views on theology, metaphysics, human nature, and so on, would come to an agreement on certain norms that ought to govern human behavior. Each would

---

3. Rawls has a consequentialist understanding of human rights; Rawls uses overlapping consensus on human rights as a condition of a People being in what he calls the Society of Peoples. For another consequentialist account of human rights see Talbott 2005.

have its own way of justifying this from out of its profound background conception. We would agree on norms [of conduct] while disagreeing on why they were the right norms, and we would be content to live in this consensus, undisturbed by the differences of profound underlying belief. (1999, 124)

For Taylor, such agreement may set the ground for future development of greater shared background justificatory schemes (1999, 140).

Taylor treats respect for different ways of knowing across cultures as a principal "condition of an unforced consensus on human rights." Yet, despite giving many examples of different ways of knowing *within* contexts, Taylor does not explore the political implications of these observations for his argument. His argument requires cross-cultural but not intra-cultural respect for differences. Within their communities, many are politically marginalized by a cross-cultural dialogue that treats cultures as distinct and the "responsibilities [that people] owe to the whole community or to its members" (1999, 130) as apolitical. In fact, the boundaries between and within communities are dynamic. However, an agreement premised on the understanding of communities as bounded and internally homogeneous functions as a social contract that privileges some within each community, as Pateman contended. Agreement to treat communities as bounded and internally homogeneous is an agreement to suppress the freedom and autonomy of individuals within communities to express dissent.

Despite an interest in the reforming movement within Buddhism and references to communitarian and liberal perspectives within the West, despite attention to changes in identities within the West (Taylor 1999, 139–40), despite discussion of "the possibilities of reinterpretation and reappropriation that the tradition itself contains" (142), Taylor's theory of human rights is inattentive to the politics of these reforms, changes, reinterpretations, and reappropriations. Because Taylor's approach does not explicitly foster the freedom and autonomy within communities necessary to think about whether their social, economic, and political institutions foster human rights, Western and feminist critiques of "Western" rights are oddly missing from Taylor's account.[4] The rights framework has been the subject of criticism from within

---

4. In his criticism of individualism and deterioration of social fabric and political trust in Western countries, he takes as axiomatic the relationship between this deterioration and individual rights. However, it is not clear from his discussion that individual *rights* rather than individualism is to blame.

the West for its failure to recognize structural forms of rights violations. Cultural patterns *in the West* create contexts of rights violations. And these can prove difficult to change even with significant legal reforms (Manfredi 1993; Jhappan 2002). Feminist critics have argued that when a human rights argument focuses on individual actors and legal mechanisms at the expense of criticizing the broader structural contexts in which rights violations take place, such argument is not contributing to a *universal* human rights framework. A notion of human rights based on liberal individualism (and its myths of equality, freedom, agency, and consent) are the subject of feminist critiques of human rights from within and outside the West.

A deliberative *universal* human rights theory that could be used to assess critically not only failure to conform to existing norms, but also the norms themselves would need an account of 1) who deliberates, 2) who they represent, 3) how they come to represent those they represent, and 4) the cultural, social, political and economic contexts and relationships of each of these. The politics of each of these provides evidence that the process of identifying an overlapping consensus on human rights should be ruled by the norms of *dissensus* not consensus. Marginalized potential deliberants, those promoting rights claims that fall outside the terrain of consensus, need a basis from which to adjudicate their rights claims. That basis itself is a terrain of contestation.

Methodologically, it does not have to be wrong to defend a view of universal human rights justified through practice, as Taylor's overlapping consensus approach attempts. The overlapping consensus Taylor envisioned could be the result of sustained global engagement (echoed by Etzioni 2004). This engagement would involve learning and mutual transformation of ideas around what constitutes the list of human rights protected, their philosophical foundations, and the legal and social institutions that best secure them. However, because *human rights* are in question, our methodology should also require us to *question* the ways in which power inequalities may generate a particular overlapping consensus and be deployed to minimize the substantive scope of the overlapping consensus on rights. Alone, an overlapping consensus approach to human rights can be used to criticize failure to conform to the established system of power, but not to criticize that system's abuse of its authority. Attention to varieties and to competition within cultures and political contexts is an important methodological modification for redeploying the study of overlapping consensus as a resource for understanding human rights.

Nondiscrimination Arguments about Human Rights

Of course, not all human rights theories use an overlapping consensus to justify the extent to which human rights can be used as a tool for political, social, and economic criticism. However, like overlapping consensus theories, much human rights theory is premised on an agreement about how we are to *think* about rights. As in overlapping consensus human rights theory, that premise is an "epistemological contract" as Mills calls it, a social contract about what meanings we share and what kinds of arguments should be heard (1997). Much human rights practice and international law deploy the underlying epistemology of social contract theory by assuming an epistemological contract. Even while they challenge the notion of *who* is owed human rights, nondiscrimination arguments reinforce the notion that *some* people are owed *some* human rights.

In this section, I argue that certain human rights arguments—those that apply themselves against *discrimination*—replicate the epistemological contract's tool for concealing the exercise of power. While the intent of these approaches may be emancipatory, the effect is not. Just as Pateman argues that social contract theory cannot be emancipatory even in the hands of feminists, so too I argue that antidiscrimination approaches to human rights have an exclusionary logic that depends on an exercise of power such that they *cannot* be emancipatory even when women and minorities campaign against discrimination.

Nondiscrimination is a familiar way in which people often think about rights and one that does not appear to be a product of social contract reasoning, but it is such a product in that it reflects an epistemological contract. But the epistemological contract implicit in nondiscrimination approaches to human rights gives us no basis from which to challenge the relations of power that determine the scope of human rights.

Judith Stiehm (1983) and Catharine MacKinnon (1993) have argued that the nondiscrimination paradigm is a problematic basis from which to advocate for equality. Reified in antidiscrimination claims in U.S. and international law, this view brings into constitutional law Aristotle's notion of equality: that we should treat those who are alike, alike and those who are different, differently. Aristotelian equality puts the political burden on the mistreated (or their representatives) to show that they are in fact *like* those who are not mistreated. This challenge is made particularly difficult by the social, economic, and political practices that are both a consequence of, and a cause of, their differential treatment (Hirschmann 2003). In fact women, black men, indigenous people, and gays have very different life experiences from those privileged in the epistemological contract *because* they are not considered persons *in the same way.*

The nondiscrimination paradigm is particularly pernicious because in order to make an argument against a form of discrimination, one must accept the premise that what equality requires is being similar. In order to argue from within the nondiscrimination paradigm that members of a particular group deserve to be treated as persons, one must argue that being *like* the other group is the just basis for equal treatment, that groups of "subpersons" must be treated as "persons." The logic of the nondiscrimination paradigm is that in order to criticize discrimination, one must argue that *these* people (women, black men, indigenous people, lesbians, etc.) are no different than those who are privileged. Ironically, the underlying epistemology—equality means treating similar people similarly—enables human rights violations to go unnoticed.

To phrase the problem in Pateman's language, "'Equality,' like other central political categories, is a contested term; but whereas 'equality' in some of its possible meanings can encompass 'difference,' no sense of 'equality' compatible with a genuinely democratic citizenship can accommodate subordination. . . . For that to be the case, the meaning of sexual difference has to cease to be the difference between freedom and subordination" (1992, 28). No sense of equality *should* mean subordination of some people, and yet the logic of the antidiscrimination paradigm enables the treatment of *some* subordination as "difference," not inequality. To challenge this possible interpretation of nondiscrimination, a human rights theory should guide critical reflection about the background conditions of society that legitimate the epistemological foundations of antidiscrimination.

The Convention for the Elimination of all forms of Discrimination against Women (CEDAW) is an international legal instrument that does just that. Although the antidiscrimination paradigm is reiterated in the CEDAW, the CEDAW also challenges the epistemology that would allow human rights to be discussed without reference to women's social and economic subordination.

> For the purposes of the present Convention, the term "discrimination against women" shall mean any distinction, exclusion or restriction made on the basis of sex which has the effect or purpose of impairing or nullifying the recognition, enjoyment or exercise by women, irrespective of their marital status, on a basis of equality of men and women, of human rights and fundamental freedoms in the political,

economic, social, cultural, civil or any other field. (United Nations 1979, Article 1)

While working within the nondiscrimination paradigm, the document also expands the notion of human rights by focusing on the role of culture in limiting the realization of the human rights of women. It sets out in the preamble that "a change in the traditional role of men as well as the role of women in society and in the family is needed to achieve full equality between men and women" (United Nations 1979, Preamble). In the body of the convention, the means of achieving these goals are spelled out in articles in which certain social, economic, and political outcomes would be the measures of nondiscrimination. States Parties must secure for men and women "The same conditions for career and vocational guidance, for access to studies and for the achievement of diplomas in educational establishments of all categories in rural as well as in urban areas; this equality shall be ensured in pre-school, general, technical, professional and higher technical education, as well as in all types of vocational training" (Article 10 [a]). States Parties must work toward "The reduction of female student drop-out rates and the organization of programmes for girls and women who have left school prematurely" (Article 10 [f]).

These and similar provisions of the CEDAW attempt to change the background conditions of societies. The CEDAW challenges the social contract logic of human rights by acknowledging that females have not been part of the social contract that heretofore has excluded them from politics and enabled their human rights violations. States parties are

> Concerned, however, that despite these various instruments extensive discrimination against women continues to exist.
>
> Recalling that discrimination against women violates the principles of equality of rights and respect for human dignity, is an obstacle to the participation of women, on equal terms with men, in the political, social, economic and cultural life of their countries, hampers the growth of the prosperity of society and the family and makes more difficult the full development of the potentialities of women in the service of their countries and of humanity,
>
> Concerned that in situations of poverty women have the least access to food, health, education, training and opportunities for employment and other needs . . .

States Parties' concern acknowledges this discrimination. However, they believe that dealing with discrimination against women without challenging the underlying logic of discrimination will not be adequate to create equality between men and women. States Parties are further "Convinced that the establishment of the new international economic order based on equity and justice will contribute significantly towards the promotion of equality between men and women." They also believe that "emphasizing that the eradication of apartheid, all forms of racism, racial discrimination, colonialism, neocolonialism, aggression, foreign occupation and domination and interference in the internal affairs of States is essential to the full enjoyment of the rights of men and women." The CEDAW casts human rights in the familiar *language* of nondiscrimination but deploys the *logic* of nondomination. In the nondomination account of equality, equality exists when hierarchies that exploit are undermined (not perpetuated) by the basic institutions of society (Okin 1989; MacKinnon 1993; Young 2000; Young 2006).

The nondiscrimination paradigm is about defining the boundaries of the right to make a claim. The authors of CEDAW assert an alternative human rights epistemology, one that recognizes rights as enabling conditions. Though the language of rights as capabilities is not found in the CEDAW, the CEDAW offers a draft alternative paradigm that philosophers would develop twenty years later (Nussbaum 1997; Sen 2004). The nondomination and capabilities paradigms offer different bases for human rights, ones that are not premised on a shared view (an epistemological contract) about what constitutes domination, capability, or human rights.

Entitlement-centric Arguments about Human Rights

Another common way of thinking about human rights is as entitlements, metaphorically analogous to property, and this way of thinking likewise entails an epistemological contract. Familiar accounts of human rights treat rights as "entitlements" with corresponding "duty-bearers."

> A claim about rights generally involves a fourfold assertion about the *subject* of entitlement, the *substance* of entitlement, the *basis* for entitlement, and the *purpose* of entitlement. (Shapiro 1986, 14; emphasis in original).
>
> A right in this sense can be thought of as consisting of five main elements: a right-holder (the subject of a right) has a claim to some

> substance (the object of a right), which he or she might assert, or demand, or enjoy, or enforce (exercising a right) against some individual or group (the bearer of the correlative duty), citing in support of his or her claim some particular ground (the justification of a right) (Vincent 1986, 8).
>
> Historically, the idea of rights has embodied two foundational claims. First, that there is an identifiable subject who has entitlements; and secondly, that to possess a right presupposes the existence of a duty-bearer against whom the right is claimed (Dunne and Wheeler 1999, 3–4)

According to this epistemology—this way of knowing what rights are—rights take a narrow form. Even if we all agree that no men, women, or children should be subordinated, the model of rights as *entitlements* severely limits the scope of rights and narrowly delimits responsibilities to those identifiable duty-bearers.

However, many human rights claims are best understood in relation to the social and economic *conditions* of the claimants. As both Donnelly (1989, 26–27) and Shue ([1980] 1996, 29–34) argue, human rights claims are made in response to "standard threats" to human dignity in a given time and place. The problem with using an "entitlements" metaphor to describe these claims is that such claims would rely on a shared understanding of what constitutes the "standard threats." However, many social conditions function to render some threats invisible. If some threats are invisible, human rights are not best understood as analogous to property that we can *have* and are better understood realized in conditions we can *experience.*

For example, domestic violence and human trafficking are rights violations that many people experience, but due to gendered social conditions they have been invisible rights violations (Bunch 1990; Charlesworth 1994; Mayer 1995). The crimes associated with battery and trafficking would constitute human rights violations were it not for the enabling basic political, economic, and social structures. These same conditions make these violations common but not "standard." Holding individuals and states more responsible might constitute a change in the basic structure, but alone would not be sufficient for ending rights violations related to domestic violence or human trafficking. Entitlement-based theories of human rights have difficulty articulating the political obligations implicated by such rights claims. Even when rights *can* be articulated as "entitlements," so articulated, rights related to the background conditions of social, political, and economic life generate collective responsibility that is not well-described by "duty-bearers."

Rights claims that require a transformation of enabling conditions are not well articulated as entitlements analogous to property not only because enabling conditions are not well conceptualized as metaphorically analogous to property, but also because enabling conditions do not have corresponding, identifiable duty-bearers. Rights claims to enabling conditions such as a public media environment that not only has a free press, but that also fosters cultural images that discourage rather than validate women's subordination do have some specific duty-bearers but these alone could not bring about the social change necessary to create the enabling conditions.

Further, the right to enabling conditions generates collective obligations that need to be defined through collective discussions about these obligations and realized through individual and group practices. The social conditions that enable rights recognition are themselves conditions for fulfilling these obligations. They are two sides of the same coin, two ways of thinking about the conditions of society. In the entitlement metaphor rights and duties are different. In the capabilities metaphor the conditions that enable rights recognition and fulfilling obligations to foster human rights conditions are the same.

As with the critique of the nondiscrimination paradigm, women's human rights activists have made an important contribution to the theory of universal human rights by challenging the entitlement understanding of human rights. Their activism thus helps us see that the epistemology of rights-as-entitlements obscures the rights-violating impact of many social, economic, and political structures (Ackerly 2001). As Young argues, the liberal model of rights as entitlements is based on a particular historical view of the world that is not good for challenging all forms of exploitative hierarchies (1990, chapter 2). It is particularly unhelpful in that the entitlement model makes us assume that rights are violated by individual action or inaction. In fact, many rights are realized through the enabling conditions created by background social, political, and economic institutions and reified through our daily practices.

Many human rights scholars have helped us think about the social conditions of human rights (Shue [1980] 1996; Donnelly 1989; Nussbaum 1997; Gould 2004; Sen 2004; Talbott 2005). Such views are inconsistent with understanding rights as exclusively metaphorically analogous to "entitlements." Understanding rights as "capabilities" makes it easier to see social, economic, and political factors—some visible, some less visible—that contribute to the autonomy (exercised individually or in relationship with others) of people.

Some of these rights have conceivable individual or institutional duty-bearers (like the police, or the government), but many do not. Many are instead realized in the terrain of political and social relationships that Pateman defended as the basis for autonomy and modern civil society (1988, 232). Likewise, the human rights theorists and activists who offer an understanding of rights as securing a context in which people can exercise their capabilities challenge the epistemological authority of the rights-as-entitlements conceptualization of rights (Nagel 1979; Nussbaum 1997; Sen 1999; Ackerly 2001; Hirschmann 2003; Talbott 2005). Of these, Talbott (2005) comes the furthest in articulating what such a theory requires of whom. "Not only your *opinion* matters. Your *actions* are needed to make progress in promoting basic human rights. Not necessarily heroic actions. Although heroic actions can be important, in the long run, what is most important is for enough people to be willing to incur small costs to promote fairness" (2005, 186; emphasis in original). According to Talbott, human rights as capabilities are secured not only through the actors most able to do something, but also through the incremental actions of all of us (cf. Sen 2004).

What a Theory of Human Rights Can Be

The myth that free and equal people consent to the terms of "a system of social cooperation between free and equal citizens" masks the nonideal political reality that the system of social cooperation is really a system of oppression, that equal treatment is really only for those who are already free and equal, and that secure entitlements are really secure only for those whose entitlements are already secure. These problems to which Pateman draws our attention in the *Sexual Contract* and develops in her contribution to the racial contract (Pateman and Mills, 2007) make it clear that three major theoretical approaches to human rights embody a domination contract in the form of an epistemological contract. This is true of theories that rest on a notion of overlapping consensus about human rights, that treat rights violations as a matter of discrimination, or that treat respecting rights as a matter of respecting entitlements.

Pateman and Mills share a critique of the social contract as the domination contract (Pateman and Mills, 2007). They argue that while a social contract is *for all* (the free and the dominated), it is not a contract *among all*. Through the social contract, some are included on unequal terms that are characterized as equal freedom, some are excluded, and some are members of the fraternity of whiteness (Pateman 1988, 60, 221; Mills 1997, 11–12ff., 20, 122, 137–38n3). In Mills's words, "Whereas the ideal contract explains how a just society would be formed, ruled by a moral government, and regulated by a defensible moral code, this nonideal/naturalized contract explains how an unjust, *exploitative* society, ruled by an *oppressive* government and regulated by an *immoral* code, comes into existence" (1997, 5; emphasis in original). Pateman defines the social contract moment as a political moment in which the separation of public and private are characterized as apolitical, and Mills defines the social contract moment as a political moment in which the authority of knowledge is characterized as apolitical. Both are critical of the epistemological basis of ideal social contract theory.

Only Mills attempts to rework social contract theory as nonideal theory: "If the ideal contract is to be endorsed and emulated, this nonideal/naturalized contract is to be demystified and condemned. So the point of analyzing the nonideal contract is not to ratify it but to use it to explain and expose the inequities of the actual nonideal polity and to help us see through the theories and moral justifications offered in defense of them" (1997, 5). He argues that having revealed the domination contract, we can use the imperfection of the social contract to guide our critical assessment of laws and practices and of the basic structure of society on which they rely (Mills 1997, 129; see also Mills's essay in this volume). He argues that by revealing that the "social" contract is really a domination contract (as both Pateman and he do), the critical function of the social contract device for political theory does not fall prey to the same criticisms as its ideal cousin. Both Pateman and I disagree that social contract theory can be rescued in the way Mills suggests.

Despite the fact that the world can well use many approaches to promoting justice, the discussion of the social contract and the epistemological contract reveals that the social contract mechanism is not adequately attentive to a common seed of injustice: the power to make an *effective* argument. I argue with Pateman that attention to social conditions is incompatible with the epistemology of social contract theory. Attention to social conditions requires a dynamic epistemology, critical of the ways of knowing that render some experiences invisible or treat them as apolitical. The logic of social contract theory is inconsistent with a dynamic epistemology that systematically reexamines its own assumptions.

Iris Young offers us a framework for theorizing about justice that includes an account of how the theory fosters reassessment of theoretical claims *and* of the theory itself.

> To the extent that people require justification from one another for their claims and proposals, they must often appeal to principles and values of justice. To the extent that some people doubt or disagree with the principles that others appeal to, reasonable political discussion also calls for justifying principles, theorizing their coherence with one another, or arguing that some take precedence over others. Appeals to principles of justice have a more pragmatic function in political interaction than many theories of justice attribute to them. Where practical judgements are the result at which discussants aim, appeals to principles of justice are steps in arguments about what should be done. . . . If all significantly affected by problems and their solutions are included in the discussion and decision-making on the basis of equality and non-domination, and if they interact reasonably and constitute a public where people are accountable to one another, then the results of their discussion is [*sic*] likely to be the most wise and just. (2000, 29–30)

Young's is a democratic theory that entails a commitment to inclusion. Even as an ideal theory (that is, a theory that does not also include an account of the processes that would bring it to fruition), the theory invites its own critical assessment. As practiced, participants might bring in principles for consideration that would challenge the privilege of inclusion in her theory. The theory does not epistemologically exclude views that could criticize its very core.

Human rights theory is necessary at moments of democratic or human rights crisis, when the norms of consensus and standards of justification are not shared. As Gary Shiffman (2002) argues, such crises occur when citizens contest norms of social cooperation (cf. Douglass 1852). And as Pateman argues, the premise of social contract theory itself suppresses such conflict and casts the oppression of some as the exercise of *their* freedom.

Human rights theory, written for a context of injustice *in* a context of injustice, needs an account of the theory *and* of how to assess critically the possibility that some injustices of the context may have been or may become embedded in the theory through the epistemology of the theory itself. For human rights theory to have a universalizable critical capacity, it needs to have the critical capacity to interrogate the epistemological basis of the theory itself.

Guided by such epistemological humility, the nonideal theory of human rights requires a methodology that enables the theory to be informed continually by experiences of subordination (public and private, visible and invisible, "standard" and unfamiliar) and to be particularly attentive to political, social, and economic conditions that enable these or that treat them as apolitical. The methodology of a nonideal theory of human rights needs to be systematically attentive to the power of epistemology. A nonideal universal theory of human rights needs to be as attentive to the process of theorizing as it is to the political commitments to which it leads.

References

Ackerly, B. A. 2001. "Women's Human Rights Activists as Cross-Cultural Theorists." *International Feminist Journal of Politics* 3 (Autumn): 311–46.

Bunch, C. 1990. "Women's Rights as Human Rights: Toward a Re-vision of Human Rights." *Human Rights Quarterly* 12 (November): 486–98.

Charlesworth, H. 1994. "What Are 'Women's International Human Rights?'" In *Human Rights of Women: National and International Perspectives*, edited by R. J. Cook, 58–84. Philadelphia: University of Pennsylvania Press.

Donnelly, J. 1989. *Universal Human Rights in Theory and Practice*. Ithaca: Cornell University Press.

Douglass, F. 1852. "What to the Slave is the Fourth of July?" Available at http://douglassarchives.org/.

Dunne, T., and N. J. Wheeler. 1999. "Introduction: Human Rights and the Fifty Years' Crisis." In *Human Rights in Global Politics*, edited T. Dunne and N. J. Wheeler, 1–28. Cambridge: Cambridge University Press.

Etzioni, A. 2004. "The Emerging Global Normative Synthesis." *Journal of Political Philosophy* 12, no. 2:214–44.

Gould, C. C. 2004. *Globalizing Democracy and Human Rights*. Cambridge: Cambridge University Press.

Hirschmann, N. J. 2003. *The Subject of Liberty: Toward a Feminist Theory of Freedom*. Princeton: Princeton University Press.

Jhappan, R. 2002. *Women's Legal Strategies in Canada*. Toronto: University of Toronto Press.

Lukes, S. 1993. "Five Fables about Human Rights." In *On Human Rights: The Oxford Amnesty Lectures*, edited S. Shute and S. L. Hurley, 19–40. New York: Basic Books.

MacKinnon, C. A. 1993. "Crimes of War, Crimes of Peace." In *On Human Rights: The Oxford Amnesty Lectures*, edited by S. Shute and S. L. Hurley, 83–109. New York: Basic Books.

Manfredi, C. P. 1993. *Judicial Power and the Charter: Canada and the Paradox of Liberal Constitutionalism*. Norman: University of Oklahoma Press.

Maritain, J. 1949. Introduction to *Human Rights: Comments and Interpretations*, 9–17. New York: Columbia University Press.

Mayer, A. E. 1995. "Rhetorical Strategies and Official Policies on Women's Rights: The Merits and Drawbacks of the New World Hypocrisy." In *Faith and Freedom: Women's Human Rights in the Muslim World*, edited by Mahnaz Afkhami, 104–32. Syracuse: Syracuse University Press.

Mills, Charles W. 1997. *The Racial Contract*. Ithaca: Cornell University Press.

Nagel, T. 1979. *Mortal Questions*. Cambridge: Cambridge University Press.

Nussbaum, M. C. 1997. "Human Rights Theory: Capabilities and Human Rights." *Fordham Law Review* 66:273–300.

Okin, S. M. 1989. *Justice, Gender, and the Family*. New York: Basic Books.

Pateman, C. 1988. *The Sexual Contract*. Stanford: Stanford University Press.

———. 1992. "Equality, Difference, Subordination: The Politics of Motherhood and Women's Citizenship." In *Beyond Equality and Difference: Citizenship, Feminist Politics and Female Subjectivity*, edited by G. Bock and S. James, 17–31. London: Routledge.

Pateman, C., and C. Mills. 2007. *Contract and Domination*. Cambridge: Polity Press.

Ramadan, T. 2004. *Western Muslims and the Future of Islam*. Oxford: Oxford University Press.

Rawls, J. 1993. *Political Liberalism*. New York: Columbia University Press.

———. [1971] 1999. *A Theory of Justice*. Cambridge, Mass.: Belknap Press of Harvard University Press.

———. 1999. "The Law of Peoples." In *The Law of Peoples with "The Idea of Public Reason Revisited,"* 3–128. Cambridge, Mass.: Harvard University Press.

Sen, A. 2004. "Elements of a Theory of Human Rights." *Philosophy and Public Affairs* 32, no. 4:315.

Sen, A. K. 1999. *Development as Freedom*. New York: Oxford University Press.

Shapiro, I. 1986. *The Evolution of Rights in Liberal Theory*. Cambridge: Cambridge University Press.

Shiffman, G. 2002. "Construing Disagreement: Consensus and Invective in "Constitutional" Debate." *Political Theory* 30, no. 2:175.

Shue, H. [1980] 1996. *Basic Rights: Subsistence, Affluence, and U.S. Foreign Policy*. Princeton: Princeton University Press.

Stammers, N. 1993. "Human Rights and Power." *Political Studies* 41, no. 1:70–82.

Stiehm, J. H. 1983. "The Unit of Political Analysis: Our Aristotelian Hangover." In *Discovering Reality: Feminist Perspectives on Epistemology, Metaphysics,*

Methodology, and Philosophy of Science, edited by S. G. Harding and M. B. Hintikka, 31–43. Dordrecht, Holland: D. Reidel.

Talbott, W. J. 2005. *Which Rights Should Be Universal?* New York: Oxford University Press.

Taylor, C. 1999. "Conditions of an Unforced Consensus on Human Rights." In *The East Asian Challenge for Human Rights*, edited by J. R. Bauer and D. Bell, 124–44. Cambridge: Cambridge University Press.

United Nations. 1979. Convention on the Elimination of All Forms of Discrimination against Women, Declarations, Reservations, and Objections. United Nations, Division for the Advancement of Women. Available at http://www.un.org/womenwatch/daw/cedaw/text/econvention.htm.

Vincent, R. J. 1986. *Human Rights and International Relations*. Cambridge: Cambridge University Press.

Young, I. M. 1990. *Justice and the Politics of Difference*. Princeton: Princeton University Press.

———. 2000. *Inclusion and Democracy*. Oxford: Oxford University Press.

———. 2006. "Taking the Basic Structure Seriously." *Perspectives on Politics* 4, no. 1:91–97

SECTION II

Autonomy and Consent

Free to Decide for Oneself
Anne Phillips

The freedom to decide for oneself has been both aspiration and worry for feminists. The worry stems mostly from the emphasis on deciding "for oneself," which seems to associate freedom with the ability to separate oneself from others. This has been felt to reflect an egotistical and overindividuated conception of the self, and a large and varied literature on maternal feminism, relational feminism, and care feminism has developed alternative formulations (Jaggar 1983; Nedelsky 1989; MacKenzie and Stoljar 2000; Friedman, 2003). Others defend the focus on the individual as a crucial part of the feminist project (e.g., Nussbaum 1999a). Whatever position one adopts on these debates, it is clear that some version of autonomy is going to remain a defining element in feminism. Through the centuries, women have been required to submit to husbands chosen by fathers, to religious injunctions regarding the appropriate forms of sexuality and motherhood, to paternalistic legislation claiming to "protect" them from their own frailties, or just to the expectation that a good woman will sacrifice her own needs or ambitions to the needs of those she loves. Generations of feminists have argued that women need a stronger sense of self in order to challenge the many constraints on their lives.

They have also explored, in subtle and complex ways, the difficulties in achieving this. Writing in the 1940s, and through the prism of existentialist philosophy, Simone de Beauvoir was particularly concerned by the "bad faith" that comes with women's lack of freedom. In a passage that still rings disturbingly true, she describes the way women may compound their own impotence by refusing to accept responsibility for their lives: "A free individual blames only himself for his failures, he assumes responsibility for them; but every thing happens to woman through the agency of others, and therefore these others are responsible for her woes. Her mad despair spurns all remedies; it does not help to propose solutions to a woman bent on complaining: she finds none acceptable. She insists on living in her situation precisely as she does—that is, in a state of impotent rage" (de Beauvoir 1969, 338). From de Beauvoir's perspective, no one ever really loses the freedom of action and choice. But the constraints that mold women into "women" can make it virtually impossible for them to exercise this freedom in the world, leading to narcissism, masochism, or that state of impotent complaint.

Writing in the 1990s, and with a particular focus on India, Martha Nussbaum was more struck by the failure to rage against the world, by the way women can become so habituated to an unequal division of income and resources that they end up thinking themselves as of lesser worth than men (2000, esp. chap. 2). As the literature on adaptive preferences has stressed, people have an extraordinary capacity to ignore those things they feel they cannot change, or undervalue those opportunities they know to be closed to them (Elster 1983; Sunstein 1991; Sen 1995). So while some (like de Beauvoir's women) will indeed rail against the injuries done to them, others quietly adjust their sights to what they perceive as possible. For Nussbaum, the exercise of freedom therefore depends on the development of certain capabilities. It is only when public policy promotes bodily health, bodily integrity, and the capacity to reflect critically on our lives (to list only three of her central human capabilities), that the "freedom to decide for oneself" becomes meaningful.

These are two examples from a wide range of perspectives, but already they indicate some of the problems in distinguishing a "free" from an "unfree" decision. The woman described by de Beauvoir feels very strongly that she is *not* free. She blames everyone but herself for her impotence; she refuses to accept responsibility for the choices she has made; it is always her husband or society or fate that is to blame. De Beauvoir is not unsympathetic to this predicament—she is not saying the woman should simply pull herself together and take responsibility for her own life—but she does see the inability to recognize oneself as a free person as one of the markers of women's oppression. For Nussbaum, by contrast, too many women think they are free when in fact they are not; they take for granted a particular ordering of society or family and fail to see that the order is unjust. This is putting it too crudely, but it is as if de Beauvoir wishes women could get beyond the complaining to acknowledge themselves as free beings, and Nussbaum that they could get beyond the resignation to acknowledge the extent to which they are unfree.

An alternative route—not much followed by feminists—is to define a free decision as one that was not physically forced.[1] It would then be evident enough, from the bound hands or pistol to the head, when people were *not* acting freely; and in the absence of overt force, it would be safe to assume that people did what they wanted to do. The fact that some people enjoy a wider range of options than others—perhaps because they are wealthier or have accumulated more qualifications, perhaps because they are male, or white, or young—would have no bearing on whether their decisions were freely made. Nor would it be considered relevant that some people are more subject than others to the pressures of family, religion, or community. Anyone who lives in the world (that is, everyone) is subject to pressures and constraints, but precisely because this is true of everyone, it makes no sense to try to disentangle the things we "really" want from those we were coerced to do. If we give in to the enticements of a successful advertising campaign, does this mean we were "forced" to smoke? If we succumb to the attractions of a higher income, does this mean we were "forced" to work in the private sector? Or to take the example I want to address in this essay, if young people give in to parental blackmail and the threat of ostracism by their community, does this mean they were "forced" into marriage?

I suspect that most readers will balk at an understanding of freedom that equates it with "not physically restrained" and will want to introduce some distinction between decisions actively embraced and those to which people resign themselves because of a lack of alternatives or pressure to conform. But people have debated the conundrums of freedom for centuries and not come much closer to settlement, and even if we take as our starting point that the freedom to decide for oneself implies something more substantial than not being legally prevented or not being physically restrained, many of the problems remain. My concerns in this essay arise from some considerations regarding gender equality in a context of cultural diversity; more specifically, they arise from the contrast between voluntary and coerced that is implied in the distinction between arranged and forced marriage. As indicated in the next section, there are a number of difficulties in the way this distinction is currently being mobilized. I argue that Carole Pateman's enormously innovative discussion of freedom and subordination in *The Sexual Contract* offers the necessary insights for resolving these.

To anticipate, Pateman notes that assessments of the validity of contract tend to revolve around the conditions under which people enter an agreement.

---

1. I take this to be the position adopted by Chandran Kukathas (2003). Kukathas argues that what matters is not so much whether decisions are voluntary (in the Nussbaum sense of informed and reflective acceptance), as that they should not be forced.

Many have argued that what looks like a free agreement is in reality often coerced, because the person entering it had no real alternatives. Standard examples in the literature include the worker who "agrees" to work for below-subsistence wages, because all the employers in the area have formed a cartel and none will offer higher wages; or the woman who "decides" to become a prostitute, because all the more respectable forms of employment are closed to her once employers learn about her illegitimate child. Though no one technically forced these individuals, it seems inappropriate to say they freely agreed, and it is widely felt that their lack of alternatives undermines the validity of their contracts. The key innovation in *The Sexual Contract* is that it focuses our attention on a second aspect: that even when nothing is awry in the conditions under which people made their decision, the agreement might still be problematic if it involves submission to another person's power. As Pateman puts it:

> A great deal of attention has been paid to the conditions under which contracts are entered into and to the question of exploitation once a contract is made. Proponents of contract doctrine claim that contracts in everyday life match up well enough to the model of the original contract in which equal parties freely agree to the terms; actual contracts thus provide examples of individual freedom. Their critics, whether socialists concerned with the employment contract, or feminists concerned with the marriage contract or prostitution contract, have countered this claim by pointing to the often grossly unequal positions of the relevant parties and to the economic and other constraints facing workers, wives and women in general. *But concentration on coerced entry into contracts, important though this is, can obscure an important question: does contract immediately become attractive to feminists or socialists if entry is truly voluntary, without coercion?* (1988, 7–8; my italics)

According to Pateman, it is not just the "bad" contracts we must be wary of, for we need to recognize that contract itself can be inimical to freedom. I argue that this deeper critique of contract helps clarify what is at issue in the distinction between forced and arranged marriage.

The Problem: Arranged and Forced Marriage

The right to determine one's own choice of marriage partner is increasingly recognized in schedules of human rights. Yet many young people are forced into marriage against their will, not (as in the staple of nineteenth-century European literature) because they can see no other means of subsistence, but because their families insist on them accepting a particular marriage partner, chosen for reasons of property, religion, family status, or caste. Familial pressure to marry within one's own ethnic or religious group operates across all cultures, and the statistics on the proportion of marriages that cross class or ethnic boundaries (very few) make for depressing reading.[2] The chances of being *forced* into an unwanted marriage are, however, especially high in societies that practice arranged marriage, for it is when it has become the norm for parents to make the decision about the choice of marriage partner on behalf of their children that the temptation to insist is most likely to arise. Paradoxically, the chances of being forced into marriage against one's will may also increase as the practice of arranged marriage wanes, for parents may become more strident about their right to dictate the choice of spouse precisely because the young people are becoming more insistent on their own right to choose. There is some evidence that this may be the case among second and third generations settled in Europe. Families often spring into action on the marriage front when they discover that their young people have formed what they regard as inappropriate relationships—perhaps with someone of a different religion or ethnicity, perhaps just someone felt to be of bad character—and the parents then start searching for what they hope will be a more "traditional," less westernized spouse, very often from their own countries of origin (Samad and Eade 2000). In such cases, the insistence of the parents may grow in direct proportion to the reluctance of their children, and what was initially conceived as an arranged marriage becomes forced. It is not easy to estimate the scale of this problem, for as with rape and domestic violence, the reported figures largely depend on whether people think public authorities are acting effectively to address it. The material discussed here derives from initiatives against forced marriage in the United Kingdom, where the figure commonly cited is one thousand young people forced into marriage each year. This is widely regarded as an underestimate. (For a fuller discussion of the U.K. initiatives, see Phillips and Dustin 2004.)

Documented cases include ones where parents or other family members

---

2. In the United Kingdom, marriages between partners from different ethnic groups account for only about 1 percent of the total. The willingness to marry "out" of one's own group is considerably higher among those in minority ethnic groups. A survey from the mid-1990s showed 20 percent of African Caribbeans married to or living with a white partner, 17 percent of Chinese, and 4 percent of Indians (Modood and Berthoud 1997, 29–30).

have kidnapped an underage girl, taken her out of the country, and held her in captivity until she "agrees" to the marriage. Though a really determined minimalist might quibble that no one was manhandling the girl when she went through the ceremony, these cases come as close as one can imagine to the bound hands or pistol to the head, and would be recognized by most as instances of forced marriage. Others are less clear-cut, and part of the difficulty in developing an effective public strategy against forced marriage is that it is not always evident whether a marriage is forced or arranged. Coerced entry into a marriage contract can take many different forms and would not always be described as such even by those most affected. The language used by a group of young South Asian women in London to describe their marriages makes it pretty clear that most of them felt they had no power to refuse. "[Y]ou just have to go along with it," says one, "if you didn't there would be just hell to pay from your parents and all your relatives" (Bhopal 1999, 121). But none of these interviewees described her marriage as "forced." They may have succumbed to emotional blackmail, they may have gone along with their parents' preferences because they felt they had no other choice, but they did in the end "agree." Given the almost inevitable gray areas between coercion and persuasion, how are we to distinguish between marriages arranged by parents on behalf of their children, but voluntarily accepted by the children, and those arranged by parents *against* their children's wishes, that should more rightly be regarded as forced?

In principle, the distinction is clear and revolves around consent: "In the tradition of arranged marriages, the families of both spouses take a leading role in arranging the marriage, but the choice whether to solemnise the arrangement remains with the spouses and can be exercised at any time. The spouses have the right to choose—to say no—at any time. In forced marriage, there is no choice" (Home Office 2000, 10). But of course people say no, and later agree, or say yes because they cannot face the consequences of refusal: are we to say that all such marriages are therefore voluntary? The notion that marriage should be based on consent is common to all religions, and it is hard to imagine any cleric conducting a marriage ceremony with one or other of the potential spouses held under restraint or refusing to go through the forms of agreement. So if the marriage happens, then at one level, the spouses must have agreed. The question is what kind of pressure was exerted on people to make them agree, and at what point this might be said to vitiate the consent.

The largest survey currently available in Britain was carried out in the mid-1990s as part of an investigation into ethnic minorities in Britain (Modood and Berthoud 1997). Those surveyed were of South Asian origin (this being the largest group in Britain practicing arranged marriage) and comprised Hindus, Muslims, and Sikhs. The investigation was undertaken, however, before there was much public awareness of the phenomenon of forced marriage, and the questions were framed in ways that make it difficult to get at a distinction between forced and arranged. Several levels of parental involvement were distinguished: "Parents made the decision"; "I had a say but parents' decision"; "Parents had a say but my decision"; "I talked to my parents but my decision"; "I made decision on my own"; and a category for those who "can't say" (Modood and Berthoud 1997, 318). Parental involvement remained high for all groups, with only 20 percent of younger Indian respondents and 8 percent of younger Bangladeshis and Pakistanis saying they made the decision on their own. For a majority of the older respondents, the parents were not just involved but actually made the decision; but this had become a minority experience for most of those under thirty-five, the exception being Muslim women, two-thirds of whom still reported that their parents made the decision. Parental *involvement* seems too large a category even to qualify a marriage as arranged, for it potentially catches in its net any family where young people discuss current boyfriends or girlfriends with their parents, and seek their opinions on who might make a good spouse. Parental *decision*, on the other hand, must include a mixture of arranged and forced. If the parents made the decision, this could mean that the young people had no strong opinion on the matter (unlikely but not impossible); that they initially disagreed but were eventually persuaded to their parents' point of view; or that they continued to disagree but were overruled. For those falling into the last two categories, there has to be a question mark over the degree of consent.

This is, in fact, increasingly recognized in the courts, where there has been a growing awareness of the complexities surrounding consent. Up until the early 1980s, petitioners to the English and Welsh courts seeking the annulment of what they claimed to be a forced marriage had to establish that they had been frightened into agreement by a "genuine and reasonably held fear" of danger to "life, limb or liberty." The courts operated, in other words, with a robustly self-sufficient notion of responsibility, and petitioners had to establish some version of the pistol to their heads. The principle had been established in 1971 in the influential case of *Szechter v Szechter*, which involved a marriage of convenience, entered into in order to extricate the woman, who was in poor health, from a Polish prison where she was being held for antistate activities. Though the petition was successful, the judge was careful to stress that it was "insufficient to invalidate an otherwise good marriage that a party has entered into it in order to escape from a *disagreeable* situation" (my italics). There had to be—as in this case there was—a more substantial threat to liberty or life. When subsequently applied to cases of forced marriage, this ruling had predictably harsh effects, for the kind of pressure parents exert on children in order to get them to accept a favored marriage partner is more commonly emotional than physical.

From the early 1980s onward, the courts have increasingly acknowledged this, and have eased up on their initially robust view of coercion to recognize the diffuse ways in which vulnerable young people can be forced into marriage against their will. In *Hirani v Hirani* (1983), the court took into account the applicant's age (she was nineteen at the time of the marriage) and her financial dependence on her parents, as well as the evidence that her (Hindu) parents had arranged the marriage in order to prevent her association with a young Muslim man. Concluding that the crucial question was not whether she was in fear of her life or liberty, but whether her mind had been overborne, the court granted a decree of nullity. In *Mahmood v Mahmood* (1993), the court took the young woman's age and "cultural background" into account in assessing whether her parents' threat to cut off financial support and send her to live in Pakistan could be seen as overriding her will. In *Mahmud v Mahmud* (1994), it decided there was "no general basis for expecting the male to be stronger than the female or the thirty-year-old to be less swayed by conscience than the twenty-four-year-old"; and granted a decree of nullity to a thirty-year-old man who had been made to believe that his persistent refusal to marry had brought about the death of his father.[3] In *Sohrab v Khan* (2002), the video of the wedding ceremony, showing the bride's unhappiness, was used as evidence that she had not freely given her consent. All these judgments recognize that there is more to free consent than simply the absence of physical force. On the interpretation of duress being employed in these decisions, many of the marriages currently described as arranged would more properly be regarded as forced.

I applaud the legal developments, but they still leave tricky questions about the nature of free decision and the meaning of consent. In part, they recognize that decisions can come with almost unbearably high costs attached: the cost to a vulnerable young woman of losing her family's financial and emotional support; or the cost to a loving son of carrying the blame for his father's death. In such cases, the costs of continuing to reject the proposed marriage were

---

3. The man had been living for some years with a non-Muslim woman, with whom he already had one child and was expecting another, and the cousin brought over from Pakistan for the marriage had already been deported by the immigration authorities at the time of the case. These circumstances help explain the liberality of the judgment.

indeed high. But what made them so overwhelming as to invalidate the apparent consent? We would not, presumably, wish to invalidate *every* decision arrived at under emotional or financial pressure, so what is it that marks these ones out as different? Chandran Kukathas (2003, 107) has argued that the fact that certain decisions come with high costs attached is irrelevant, for while "[c]ost may have a large bearing on the decision taken . . . it has no bearing on the individual's freedom to take it." "No bearing" is surely too cavalier, but it is true that there is a cost attached to every decision (you have to give up something, if only time, in order to do something else); and that the size of the cost does not seem to be the deciding factor. His own example is the CEO who is offered a billion dollars not to leave his position to become a university professor; this makes the decision to leave extremely costly, but we would hardly conclude that it makes him less free to go. Or we might consider the more commonplace example of the highly paid company executive who is deciding whether to give up her career in order to look after her child full time. Measured in terms of loss of income and loss of social status, it will be more "costly" for her to do this than for her sister, who works for low wages in the local supermarket, to make the same decision. All other things being equal, the two women could find themselves living a similarly precarious existence; since one gave up so much more than the other to be with her child, we can say that the costs attached to her decision are considerably higher. But this does not seem enough of a reason to say she had *no* choice, nor is it so obviously a reason to say she had *less* of a choice. Indeed, when the higher cost reflects a position of privilege (the company executive has been earning more than her sales assistant sister for years), it seems odd to represent it as reducing her freedom of choice.

This is one concern. The other is that arguments that depend on vulnerability to cultural norms and expectations can perpetuate stereotypes of minority cultural groups. In the cases noted above, the legal judgment was informed by a perception of the typical South Asian family as more close-knit than is the norm across Western Europe, and correspondingly harder for its members to challenge. This is most explicit in *Mahmood v Mahmood*, where the young woman's "cultural background" was cited as explaining why she might have been particularly vulnerable to her parents' threats. She was, by implication, less able than a girl from a different background to assert herself against her parents, and more likely to succumb to their pressure. This may or may not be sociologically plausible, but it says, in effect, that "culture" makes people less capable of autonomous action, and less responsible for what they do. Note that when this kind of argument is attempted on behalf of male defendants in criminal cases, feminists mostly want to reject it (Phillips, 2007). "My culture made me do it" is not regarded as an acceptable defense for a man who has killed an unfaithful wife or a father who has killed what he viewed as a sexually wayward daughter; and with a few disturbing exceptions, the courts in Europe have not been sympathetic to this type of defense. So is there a potential inconsistency here? If "cultural background" can be used to explain away a woman's seeming consent to a marriage, can it not also be used to explain away a man's violent reaction to his wife's infidelity? If vulnerability to cultural expectations and family pressure can cast doubt on the significance of a consent to marry, why not extend the same compassion to defendants in so-called "honor crime" cases?

We can, perhaps, extricate ourselves from the seeming inconsistency by insisting that criminal cases be judged by more stringent criteria than those involving the dissolution of a marriage, but even if we do so, we are left with the worrying implication that women from a minority ethnocultural group are less capable than others of giving their consent. One of the points repeatedly highlighted by Carole Pateman in her analysis of patriarchy is the tendency to treat a woman's consent as inherently unstable. The most notorious examples come from rape cases, where defendants have successfully argued that they understood the woman's "no" as really a "yes." We have not yet seen the last of this, but the once widespread perception of women as less than autonomous beings is no longer so pronounced. It lingers on, however, in the treatment of women from minority or non-Western cultures. When "cultural background" is offered in the American or European context as a reason for thinking that seeming consent was in reality enforced submission, the move is almost entirely reserved for women from minority cultural groups; one might go further and say it is almost entirely reserved for women from racialized minorities (see also Volpp 2000). Compare what happens when someone socialized within a Christian, Jewish, or secular culture takes a marriage partner. We may find ourselves puzzled by their choice. We may, on occasion, observe that they ended a previous relationship with a partner disliked by their parents and settled for someone more in tune with the class, religious, or "racial" preferences of their family. (This is not, after all, an unusual occurrence.) But we still, on the whole, regard it as *their* choice, and do not describe the decision to marry as submission to an all-powerful family. The marital choices of women from minority or nonhegemonic cultures are, by contrast, more likely to be regarded as inauthentic. It is when Muslim or Hindu or Sikh women take a marriage partner favored by their families that it becomes more common to question whether they really gave their consent.

The presumption that young people from minority cultural groups are less able to act autonomously has already had some disturbing consequences in public policy. As the phenomenon of forced marriage becomes more recognized in official circles, governments have increasingly looked to immigration control as their way of containing it: they have focused, that is, on cases that involve spouses brought in from abroad and have introduced immigration restrictions in the name of protecting vulnerable young girls. In 2002, Denmark amended its Aliens Act to make it impossible to bring an overseas spouse or cohabitee into the country when either party is under twenty-four.[4] Though the legislation was framed in race-neutral terms, applying to everyone except citizens of the European Union and other Nordic countries, there is no doubt that it was conceived with ethnic minority Danes in mind, and it effectively establishes a minimum age of twenty-four for anyone seeking an overseas partner. Similar regulations have been adopted in Netherlands and the United Kingdom, though not with such a high age limit. The declared object is to protect vulnerable young people from coercion into unwanted marriages, the argument being that they will be better able to withstand family pressure when they are older. The effect, however, is to infantilize ethnic minority women. In the Danish instance, a woman planning to marry an overseas partner has to reach the ripe age of twenty-four before she will be regarded as acting on her own initiative. Under the less draconian U.K. regulations, she has to be two years older than her counterpart marrying a U.K. partner before she can be trusted to know her own mind. Without in any way understating the pressures that can be brought to bear on young people to get them to submit to an unwanted marriage, I find the blanket tendency to discount decisions made by younger people in minority cultures deeply worrying. Public policy does not, on the whole, ban an entire practice because of evidence that some individuals are being coerced into it. This becomes the standard response only when it is presumed that certain groups of people do not (or cannot) know their own mind (for further elaboration of this point, see Phillips 2007).

Sawitri Saharso has addressed this tendency to deny women's autonomy in

---

4. The minimum age before 3 June 2000 had been eighteen; at that point, new regulations came into force, abolishing the automatic right to family reunification for spouses aged eighteen to twenty-five, and replacing it by a discretionary right that depended, among other things, on establishing that the marriage was "undoubtedly contracted at the resident person's own desire." The Aliens (Consolidation) Act 2002 eases up a bit on age (twenty-four instead of twenty-five), but significantly reduces the scope for discretion. Other elements of the new legislation include a requirement that the spouses' aggregate ties with Denmark must be stronger than their aggregate ties with another country.

her analysis of multicultural policy in the Netherlands (Saharso 2003). She gives as one illustration a public discussion that took place in the late 1990s over the supposed use of sex-selective abortion, and whether the Dutch legislation should be tightened to prevent abortion on the grounds of sex. The presumption was that certain minority groups in the Netherlands had a cultural preference for boys, were using ultrasound scanning to identify female fetuses, and then arranging for their abortion. (Saharso notes that there is no evidence that this was a widespread practice.) In one revealing contribution, a newspaper journalist suggested that a Muslim woman requesting the abortion of a female fetus could not be regarded as expressing her own desire or choice, but only as reflecting a culturally imposed requirement for boys. This being so, her "wishes" should be discounted. Ceding to the request would mean capitulating to a misogynist culture.

Saharso notes the danger in this way of approaching the issue. In most circumstances where a woman requests an abortion, she is responding in some way to social constraints: perhaps to the difficulties in her society of bringing up a child in poverty, or without a partner; perhaps to the difficulties in her society of combining motherhood with a career. That she might have reached a different decision had the circumstances been more favorable, is not, on the whole, taken as invalidating her choice. Why, then, is the decision treated as less authentically "hers" when she is responding to the difficulties in her social/cultural group of having another girl? There seems to be a rather shaky distinction here between choosing not to have another child because the social inequalities of contemporary capitalism mean the family will be condemned to poverty (regarded as a sad but legitimate choice); and choosing not to have another *girl* child because the gender inequalities of one's culture mean the family will be condemned to poverty (an unacceptable capitulation to misogyny). The point—for both Saharso and myself—is not that sex selective abortion is fine. But it is problematic to make the case against it depend on denying the moral agency of women from minority cultures, on denying the validity of women's consent.

This, then, is the worry. Forced marriage is an undoubted harm. Initiatives to prevent it should not focus exclusively on instances that involve the use of physical force but should address the many other ways in which pressure can be exerted on people to extract a semblance of consent. Public authorities clearly have a responsibility to assist citizens who have been kidnapped, tricked into traveling overseas, or held under house arrest until they "agree" to a marriage; and there has been promising action on this front in recent years in the United Kingdom, India, Bangladesh, and Pakistan. Public authorities also have a responsibility to address the more covert instances of forced marriage, cases where the agreement is extracted through months of emotional blackmail, from young people who can see no other way out. The difficulty is that extending the initiative in this way seems to depend on querying the status of "consent," and could easily encourage a wholesale denial of the moral agency of people from minority cultural groups. Imagine the subsequent scenario, with each and every minority "choice" scrutinized for the overweening power of culture, and each and every arranged marriage brought under public suspicion. In a political context that is all too ready to contrast the liberated individualism of the West with the oppressive closure of the Rest, this threatens a disturbing hierarchy of cultures.

Pateman on Property in the Person

The argument Carole Pateman develops in *The Sexual Contract* is illuminating here, for it offers an alternative way of querying the validity of the marriage contract that does not rely on denying the capacity to consent. As noted above, Pateman distinguishes between the conditions under which a contract is entered into (where one party might be under immense pressure to agree to unfavorable terms), and the possibly exploitative nature of the contract once it has been made. Where others have focused on the first, she is more interested in the second. Drawing inspiration from Marx's analysis of the wage contract, she argues that even the fairest of contracts can still be exploitative, if its very purpose is to establish a relationship of subordination. As lawyers will tell you, the point at which a contract bites is the point where it commits you to something you no longer wish to do. Up till then, there is no need for a contract; you happily do what the other wishes, perhaps because it is also what you wish, perhaps because you think it the right thing to do. It is when the action becomes less voluntary that the existence of the contract matters, and this is when it becomes apparent that the contract establishes a relationship of power. As Marx put it in a famous passage from *Capital* where he shifts our attention from the sphere of exchange to that of production, "a certain change takes place, or so it appears, in the physiognomy of the *dramatis personae*." What had earlier been "a very Eden of the innate rights of man," with buyer and seller contracting as free and equal persons, now becomes a relationship of subordination: "He who was previously the money-owner now strides out in front as a capitalist; the possessor of labour-power follows as his worker. The one smirks self-importantly and is intent on business; the other is timid and holds back, like someone who has brought his own hide to market and now has nothing else to expect but—a tanning" (Marx 1976, 280). As Pateman describes it, this kind of contract establishes a condition of *civil subordination*, for what we have "freely" given up is some of our power to govern ourselves.

In Pateman's analysis, the exploitation built into the contract is particularly stark when the contract involves property in the person—"[c]ontracts about property in the person inevitably create subordination" (1988, 153)— and much of the subsequent feminist discussion of her work has revolved around this (e.g., Schwarzenbach 1990–91; Brown 1995; Gatens 1996; Fraser 1997). Some have raised doubts about her analysis of the prostitution contract and the suggestion that it is impossible to separate out the sale of sexual services from the sale of the body itself. They have argued that treating the prostitute as engaged in something intrinsically different from others who sell their "bodily services"—the dancer, the nightclub singer, or, in Martha Nussbaum's odd example (1999b), the professor of philosophy—helps sustain the social stigma surrounding prostitution, and thereby the exploitative conditions under which prostitutes work. Others have taken issue with the critique of the surrogate motherhood contract as extending to women "the masculine conception of the individual as owner, and the conception of freedom as the capacity to do what you will with your own," and thereby sweeping away "any intrinsic relation between the female owner, her body and reproductive capacities" (Pateman 1988, 216). This has been felt to buy into a sentimentalized notion of woman as peculiarly bound up with her body, in ways that exaggerate the differences between women and men. Oddly, many of the criticisms depend on a point Pateman herself makes central to her argument: that what is true of prostitution or surrogate motherhood is also true of any kind of waged work. The curious misreading is, I think, revealing, for it confirms how difficult it has become for people to think of contract per se as bad.

Pateman does stress that the peculiar twist to the prostitution or surrogate motherhood contract is that the body is not just incidental but the whole point of the deal; and she argues that this marks these contracts out as different from the standard wage-labor contract, which requires a body but is only really concerned with the services that body performs. There is some suggestion here that men want power, not just over women, but specifically over their bodies. In other parts of the *Sexual Contract*, there is also some suggestion that women are bound up in their bodies in ways that differ from men. But in most ways, Pateman's analysis of "body-contracts" follows the contours of Marx's analysis of wage labor, making similar points about the impossibility of separating out any worker from his or her services. As she puts it in a later essay, "A worker cannot send along capacities or services by themselves to an employer. The worker has to be present in the workplace if the capacities are to be 'employed,' to be put to use" (Pateman 2002, 33). The point, as I understand it, is not that contracts regarding marriage, prostitution, and surrogate motherhood are qualitatively different from any other kind of contract, because of some weird way in which women (but only women) relate to their bodies and selves. The point is that *all* contracts regarding property in the person (hence, also, all wage-labor contracts) involve handing oneself over to someone else's power.

This perception that freedom is not only about the conditions on which we enter an agreement, but also what kind of agreement it is, provides the extra dimension needed to address the issue of forced marriage. When attention is focused exclusively on the conditions under which people agree to marry (the more familiar way in which critics query the freedom of contract), we seem to face an unhappy choice between condoning as voluntary a number of marriages that ought to be regarded as forced, or discounting as inauthentic the supposed consent of individuals from minority cultural groups. Either we restrict the category of forced marriage to the dramas of overt compulsion (thereby denying public assistance to those who suffer "only" from emotional blackmail). Or we regard all arranged marriages with suspicion, all young women from minority cultural groups as victims, and refuse to consider them as moral agents. This second route reeks of cultural hierarchy. If we take it, moreover, it becomes hard to develop a consistent critique of cultural defense.

Drawing our attention to the content of the contract as well as the conditions under which it is entered, Pateman offers a way forward from these dilemmas. The crucial point about marriage is that it falls into that category of agreement in which individuals concede some element of personal, bodily, autonomy. It is not a one-off agreement (I'll swap you this for that); nor is it an agreement whose performance can be delegated to somebody else (I'm sorry, I can't after all drive you to the airport, but I'll pay for a taxi instead). Marriage is a contract involving property in the person, and as such requires one's presence in order for the contract to be fulfilled. This is why the right to divorce is so important, for while we may think people should continue to be bound to a promise to pay us a million dollars even when they no longer find it so convenient, this is of a different order from being bound to share someone's life, home, and bed even when you no longer love or respect them. It is also, I suggest, why "reluctant" agreement is particularly problematic in the case of marriage. If I reluctantly agree to sell my house for less than I feel it is worth—perhaps because circumstances make it impossible for me to wait for another buyer—the reluctance does not give me the right to turn up on what is now your doorstep and tell you the deal is off. Reluctantly agreeing to marry is, however, of a different order, for while the reluctance may dissolve after marriage (and many people do talk of how they came to know and respect their partners after marriage, not before), marriage is not the sort of contract that should be based on reluctant consent.

This is graphically illustrated in the advice given by the United Kingdom's Forced Marriage Unit to young people who fear they are about to be taken abroad for marriage purposes. Though anxious enough to have contacted the unit for advice on what to do, many remain reluctant to cause a rift in their family by refusing to join them on the proposed trip, and they often decide to swallow their anxieties and just trust that the fears are misplaced. Staff counseling the young people sometimes make the point that if they do find themselves forced into marriage, they will thereby find themselves exposed to rape, for agreement to marry will be taken as agreement to sex and may well end up with agreement to become a mother. This is a very Pateman-like point. It relies on the fact that a contract to marry is an unusual kind of contract, dealing with property in the person. As such, it is the kind of contract that hands *you* (not your money or car or house) over into someone else's power.

In the twenty years since *The Sexual Contract* was published, domestic violence has become more vigorously pursued by the police, and marital rape is more widely recognized as a prosecutable offence. In many legal jurisdictions, divorce is more readily available and divorce settlements have become more equitable; indeed, in quite a few jurisdictions, men now complain that they are treated less well than women. Women have more protections within marriage, and find it easier, on the whole, to leave, and the loss of autonomy associated with an agreement to marry has been correspondingly reduced. It would be risky, however, to exaggerate the implications of this, and excessively optimistic to suggest that the marriage contract no longer involves any relationship of power. Like an agreement to work for someone, an agreement to marry involves suspending some of the powers of self-government. Focusing only on the moment of consent (was it free or forced?) is therefore particularly misleading when it comes to marriage, for we also need to take account of the kind of agreement that marriage entails. I noted earlier that we would not want to invalidate every decision arrived at under emotional or financial pressure, and asked what, if anything, marks out decisions regarding marriage as different. Well, perhaps it is this. Agreeing to marry is not just any old agreement. It is an agreement to give up on some of your future freedom to decide for yourself.

Pateman says at one point that "[a] free social order cannot be a contractual order" (1988, 232). I have never been entirely sure how to take this: as an encouragement to create a social order with no contracts at all? to create a social order with no contracts in the person? or as a reminder that freedom is always under threat in a contractual order, and needs to be underpinned by a strong democracy in order to keep the dangers at bay? Whichever interpretation one adopts, Pateman is surely right to point out the fallacy of contract, the false belief that if you have freely agreed, you cannot then say that fulfilling the contract makes you unfree. There may be cases where this once-and-for-all agreement is plausible, but not marriage. Pateman's critique of the marriage and other "body contracts" then provides us, I think, with some of what we need to differentiate the kind of agreement necessary to marriage from other kinds of agreement. In doing so, it helps us avoid the pitfalls in discussions of forced and arranged marriage, and, specifically, the suggestion that the "consent" of a young Muslim, Hindu, or Sikh is less valid than the consent of a young Christian, atheist, or Jew. The point about forced marriage is not just that people are forced into it, but that what they are forced into is marriage. The extra vigilance required in relation to marriage is dictated by the nature of the marriage contract, not by a lesser capacity for decision-making among individuals from minority cultural groups.

References

Beauvoir, Simone de. 1969. *The Second Sex*. London: New English Library. (First published in France in 1949; first English translation, 1953.)

Bhopal, Kalwant. 1999. "South Asian Women and Arranged Marriages in East London." In *Ethnicity, Gender, and Social Change*, edited by R. Barot, H. Bradley, and S. Fenton, 117–34. London: Macmillan; Basingstoke: St. Martin's.

Brown, Wendy. 1995. "Liberalism's Family Values." In *States of Injury*, 135–65. Princeton: Princeton University Press.

Elster, Jon. 1983. *Sour Grapes: Studies in the Subversion of Rationality*. Cambridge: Cambridge University Press.

Fraser, Nancy. 1997. "Beyond the Master/Subject Model: On Carole Pateman's *The Sexual Contract*." In *Justice Interruptus: Critical Reflections on the "Postsocialist" Condition*, 225–35. London: Routledge.

Friedman, Marilyn. 2003. *Autonomy, Gender, Politics.* Oxford: Oxford University Press.

Gatens, Moira. 1996. *Imaginary Bodies: Ethics, Power, and Corporeality.* London: Routledge.

Home Office. 2000. *A Choice by Right: The Report of the Working Group on Forced Marriage.* London: Home Office Communications Directorate.

Jaggar, Alison. 1983. *Feminist Politics and Human Nature.* Totowa, N.J.: Rowman and Allanheld.

Kukathas, Chandran. 2003. *The Liberal Archipelago: A Theory of Diversity and Freedom.* Oxford: Oxford University Press.

MacKenzie, Catriona, and Natalie Stoljar, eds. 2000. *Relational Autonomy: Feminist Perspectives on Autonomy, Agency and the Social Self.* Oxford: Oxford University Press.

Marx, Karl. 1976. *Capital.* Vol. 1. London: Penguin. First published 1867.

Modood, Tariq, Richard Berthoud, et al. 1997. *Ethnic Minorities in Britain: Diversity and Disadvantage. Fourth National Survey of Ethnic Minorities.* London: Policy Studies Institute.

Nedelsky, Jennifer. 1989. "Reconceiving Autonomy: Sources, Thoughts, and Possibilities." *Yale Journal of Law and Feminism* 1, no. 1:7–36.

Nussbaum, Martha C. 1999a. "The Feminist Critique of Liberalism." In *Sex and Social Justice,* 55–80. Oxford: Oxford University Press.

———. 1999b. "'Whether from Reason or Prejudice': Taking Money for Bodily Services." In *Sex and Social Justice,* 276–98. Oxford: Oxford University Press.

———. 2000. *Women and Human Development: The Capabilities Approach.* Cambridge: Cambridge University Press.

Pateman, Carole. 1988. *The Sexual Contract.* Cambridge: Polity Press.

———. 2002. "Self-ownership and Property in the Person." *Journal of Political Philosophy* 10, no. 1:20–53.

Phillips, Anne. 2003. "When Culture Means Gender: Issues of Cultural Defence in the English Courts." *Modern Law Review* 66:510–31.

———. 2007. *Multiculturalism without Culture.* Princeton: Princeton University Press.

Phillips, Anne, and Moira Dustin. 2004. "UK Initiatives on Forced Marriage: Regulation, Exit, and Dialogue." *Political Studies* 52:531–51.

Saharso, Sawitri. 2003. "Feminist Ethics, Autonomy, and the Politics of Multiculturalism." *Feminist Theory* 4, no. 2:199–215.

Samad, Yunas, and John Eade. 2002. *Community Perceptions of Forced Marriage.* London: Community Liaison Unit, Foreign and Commonwealth Office. Available at http://www.fco.gov.uk.

Schwarzenbach, Sibyl. 1990–91. "Contractarians and Feminists Debate Prostitution." *Review of Law and Social Change* 18:103–30.

Sen, Amartya. 1995. "Gender Inequality and Theories of Justice." In *Women, Culture, and Development*, edited by M. Nussbaum and J. Glover, 259–73. Oxford: Clarendon Press.

Sunstein, Cass. 1991. "Preferences and Politics." *Philosophy and Public Affairs* 20:3–34.

Volpp, Leti. 2000. "Blaming Culture for Bad Behavior." *Yale Journal of Law and the Humanities* 12:89–116.

Cases

Hirani v Hirani [1983] 4 F.L.R. 232
Mahmood v Mahmood [1993] S.L.T 589
Mahmud v Mahmud [1994] S.L.T. 599
Sohrab v Khan [2002] SCLR 663
Szechter v Szechter [1971] 2 W.L.R. 170

Women's Work: Its Irreplaceability and Exploitability
Robert E. Goodin

> Only during the last fifty years in Britain has
> a wife become the sole servant in the family
> —*Carole Pateman (1988b, 127)*

Throughout her distinguished career, Carole Pateman has been sensitizing us to the importance of economic security in underwriting people's full participation in the political and social life of their community.[1]

A precondition for securing economic security for women, in particular, is the recognition of the peculiar nature and value of the work that they do in society: a recognition, as Pateman puts it in her essay "The Patriarchal Welfare State," "that *as women* they have specific capacities, talents, needs and concerns"; that "their unpaid work providing welfare could be seen, as Wollstonecraft saw women's tasks as mothers, as women's work *as citizens,* just as their husband's paid work is central to men's citizenship" (1988b, 198, 197).

It is important that women's unpaid work be recognized as work—as productive labor—and valued as such. But it is equally important to recognize the *distinctiveness* of the productive contributions often lumped together under the category of "women's work."

Important though it is to get women's unpaid household labor properly counted in the national accounts or gross national product, it is important also to recognize that merely bringing those contributions under the measuring rod of money misses much that matters. It is not just that that metric miscounts the value of that work. It also inevitably mischaracterizes that work in certain ways, ways that are crucial to the dynamics of household formation

---

This chapter is in many ways a companion to my earlier collaborations with Nancy Folbre (Folbre and Goodin 2004) and Diane Gibson (Goodin and Gibson 2002). For conversations on these themes over many years, I am grateful to them, to Eva Kittay—and of course to Carole Pateman.

1. Represented, most recently, in her work in support of "basic income": Pateman 2004.

and functioning, and even more crucial (as I shall show) in household dissolution.

This in a nutshell is my central claim: The same features that make households valuable (to both the men and the women in them) make women exploitable within them. And I think I can show that in a way that even the most hard-bitten "Chicago economist" would have to accept.

"Chicago economics" is of course just shorthand for the market liberalism that has dominated mainstream social policy discourses for a quarter century, dating from the rise of Reagan and Thatcher. Its ethos is starkly individualist and radically subjectivist, with preferences and choices based on them driving social behavior (Hakim 2000). The slogan of the Chicago School in general is "free to choose" (Friedman and Friedman 1980), parodied by Roemer (1988) as "free to lose." But there is a distinctively "Chicago economics" way of looking at the family that I shall here be particularly concerned to critique. Its chief exponent, Gary Becker (1976, chap. 11; 1981), argues for a sharp division of labor within the family, in which the higher paid spouse (usually the husband) does all the household's paid labor while the lower paid spouse (usually the wife) does all the household work. Becker and his "Chicago economics" followers think that that is a "rational" way to organize your household, on the grounds that that way of organizing the family minimizes the total number of hours the household as a whole spends on paid plus unpaid work. But such ways of thinking misrepresents the distinctive nature of women's caring work within the family, which is irreplaceable and exploitable in ways to which Carole Pateman is sensitive but market liberals and Chicago economists are not.

Unpaid Household Labor

A major portion of women's labor is unpaid household labor. Being unpaid, it is unpriced. Being unpriced, it is uncounted in ordinary national-accounting conventions and undervalued by the standards of commercialized society, according to which only the countable counts, or anyway it counts for far more than the uncountable (Waring 1988; Schor 1992, chap. 4).

Natural though that now seems to some, it was not always so (Folbre 1991; 1994, pt. 2). As Carole Pateman reminded us in her discussion of "Wives, slaves and wage slaves" in *The Sexual Contract:*

> The construction of the male worker as "breadwinner" and his wife as his "dependent" can be charted in the classifications of the Census

> in Britain and Australia. In the Census of 1851 in Britain, women employed in unpaid domestic work were "placed . . . in one of the productive classes along with paid work of a similar kind." This classification changed after 1871, and by 1911 unpaid housewives had been separated from the economically active population. . . . The Australians divided up the population more decisively than the British, and the 1891 Census was based on two categories of "breadwinner" and "dependent." Unless explicitly stated otherwise, women's occupation was classed as domestic, and domestic workers were put in the dependent category. (Pateman 1988b, 137)

Thus was cast in statistical cement the view that "housework is not 'work'": the view that "work takes place [only] in the men's world of capitalism and workplaces" (Pateman 1988b, 136).

Accounting for All *of Women's Work*

Feminist economists have launched a campaign to crack that statistical cement, reforming national accounts statistics on precisely this point (Waring 1988). They have made some real headway, enlisting the support of the Organization for Economic Cooperation and Development (OECD) no less (Beckerman 1978; Goldschmidt-Clermont and Pagnossin-Aligisakis 1995). Several countries are now attempting to produce "satellite accounts" designed to include, first and foremost, the value of "home production" (unpaid household labor) alongside more marketized measures of economic activity in fuller national accounts (Holloway et al. 2002).

These measures are problematic in myriad ways, of course. Not least among them is how to fix a monetary value for activities, like unpaid household labor, that do not fall under the measuring rod of money in the ordinary course of events. It is ordinarily thought that there are fundamentally just two options: an "opportunity cost" method that values the time spent in unpaid household labor at the rate of pay that that person could (given her human capital characteristics) command in the paid labor market; or a "replacement cost" method that values unpaid household labor at the price the household would have to pay to hire in someone else to perform the same services.[2]

---

2. Those two are both input-based valuations. There is a less-discussed output-based alternative: take what it would cost to purchase the service (a restaurant meal, for example), subtract the costs of capital and raw materials required to provide that service, and assign the residual as the value of the labor input. Under this approach, the value of labor is unconnected to actual wage rates. I am grateful to Nancy Folbre for this explication (cf. Ironmonger 1996; Holloway, Short and Tempkin 2002).

These two approaches differ in many respects, not least in "cost to whom?" "Opportunity cost" represents the cost to the individual herself: the earnings she has to forego in order to provide the service. "Replacement cost" represents more the "cost to society" of her doing it, rather than buying in substitutes (Folbre 2005).

Unsurprisingly, therefore, two methods can differ dramatically in the values that they assign to the same activity. Imagine a corporate lawyer who spends five hours a week cooking and cleaning her house—activities that she could in principle contract out to hired help. On the "opportunity cost" method, her five hours a week of unpaid household labor would be valued at her hourly wage rate net of tax (say, $200 per billable hour, or $1,000 in total). On the "replacement cost" method, those five hours a week would be valued only at what it would cost to get the cheapest cook-housekeeper to perform the same services ($20 an hour, say, or $100 in total).

There are things to be said for each way of doing the calculation (more of which shortly). But from the hardheaded Chicago economist's point of view, the choice might be thought to be easy. By a simple extension of Becker's (1976, chap. 11; 1981) basic logic sketched above, if the woman could earn the cost of a maid's wages in less time than it would have taken her to do the jobs the maid does for her, then the total number of hours she (and her household, as a whole) spends in paid and unpaid labor would be minimized.[3]

In cases like the corporate lawyer's, where "opportunity cost" exceeds "replacement cost," the Chicago economist would think that the "replacement cost" method of valuing her unpaid household labor simply *has* to be the right method, given the purposes of national accounts statistics. Here is the Chicago economist's reasoning: if the corporate lawyer could have purchased the same (*exactly* the same) services from someone else at lower cost than providing them herself, then bearing the extra cost of providing them herself was a "pure consumption act" on her part. National accounts statistics count production, not consumption.[4]

People always value what they have more than its market price. (Otherwise

---

3. Note the National Academy panel (Abraham and Mackie 2004, 28–34) takes a more moderate line, discussed below.

4. Conversely, in cases where "opportunity cost" is below "replacement cost," the Chicago economist would reckon that "opportunity cost" is the obviously right method, instead. To the Chicago economist's way of thinking, if women who could do the job more cheaply themselves choose to hire it out nonetheless, the difference (what they paid for those replacement services, less what it would have cost them to provide those services themselves) is once again a "pure consumption" act on the part of the women involved. That does not belong in the national accounts, either.

they would have sold it at that market price.) But no one thinks that national accounts statistics should try to figure in the value of all the extra pleasure, above and beyond their market price, that people's cars and homes give them. National accounts are a measure of *production*, and economic activity more generally—of the national capacity to enjoy welfare, not of the levels of welfare actually enjoyed.[5]

So what's wrong with that analysis? Well, one thing might be a general worry about "self-exploitation" (or worse). One cannot help but wonder why a corporate lawyer who spends almost every hour God gives her slaving away at the office should *also* put in lots of time slaving over the stove and at the vacuum, when she could hire in help to do those tasks. Those suspicions are exacerbated by dramatic evidence of waged women doing a "second shift" at home: time-use surveys invariably show that their unpaid labor hours do not decrease by anything like as much as their paid labor hours increase; and their partners' unpaid labor hours increase only very modestly.[6] One suspects some perverse sociological-cum-psychological dynamic might be at work, such that "refusing to do the housework" or "hiring in help" are effectively not options for women even if they go out to paid work—or, anyway, they are much less eligible options, given the social or marital disapprobation attached to them.[7]

One striking piece of evidence in support of that suspicion is this. The time that a woman spends in unpaid household labor declines the more time she spends in paid labor: it declines less than hour-for-hour, as I have said; but it nonetheless declines, just as we would expect. But here is the interesting wrinkle. Once the woman's earnings exceed those of the man in the household, her unpaid household labor time declines *less quickly* as her paid labor time increases than it did when her earnings were lower than her partner's (Bittman et al. 2002).

That is just the opposite of what the Chicago School economist would expect. "The higher your market value, the more time you are spending on things outside the market rather than realizing your higher market potential? Crazy!"

---

5. The same can be said of "income" itself, even at the individual level: how much income someone has tells us her *potential* for well-being; but her actual well-being depends on how she spends it; a rich miser has a high income but an objectively low standard of living (Ringen 1988).

6. Pateman (1988b, 128–29) notes this in her discussion of the "patriarchal welfare state." For further evidence, see: Szalai 1975; Gershuny and Robinson 1988; Hochschild 1989, 1997; Baxter and Gibson 1990; Gershuny 2000, chaps. 3, 5.

7. Pateman 2004, 99. Collectively these enter Folbre's (1994, chap. 2) economic model of the family as the "structure of constraints."

While Chicago economists might be puzzled, Chicago sociologists would not be. Many men fancy themselves head of the household, and they are psychologically threatened when their womenfolk earn more than they do. To purchase domestic peace their women have to reassure them by "overachieving" in their traditional domestic roles.

Chicago economists, of course, pride themselves on expansive utility functions, capable of accommodating any awkward social fact by adding yet one more argument to the already long equation. Here, the response would presumably be simply to say, "Well, in this case the 'replacement costs' include not only the housekeeper's wage but also the disapprobation she would suffer from hiring a housekeeper" (Becker 1976, chap. 12; Brennan and Pettit 2004).

It is not only external disapprobation, from within the household or the wider society, that increases her costs if she does not provide unpaid household services herself, however. Women are sometimes also "prisoners of love," in this further sense: they value more than their partners do the household services and the affective sentiments they betoken (Folbre 2001; England and Folbre 2001). That puts them at a bargaining disadvantage within the household when it comes to any arguments over how much unpaid household work is to be done and by whom.

This does not necessarily depend on bargaining of the ordinarily sordid sense. The same disadvantage accrues in the absence of any hard bargaining. Imagine a case of completely sincere, nonstrategic preference revelation: the man simply puts in as many hours on housework as he thinks necessary and the woman puts in as many more as she thinks necessary. The woman does more because she *cares* more. And while in some sense the man benefits from that, it is not a benefit he would himself have valued highly enough to provide himself (Pollak and Watcher 1975; Lundberg and Pollak 1994).

Purely a Preference?

Chicago economist's point of view would be that the woman does more housework because she *prefers* it (or what is achieved by it) more (Hakim 2000). And that is just to say, once again, that the extra unpaid household labor she does, or the extra price she pays for it, is just a consumption act. She does it because, in her view, it makes her better off. That is at least on balance good for her, not bad: otherwise she would not have done it.[8] In short, instead of

---

8. Canvassed by Abraham and Mackie (2004, 28–32), who transcend that analysis in their final conclusions.

regarding child care and other forms of unpaid household labor as labor—as a *cost*—the Chicago economist invites us to regard "children as pets."[9]

The Chicago economist would go on to insist that the man in her household is not really taking advantage of her, either—at least assuming he is being completely sincere and nonstrategic in the expression of his preferences (though how would we, or even she, ever really know?). Although he certainly benefits from the extra unpaid labor she does in the household, it is not a benefit that he values highly enough to have paid the cost of providing it himself.

It is obviously unfair for people to impose benefits on us that we did not seek and do not want, and then simply send us the bill. Under the law of restitution or unjust enrichment, you have to give back a set of encyclopedias delivered to your house that you did not order; but under that same body of law, you cannot be made to pay for goods you did not order. Yet that is what the Chicago economist sees happening when a woman who values a tidy home more than her man expects recompense from him for doing more tidying than the man himself would have if left to his own devices.

One way to reply to the Chicago economist's insistence that the extra unpaid household labor that women do should be counted as a "pure consumption act" on their part—purely a preference, like any other—is to question where those preferences come from. Are they "really hers" or have they somehow been implanted in her (by social conditioning, manipulative advertising, and such like)? That is how Pateman (2004, 99) replies to arguments that women do more unpaid caring labor and men more paid labor "merely because of differences in individual tastes or preferences."[10]

Even accepting that all preferences (like all beliefs) have in some sense "causal origins," however, I am inclined ordinarily to say (with Lerner 1972) that "they're hers now." To refuse to respect her preferences, just because they have causal origins outside her, is to deny her identity and agency in a way she would be entitled to feel is morally offensive (Anderson 1999). Clearly

---

9. In Nancy Folbre's (2001, chap. 5) delightful phrase: as she put it in a more sober moment, "contrary to neoclassical theory, children are not consumer durables" (Folbre 1982, 325).

10. Here she is critiquing Philippe Van Parijs (1995), whose "example is that the partner who most strongly prefers tidiness will make sure that the home is tidy." But, Pateman (2004, 99) replies, "female partners do not by some quirk happen to prefer tidiness more strongly than their male partners. The institution of marriage and social beliefs about what it means to be a 'wife' or 'husband' have vanished in Van Parijs's analysis, and there are merely two individuals, indistinguishable except for their different tastes for tidy surroundings. His theoretical approach in *Real Freedom for All* precludes analysis of the structure of relations between the sexes."

there are cases—posthypnotic suggestions and the like—where we might think that it nonetheless is right to repudiate the preferences as "not really her own." But this does not seem an attractive strategy in the general case.

A stronger reply, I think, would be to mount a challenge to the "individualistic subjectivism" at the heart of the Chicago economist's theory of value.[11] That can be challenged in either (or both) of two ways. One way is to challenge that theory of value for being too "individualistic," while still accepting its subjectivism. The second way is to challenge that theory for being too "subjectivist," arguing instead for a more "objectivist" theory of value.

The second strategy is easier, and more obvious. There, we simply say that it is objectively good for more unpaid labor to be done in the household—at least of certain sorts, such as raising the children, for example—than the man would, left to his own devices, prefer to do.[12] Maybe it would even be a failure of objective moral duty for the man to neglect his children in the ways that, left to his own devices, he says he would. That is not to deny the sincerity of his protestations. Here, we are accepting that his preferences are as he says they are. We are simply saying that his subjective preferences fail to match the requirements of The Right or The Good, and that those are objective values that trump his mere preferences in cases of conflict.

The first strategy for rebutting the Chicago economist's theory of value is more subtle. This strategy involves accepting that all value is subjective, but insisting that goods can be subjectively valuable to us collectively rather than to us as isolated individuals. In extremis, this might involve notions of collective minds and irreducibly social goods (Taylor 1985). But we need not go nearly that far to mount an effective critique of the Chicago economist's theory of value on this score. We might simply say that the rest of society—understood just as various others outside your household—take a view about how much unpaid household labor your household does.[13] Clearly, we all have a collective preference over how well people raise their children, for one obvious example (Coleman 1993). And if a father proposes to spend less time than we collectively prefer seeing to it that his children are properly reared, our collective preference should trump his personal predilections in the matter (Folbre 1994; England and Folbre 1999).

---

11. Other forms of "unpaid household labor" (ironing socks, washing windows, etc.) may not generate goods that are objectively good from a social point of view.

12. This is one way of reading Pateman's (1989, 197) allusion to Wollstonecraft, quoted at the beginning of this chapter.

13. This is another reading of Pateman's allusion to Wollstonecraft, quoted at the beginning of this chapter.

Those are two perfectly good ways of explaining why a woman who does more unpaid household labor than the man in her household thinks necessary might still be said to be performing socially useful (objectively good, socially preferred) productive labor, rather than just engaging in some sort of "pure consumption act" purely for her own benefit. But it does not yet explain the accounting puzzle with which we began.

Those responses to the individualistic subjectivism of the Chicago economist's theory of value both provide reasons for thinking that more labor should be done in the household than the man would prefer. But both those arguments specify an *amount* of labor that ought be done in the household, not *by whom* it ought be done. Neither of those arguments explains why the extra labor should necessarily be done by the woman herself (or by a member of the household itself, more generally), rather than by hired help. That was the puzzle with which we began: why the corporate lawyer ought not be regarded as performing a self-indulgent act of "pure consumption" in cleaning her own home, when it would have been so much cheaper to hire commercial cleaners.

To address that question, it seems, we really do (as I foreshadowed) have to treat certain sorts of goods produced by members of the household for the household as being different in kind from those that can be procured on the open market. Then we can say that the commercial lawyer is right to produce those goods herself, because there is something in the nature of those goods that they can be produced only by her (cf. Folbre and Nelson 2000). The unpaid household activities we are inclined to code as "caring labor" are valued in part as "labors of love," and to that extent they are not labors for which there are any close market substitutes (Kittay 1998).

It is a general, but underappreciated, fact about goods in general that they rarely have literally a perfect substitute. Any given good displays a wide array of "characteristics," for which they might be valued and under which description they might be chosen (Lancaster 1966; Sen 1980, 1985). Goods that are "close substitutes" for one another under one description (in respect of one valued characteristic) will often not be close substitutes at all for one another under other descriptions (in respect of other characteristics that might be valued instead).

It should therefore come as no surprise to any moderately reflective economist that substitutability might be imperfect when it comes to goods with as many potentially salient characteristics as has labor in the intimate setting of the household (Zelizer 2000). And if the labor is such that she alone can perform it, then her own "opportunity costs" rather than the "replacement costs" of ostensible market substitutes is the right way to value her labor (Abraham and Mackie 2004, 32–34, rec. 1.4).

Why Inside the Household?

There is another reply to Chicago economists' disparagement of highly waged women doing their own housework, rather than hiring in help, that takes the argument more deeply into their home territory.

For this, recall the standard economic theory of the firm, owing to the founder of the Chicago School of "law and economics," R. H. Coase (1937). Why do we have firms at all? Why does anyone ever hire anyone else, rather than just buying all that they need on the open market? The Chicago economists' answer is that firms hire employees when it is easier to monitor the quality of the labor inputs than it would be to monitor the quality of the outputs, that is, the goods they would alternatively have to buy on the open market (Coase 1937).

The standard economic theory of the firm expresses all this in terms of information and monitoring. But the same thing would be true if there were some intrinsic quality of the good that was different, if the same thing simply could not be bought on the open market.

So play the Chicago economics game, for a moment, and think of the family as a firm. Ask the Chicago economist's question about the firm: why internalize production within the household-cum-firm, rather than just hiring in goods and services from outside? Why hire an employee (for which read, "a partner") rather than just buying in the goods and services she or he would produce?

Well, from the Chicago economics perspective, there are basically just two possible answers. One is that you could not obtain the same goods and services from the market. The other is that you could not be as sure of the quality of those goods and services if bought on the open market as you could if they were produced within the family.

But that then means that the "replacement cost" approach to valuing unpaid household labor simply has to be wrong. Replacements cannot be had, or anyway cannot reliably be had.[14]

From that it follows, by the Chicago School's own economic logic, that we cannot then say that women are just exploiting themselves, putting in more

---

14. Replacement cost is, at most, a lower bound on the value of her labor: and it is not even that, if her labor is literally irreplaceable.

hours than necessary in unpaid household labor, *merely* to satisfy their own preferences. They are doing at least some of it (the "caring labor" portion of it) in order to produce something that they could not, or not reliably, buy in from outside the household.

To be sure, they would not do it unless they wanted to do it (or wanted something that doing so does for them). The point remains that it is a productive act, an act producing something of value in the only way it can reliably be produced. It cannot be disparaged as a pure consumption act, like buying a Ferrari rather than a Ford—a preference one ought be welcome to indulge, but for which one ought reasonably expect to pay a price.

Asymmetrical Exits

So far I have been arguing that unpaid household labor is not just undervalued in the national accounts but that it is badly valued—because wrongly characterized—by either of the ways economists have for fitting it into the national accounts. Asking whether "opportunity costs" exceed "replacement costs"—whether it would be cheaper for the woman to hire in help with the housework or to do it herself—assumes that her unpaid household labor is fully replaceable by the labor of someone else from outside the household. Much of it undoubtedly is. But much of the characteristically "caring" labor of the household must, by its nature, be done by an intimate who "cares."[15] That is one important reason why unpaid household labor is different from the ordinary labor market, and indeed one important reason why the household exists at all.

You Can't Take It with You

Just as the inputs into what Chicago economists might dub the "household production function" are different, so too are its outputs. The investment of caring labor is, I have argued, a productive (not just a consumption) act. But what is thereby produced is as peculiar to the particular household as are the inputs that produced it.

Economists generally distinguish between "fixed" and "mobile" capital. An

---

15. Zelizer 2000. For the sake of the analysis I am here developing, I continue to concentrate on that limiting case. For discussions of the more complex circumstances of the real world, see Folbre 1994; Kittay 1998; England and Folbre 1999; Folbre and Nelson 2000; Folbre 2001.

example of the first is a manufacturing plant: once it has been built somewhere, it is hard to relocate elsewhere. An example of the second is human capital: once you have an engineering degree, you can take it wherever you want to build a bridge.

Now, the products of "caring labor" within a household are particular to that household and the people entwined within the caring relationships within it. A mother's investment in caring for her family is not easily transferable to some other family. In that sense, the products of "caring labor" are more like a manufacturing plant than an engineering degree.

Caring labor can also be said to be characterized by "asset specificity." You need one specific set of assets (knowledge, experiences, attitudes) in one caring relationship, which is very different from the set of such assets you need in some other caring relationship. To some limited extent "good parenting" might be a skill that is transferable from one family to another; but to a substantially larger extent, the knowledge, experiences, and attitudes that make you a good parent of one set of children cannot possibly transfer to a completely different set of children.

Economists tell us that workers would rationally invest in acquiring job-specific skills only if they have some substantial guarantee of continuity in that same job over a long period. If they have no such guarantee, it would be much more rational for them to acquire more transferable skills that they can use in any job they find themselves in (Hall and Soskice 2001). If we want to encourage cultivation of job-specific skills—the sorts of assets specific to caring well for this set of people, in the household example—we have to give workers reasonable expectations of being in those positions for a moderately long time.

Conversely, once workers are in positions characterized by high asset specificity and relatively fixed capital investments, they are substantially less mobile than they would otherwise have been. They *can* still leave, of course: we are not talking about a literal slavery contract here. But the greater the ease of leaving the greater a proportion of your capital you can take with you and use productively elsewhere.

Economists are familiar with these issues in economic settings that are more standard. They know that it is easier to impose high taxes on fixed capital than on mobile capital that could easily flee to lower-tax locales, for example. Economistic analysts of the family should simply recognize the corollary of that, as applied to the family.

Breaking Becker Families

Remember the basic Chicago economics story about the family. The rational way to organize it, Gary Becker (1976, chap. 12; 1981) tells us, is for whichever partner has the higher wage rate to do all the household's paid labor, and whichever partner has the lower wage rate to do all the household's unpaid labor. And for once, sociology tracks economics tolerably well: the woman in the household usually has the lower wage rate, and usually does indeed do the bulk of the caring labor within the household (even if she also performs paid labor.)

But consider now the consequences of this division of labor, should the household split-up. The partner who has engaged in preponderantly caring labor ends up with relatively more assets that are specific to that particular household; her investments in it are relatively more "fixed," tied to that particular household and not easily transferred elsewhere. The upshot, then, is that a household hyperefficiently following Becker's prescription ends up being more of a trap for whichever partner (typically the female) who does the bulk of the unpaid caring labor, than it does for the other partner whose paid labor experiences and skills are easily transferable to any other household (Lundberg and Pollak 2003).

There are of course many other forces tying women to unpaid household labor than are captured by Chicago economists' models of a hyperefficient division of labor within the household (Folbre 1994, pt. 2). Historically "marriage bars" (restrictions on hiring married women and antinepotism laws) and trade union resistance have limited married women's employment options outside the home (Schor 1991, 95). To their credit, Chicago economists oppose such discrimination; to their discredit, they do so on grounds of inefficiency rather than injustice (Becker 1957). But whereas Chicago economists can join in opposition to marriage bars and trade union bans as unfortunate sociological facts without any economic justification, they cannot so easily dismiss the source of women's disadvantage that I here identify as merely some "unfortunate sociological fact." Instead, it is a direct corollary of their own efficiency-maximizing prescriptions.

This argument is different from the ordinary sociological one in another way as well. The standard story is that women are trapped in the home, and in unhappy homes all too often, by the lack of opportunities in the paid labor market. Marriage bars and trade union bans prevent them from getting jobs and work experience that would enable them to secure a living wage were their marriage to break up. The lack of any realistic alternative to relying on their existing partner's breadwinning is what traps women, in the standard account.

The account I have here been offering has implications beyond that, however. Not only might women find it harder to secure employment at a living wage outside the home, and be discouraged from leaving for that reason. They are also discouraged from leaving because many of their assets are tied to their particular household, and many of the investments they have sunk into this household are fixed in it. In this account, the disadvantage that women suffer due to specializing as Chicago economists would have them do in unpaid caring labor in the household is that it leaves them with "sticky," immobile capital. And it is that, rather than (or in addition to) blocked labor options, that disadvantages women in the break-up of Becker-style families.

Exploitation, Self- and Otherwise

When Chicago economists see a woman doing unpaid household labor that she could have replaced more cheaply with hired help, they code it as a consumption act. (She must be cooking dinner herself, rather than buying takeaways, because she enjoys cooking.) When sociologists observe the same phenomenon, they are more likely to code it as socialization. (She does it because it is socially expected of her, and she cannot or will not go against those expectations.) When psychologists observe the same phenomenon, they might be tempted to code it as "self-exploitation." (Women, particularly "working women," internalize feelings of guilt that drive them to it.)

No doubt elements of all those explanations are true, in mixtures that vary from person to person and situation to situation. But there is another element of exploitation at work, beyond the narrowly psychological sense of "self-exploitation" (Bubeck 1995).

In his brilliant generalization of the basic Marxian model of exploitation, John Roemer (1982) suggests that we can differentiate a whole range of theories of exploitation, depending simply on "what you are allowed to take with you when you go." By setting the fallback position people would be in were they to withdraw from society, those withdrawal rules set the baseline for bargaining and exchanges that occur within society.

Different views about what counts as exploitation correspond to different views about what you should be able to withdraw when you go. From a capitalist perspective, the just withdrawal rule would be one that allows you to take your own labor power and your own capital with you when you go. By that capitalist standard, feudalism is exploitative because it ties serfs to lords, not allowing them to leave and take with them even their own labor power. From a socialist perspective, the just withdrawal rule would be one that allows you to take your labor power and your per capita share of social capital with you when you go. By that socialist standard, capitalism is exploitative because it allows workers to take with them only their own laor, rather than their per capita share of total social capital.

Consider now an analogous "feminist withdrawal rule." From this feminist perspective, the just withdrawal rule would be one that allows both partners to take an equal share of all that has been invested in the household when they leave.[16] By that standard, it is exploitative for the man to be able to withdraw a larger portion of his investments than the woman, simply because there are more "caring" investments in her portfolio.

People who are exploited are not physically forced to do something. When exploiting them, we certainly take advantage of them. But they are seemingly complicit in that, as well. They are given a choice: in the classically Marxian example, to work for increasingly miserable wages, or to starve outright; in the case of a woman with no marketable skills, to work in the home on whatever terms her husband sets, or to subsist on state support (Folbre 1982). The fact that housewives get what (in some sense) they chose seems to exonerate others from any blame for bad outcomes they suffer in consequence. Thus, the woman who spends more time in unpaid household labor than the Chicago economist tells her is really necessary has, on this model, only (or mainly) herself to blame.

Exploitation, on this analysis, is defined by reference to the "terms of exiting": what you can take with you when you go. The above examples all deal in terms of what you are *allowed* to take with you, how much capital, how much labor power. But there are also some other things that would be simply impossible to take with you when you go.

One such example would be assets specific to the particular household and the investments fixed in it by a woman's caring labor. Insofar as those are things that she cannot take with her when she goes, that forms the baseline for subsequent interactions within the household. She makes choices that are optimal from her own perspective, given that baseline. But what counts as "good" for her—an improvement on that baseline—obviously depends on where that baseline has been set.

16. This "symmetrical" rule governing the breakup of the family would seem to be a natural corollary of feminist prescriptions for "symmetry" within ongoing families (Thompson 1825; Young and Wilmott 1973).

The fact that that baseline allows her to take a smaller proportion of her investments in the household when she goes, compared to the man who has made fewer household-specific investments, makes her subject to exploitation (let's call it "gender exploitation"). Just as wage-laborers suffer capitalist exploitation by virtue of the fact that they cannot take their per capita share of social capital with them when they go, so too do women experience gender exploitation by virtue of the fact that they cannot take the full products of their caring labor with them when they go. Even if they take the children with them when they leave, women's heavier investments in "relationship work" will inevitably be lost with the dissolution of the relationship. If women decide not to leave as a consequence, then any bargains they strike within the household will be struck from that baseline and inflected by the fact that they could take less of their investments were they to go: just as the exploitative wage bargains struck by workers under capitalism are struck from the baseline of the capitalist withdrawal rule and the bargaining disadvantage under which that places propertyless wage-laborers.

Conclusion

A disproportionate share of women's work is in unpaid household labor. That is just as Chicago economists would recommend. At least some of that unpaid household labor is valued by those for whom it is done in part because of who is doing it rather than what is done. That is just a plain fact about the nature of caring work.

Insofar as the unpaid household labor is valued because of who is doing it rather than what is done, there are no close market substitutes for that person's unpaid labor in that household. That is not only a problem for keepers of the national accounts in trying to assess the value of that labor. It is more importantly a problem for women themselves, insofar as they cannot enjoy the full advantages of increasing participation in paid labor that they could have done in an economist's ideal world with perfect substitutes. However much they earn on the market, it cannot fully buy them out of the second shift at home.

Nonsubstitutable labor inputs often give rise to nontransferable outputs. Investments of caring labor cannot be withdrawn in the same way other investments in the household can be. Insofar as that is true, and insofar as women are the ones whose investments are more of that form, that makes women more exploitable within the household. They are disadvantaged relative to their male partners by the rules ("facts of life") governing household breakup; and (assuming with ordinary economic models of bargaining that that "nonagreement point" is the baseline from which bargaining proceeds) that disadvantage is carried over into the way life is lived within the ongoing household as well.

What the Chicago economist prescribes as a matter of efficiency feminists rightly see as a source of the exploitability of women. The gendered division of unpaid (especially caring) labor within the household renders women susceptible to exploitation and forces them into overtime. Even Chicago economists would have to admit as much, if they only noticed these peculiar features of "women's work" within the household. Caring work is different—and even Chicago economists should care.

The policy implications of all this will be familiar enough. Men and women (and indeed all adults) should share equally in caring labor; otherwise, caregivers will be exploitable and quite probably exploited, even if they are "paid." Pay is important: there should be "basic income" for all, as Carole Pateman (2004) has recently argued. But behavior change is also needed—caring labor should be more equal, as Carole Pateman (1988a; 1988b, chap. 6; 1989) has long argued. There is nothing surprising in those conclusions themselves. The surprise is only that even Chicago economists—devoted though they may be to the advantages of specialization and division of labor—ought to be committed to that cause.

In *The Sexual Contract*, Pateman (1988b, 8) wrote: "Criticism . . . has been directed at exploitation, . . . in . . . that wives are not paid at all for their labour in the home. . . . However, exploitation is possible precisely because . . . contracts about property in the person place right of command in the hands of one party to the contract. Capitalists can exploit workers and husbands can exploit wives because workers and wives are constituted as subordinates through the employment contract and the marriage contract." Even after the most brutal excesses associated with allocation of "property in the person" have been overcome, women remain importantly exploitable because of the peculiar sort of caring labor they perform and the distinctive sorts of relationship-specific human capital they build up in the process. The same thing that makes women's work within the household irreplaceable renders the women doing it exploitable. Truly they can be seen as "prisoners of love" (Folbre 2001), in ways that follow on directly from Carole Pateman's pathbreaking insights.

References

Abraham, K. G., and C. Mackie, eds. 2005. *Beyond the Market: Designing Nonmarket Accounts for the United States.* Report of the Panel to Study the Design of Nonmarket Accounts, Committee on National Statistics, Division of Behavioral and Social Sciences and Education, National Research Council. Washington, D.C.: National Academies Press.

Anderson, E. S. 1999. "What Is the Point of Equality?" *Ethics* 109:287–338.

Baxter, J., and D. Gibson, with M. Lynch-Blosse. 1990. *Double Take: The Links between Paid and Unpaid Work.* Canberra: Australian Government Publishing Service.

Becker, G. S. 1957. *The Economics of Discrimination.* Chicago: University of Chicago Press.

———. 1976. *The Economic Approach to Human Behavior.* Chicago: University of Chicago Press.

———. 1981. *A Treatise on the Family.* Cambridge, Mass.: Harvard University Press.

Beckerman, W. 1978. *Measures of Leisure, Equality, and Welfare.* Paris: Organisation for Economic Co-operation and Development.

Bittman, M., P. England, L. Sayer, N. Folbre, and G. Matheson. 2002. "When Does Gender Trump Money? Bargaining and Time in Household Work." *American Journal of Sociology* 109:186–214.

Brennan, G., and P. Pettit. 2004. *The Economy of Esteem.* Oxford: Oxford University Press.

Bubeck, D. 1995. *Care, Gender, and Justice.* Oxford: Oxford University Press.

Coase, R. H. 1937. "The Nature of the Firm." *Economica* 4:386–405.

Coleman, J. S. 1993. "The Rational Reconstruction of Society." (Presidential address) *American Sociological Review* 58:1–15.

England, P., and N. Folbre. 1999. "The Cost of Caring." *Annals of the American Academy of Political and Social Science* 561:39–51.

———. 2001. "Involving Dads: Parental Bargaining and Family Well-being." In *Handbook of Father Involvement: Multidisciplinary Perspectives*, edited by C. S. Tamis-LeMonda and N. Cabrera, 387–408. Hillsdale, N.J.: Lawrence Erlbaum Associates.

Folbre, N. 1982. "Exploitation Comes Home: A Critique of the Marxian Theory of Family Labor." *Cambridge Journal of Economics* 6:317–29.

———. 1991. "The Unproductive Housewife: Her Evolution in Nineteenth-Century Economic Thought." *Signs* 16:463–84.

———. 1994. *Who Pays for the Kids? Gender and the Structures of Constraint.* London: Routledge.

———. 2001. *The Invisible Heart: Economics and Family Values.* New York: New Press.

———. 2005. "Valuing Parental Time." Mimeo., Department of Economics, University of Massachusetts, Amherst.

Folbre, N., and R. E. Goodin. 2004. "Revealing Altruism." *Review of Social Economy* 62:1–25.

Folbre, N., and J. A. Nelson. 2000. "For Love or Money—or Both?" *Journal of Economic Perspectives* 14:123–40.

Friedman, M., and R. Friedman. 1980. *Free to Choose.* Harmondsworth, Middlesex: Penguin.

Gershuny, J. 2000. *Changing Times: Work and Leisure in Post-Industrial Society.* Oxford: Oxford University Press.

Gershuny, J., and J. P. Robinson. 1988. "Historical Changes in the Household Division of Labor." *Demography* 25:537–52.

Goldschmidt-Clermont, L., and E. Pagnossin-Aligisakis. 1995. *Measures of Unrecorded Economic Activities in Fourteen Countries.* Occasional Paper No. 20, Human Development Report Office. New York: United Nations Development Program.

Goodin, R. E., and D. Gibson. 2002. "The Decasualization of Eldercare." In *The Subject of Care: Feminist Perspectives on Dependency*, edited by E. F. Kittay and E. Feder, 246–56. Totowa, N.J.: Rowman and Littlefield.

Hakim, C. 2000. *Work-Lifestyle Choices in the Twenty-first Century.* Oxford: Oxford University Press.

Hall, P. A., and D. Soskice, eds. 2001. *Varieties of Capitalism.* Oxford: Oxford University Press.

Hochschild, A. R. 1989. *The Second Shift: Working Parents and the Revolution at Home.* New York: Viking.

———. 1997. *The Time Bind.* New York: Metropolitan Books.

Holloway, S., S. Short, and S. Tamplin. 2002. *Household Satellite Account (Experimental) Methdology.* London: Office of National Accounts, National Statistics. Available at http://www.statistics.gov.uk/hhsa/hhsa/resources/fileattachments/hhsa.pdf.

Ironmonger, D. 1996. "Counting Outputs, Capital Inputs and Caring Labor: Estimating Gross Household Product." *Feminist Economics* 2, no. 3:37–64.

Kittay, E. F. 1998. *Love's Labor: Essays on Women, Equality, and Dependency.* New York: Routledge.

Lancaster, K. J. 1966. "A New Approach to Consumer Theory." *Journal of Political Economy* 74:132–57.

Lerner, A. P. 1972. "The Economics and Politics of Consumer Sovereignty." *American Economic Review (Papers & Proceedings)* 62, no. 2:258–66.

Lundberg, S., and R. A. A. Pollak. 1994. "Noncooperative Bargaining Models of Marriage." *American Economic Review (Papers & Proceedings)* 84, no. 2:132–37.

Lundberg, S., and R. A. Pollak. 2003. "Efficiency in Marriage." *Review of Economics of the Household* 1:153–68.

Parijs, P. van. 1995. *Real Freedom for All.* Oxford: Clarendon Press.

Pateman, C. 1988a. "The Patriarchal Welfare State." In *Democracy and the Welfare State*, edited by A. Gutmann, 231–60. Princeton: Princeton University Press. Reprinted in Pateman 1989, 179–209.

———. 1988b. *The Sexual Contract.* Oxford: Polity Press.

———. 1989. *The Disorder of Women.* Oxford: Polity Press.

———. 2004. "Democratizing Citizenship: Some Advantages of a Basic Income." *Politics & Society* 32:89–105

Pollack, R. A., and M. L. Watcher. 1975. "The Relevance of the Household Production Function and Its Implications for the Allocation of Time." *Journal of Political Economy* 83:255–77.

Ringen, S. 1988. "Direct and Indirect Measures of Poverty." *Journal of Social Policy* 17:351–65.

Roemer, J. E. 1982. "Exploitation, Alternatives, and Socialism." *Economic Journal* 92:87–107

Roemer, J. E. 1988. *Free to Lose.* Cambridge, Mass.: Harvard University Press.

Schor, J. B. 1991. *The Overworked American: The Unexpected Decline of Leisure.* New York: Basic Books.

Sen, A. 1980. "Description as Choice." *Oxford Economic Papers* 32:353–69.

———. 1985. *Commodities and Capabilities.* Amsterdam: North-Holland.

Szalai, A. 1975. "Women's Time: Women in the Light of Contemporary Time Budget Research." *Futures* 5:385–99.

Taylor, C. 1985. *Philosophical Papers.* Cambridge: Cambridge University Press.

Thompson, William. 1825. *Appeal of One Half of the Human Race, Women, Against the Pretensions of the Other Half, Men, to Retain Them in Political, and Thence in Civil and Domestic, Slavery.* London: Longman.

Waring, M. 1988. *Counting for Nothing: What Men Value and What Women Are Worth.* Wellington, N.Z.: Allen and Unwin. Published in the United States under the title: *If Women Counted: A New Feminist Economics.* New York: Harper and Row.

Young, M., and P. Willmott. 1973. *The Symmetrical Family: A Study of Work and Leisure in the London Region.* London: Routledge and Kegan Paul.

Zelizer, V. A. 2000. "The Purchase of Intimacy." *Law & Social Inquiry* 25:817–48.

A Democratic Defense of Universal Basic Income
Michael Goodhart

One powerful and illuminating argument animates much of Carole Pateman's remarkably diverse work on democracy, participation, political obligation, social contract, feminism and feminist interpretation, and the welfare state: subordination and democratic citizenship are incompatible. To my mind, her particular genius has been to show how social institutions and relationships, from marriage to the capitalist organization of production, make some individuals dependent upon others; to demonstrate that such relationships pervade our political theories and our societies; and to argue forcefully for a deep democratization that would transform our theory and our practice and make us more free. Seen in light of this overarching concern, Pateman's recent interest in proposals for a basic income represents a seamless continuation of her scholarly endeavors (see Pateman 2004, 90).

A basic income (BI) is an unconditional social transfer set at a level that assures every citizen subsistence. It is payable to all individuals regardless of their economic means, family or employment status, willingness to seek paid work or accept jobs, or any other status or requirement (Purdy 1994, 33; cf. Parijs 1995). In short, BI makes guaranteed subsistence a core entitlement of citizenship. Proposals for BI have a long intellectual history (see Dowling, Wispelaere, and White 2003; Parijs 2004; Rothschild 2001); they have recently attracted considerable interest in response to grave concerns about the social, economic, and political viability of the welfare state in the age of neoliberal globalization (Offe 1992; Standing 1992).

Although this contemporary discussion of BI began as one about policy reforms that might enhance distributive efficiency, reduce poverty, and shore up the political foundations of the welfare state, the debate has largely come to be framed by considerations of social justice. Liberals (White 2003), libertarians (Steiner 1992; Parijs 1995), egalitarians (Baker 1992), and communitarians (Jordan 1992) have all offered justifications for variants of BI.[1] The duties and obligations of citizenship figure prominently in this discussion, with concerns about reciprocity and free-riding at the forefront. Such concerns explain in part why some commentators favor a scheme of basic capital over BI (e.g., Ackerman and Alstott 1999; Ackerman 2003) and why other supporters advocate imposing conditions on recipients of BI, such as willingness to work or to make a productive contribution to society (e.g., Atkinson 1996; Dore 2001; Goodin 2001; Phelps 2001; White 2003).

Carole Pateman's distinctive and characteristic contribution to the BI debate has been to demonstrate that its terms are deeply flawed. Contemporary treatments of social justice usually operate independently of specifically democratic inquiry and adopt peculiarly economistic concepts and theories (Pateman 2004, 91–92). By conceiving freedom and reciprocity in a narrowly economic way; by ignoring feminist insights about the interdependence of work, welfare, and citizenship; and by missing or misapprehending the relationship between freedom and institutional structure, advocates and critics of BI alike have neglected its potential contribution to democratization (Pateman 1998, 2003, 2004). That contribution consists in the crucial role that a properly conceived and designed BI can play in ensuring that all people "live within democratic authority structures that enhance their autonomy, and that they have the *standing,* and are able (have the opportunities and the means) to enjoy and safeguard their freedom" (Pateman 2004, 91). Put succinctly, Pateman's argument is that a BI could significantly further democratization but that it will be unlikely to do so unless we articulate and defend explicitly *democratic* arguments for it—arguments that include an insistence on its unconditionality. Following this suggestion, I intend to sketch a democratic justification for a universal basic income here. This justification differs in some respects from the one toward which Pateman has gestured, in particular in its global application, yet it is inspired by the central insights of her work: the close connection between freedom and democratization; the role of social relationships and institutions in structuring and perpetuating subordination; and the use of feminist analysis to inform our understanding of what genuine freedom requires.

The chapter is divided into four sections. In the first I briefly survey the

---

1. See also White 2003, chap. 1. for a related discussion of theories of economic citizenship.

tradition of emancipatory democratic theory that emphasizes rights to economic independence in securing and enjoying political freedom. In the second section I provide an overview of an account of democracy I call *democracy as human rights*. This account reinterprets democracy's core principles of freedom and equality in terms of human rights, an interpretation grounded in the emancipatory democratic tradition and motivated by globalization's challenge for democracy. On this account, democracy is defined as the political commitment to universal emancipation through securing the equal enjoyment of fundamental human rights for everyone. The idea of emancipation, which encompasses noninterference and nondomination in all domains of social life, captures the crucial role that relationships and institutions play in determining freedom. In the third section I demonstrate that securing the equal enjoyment of fundamental rights for everyone can best be achieved through a framework of social policies and institutions that includes BI. In the final section I argue that a democratic BI must be universal—that it must function globally. Not only is this universal scope entailed by the global character of democracy as human rights, it is, perhaps counterintuitively, vital to its practical success.

Two questions typically asked of any BI proposal are "is it desirable?" and "is it feasible?" Separating these questions suggests that even if BI proposals are found desirable on democratic or other grounds, doubts about feasibility—ranging from cost considerations to political calculations—might ultimately sink them (Solow 2001, ix). Although I will briefly discuss these practical challenges below, I want to try to frame these objections before proceeding. What BI might cost and how it might be funded and implemented are certainly important questions, yet whether we think BI is worth the cost depends in large part on the nature and the appeal of the arguments we provide. If we conclude that BI is necessary for democracy, our assessment of its costs will be radically different than if we conceive it merely as an alternative welfare policy. Similarly, whether BI can command a popular consensus cannot be considered independently of the reasons we give for supporting it. Those reasons are my subject here, and my primary concern is to show that democracy (or one interpretation of it) *requires* BI.

Freedom, Equality, and Emancipation in the Democratic Tradition

Democracy as human rights (DHR) is a reinterpretation of core democratic principles of universal freedom and equality worked out in response to the challenges globalization poses for democracy. This means it is concerned with how to realize freedom and equality not just in the traditional political sphere but in all sorts of domains where democracy is not usually thought to obtain, from the household to supranational economic management. This is one way in which DHR speaks to and extends Pateman's democratic vision. Before outlining this reinterpretation I briefly address its place within the democratic tradition; situating DHR in this way highlights its *democratic* character.

DHR belongs to an emancipatory democratic tradition that is frequently overlooked in a climate dominated by political liberalism. It is anchored in two core democratic principles, freedom and equality, that give democratization theories their distinctive leveling power. "Men being . . . by Nature, all free, equal and independent," Locke wrote, "no one can be put out of this Estate, and subjected to the Political Power of another, without his own *Consent*" (Locke 1960, II sec. 95). The simple premise that all men are free and equal undermines justifications for natural authority and subjection; as Pateman (1988, 39–40) argues, "the doctrine of natural individual freedom and equality was revolutionary precisely because it swept away, in one fell swoop, all the grounds through which the subordination of some individuals, groups or categories of people to others had been justified."

Freedom and equality thus ensure that there is no arbitrary rule, no domination or unwarranted interference, no government without consent. From the time of the Levellers and Locke, and certainly by the French Revolution, freedom, equality, and emancipation were being expressed in the language of natural or universal human rights (Soboul 1977, 160–61).[2] The French *Declaration of the Rights of Man and of the Citizen* established an ideal, a "direction of intention" that shaped the evolution of liberal and social democracy (Lefebvre 1957, 184). Although the doctrine was only partially realized in the eighteenth century—and remains only partially realized today—its implacable emancipatory logic was apprehended by women and men of the time (Hunt 2000, 12). From the beginning, democratization theorists of various stripes recognized the role of economic independence in achieving emancipation and realizing democracy and human rights for all. Rousseau, Paine, Wollstonecraft, Mill, Stanton, and others saw that without economic independence one cannot be free. Reliance on another for one's subsistence—as a spouse, a child,

---

2. The idea of natural rights meant, for many theorists, simply that everyone was born with them; here, that freedom and equality are natural or innate qualities characteristic of all people. This premise is best regarded as a political principle, not as a foundational or metaphysical claim: universality was a necessary feature of the leveling or democratizing arguments in which these principles were employed.

an employee—puts one in a state of dependence that many of these theorists viewed as equivalent to slavery and incompatible with citizenship. Thus, at least since the eighteenth century, democratic theorists have explicitly recognized the links between a right to one's subsistence and political freedom in achieving emancipation. And at least since that time they have theorized that link in terms of human rights.[3]

While democratic and feminist theorists, including Pateman, have exposed and interrogated the deep links between citizenship and independence, the rights-based tradition of emancipatory democratic thinking has been largely overlooked, for a combination of reasons. Historically, liberalism captured the discourse of rights and stripped it of its economic and egalitarian thrust. Today almost any discussion of rights is categorized as "liberal," even though democratization theorists have seen rights as the leading edge of a leveling and emancipatory program of social and political reform for centuries. Democracy in the classical liberal tradition is typically reduced to a political method, and rights are conceived as civil and political rights—with the effect that domination outside the political sphere becomes essentially invisible. Classical liberals and libertarians remain skeptical of too much democracy; they insist on a distinction between civil/political rights (including property rights), which they conceive as natural or as byproducts of self-ownership, and economic rights, which they dismiss as illegitimate. Rawlsian liberals accept the importance of economic well-being but tend to treat it as a matter of social justice rather than rights or democracy. Socialists have emphasized the material preconditions of effective freedom but have dismissed the language of rights (and sometimes of democracy), mistaking Marx's historically situated critique of bourgeois rights for a timeless general indictment of human rights. Many contemporary human rights theorists recognize the interdependence of political and economic rights (e.g., Pogge 2000; Donnelly 2003) but rarely conceive their arguments as democratic (and often remain wary of democracy, see Donnelly 2003, 199ff.; cf. Freeman 2000). So democratic theory today mainly concerns participation in collective decision making and the electoral process with an emphasis on deliberation and the requirements of inclusive discourse, which are commonly regarded as coextensive with the requirements of freedom and equality (e.g., Bohman 1997).

3. This view differs from traditional republicanism, which treated independence as a precondition for citizenship rather than a political objective and which relied on a masculine, militaristic, and thus highly exclusive, ideal of civic virtue. Some recent republican revivalists (e.g., Pettit 1997; Skinner 1998) have advanced more inclusive versions of the idea, but the democratic form remains distinctive in its emphasis on universal human rights.

DHR attempts to revitalize the emancipatory democratic tradition, emphasizing the centrality of economic independence to political freedom and reclaiming human rights as a conceptual vocabulary for democratization. The democratic political method is essential to this emancipatory program—it protects people from arbitrary rule—but it does not exhaust it. Democracy also requires substantive freedoms, including the right to subsistence; these substantive freedoms, as well as a democratic political framework, are necessary for achieving emancipation.

Democracy as Human Rights

DHR represents *a political commitment to universal emancipation through securing the equal enjoyment of fundamental human rights for everyone*.[4] I shall proceed in explicating DHR by elaborating upon elements of this definition. Once its basic premises have been fully explained, I show how DHR implies a concern with governance that facilitates democracy's horizontal and vertical extension—that is, how it expands democracy's scope to encompass many domains of social relations and its reach from local through global systems of interaction.

DHR is a political commitment to *universal emancipation.* Emancipation evokes release from subjection or slavery; it denotes both nonsubjection and the *act* of freeing or winning release from subjection. More recently the idea has come to include progressive struggles to transform society, a usage linking emancipation with left or progressive politics and with efforts to remake the social, economic, and political order (Booth 1999, 40–41). These two aspects of emancipation are closely related: creating a new and more just social order often entails eliminating structures of oppression and domination. In this sense emancipation is also closely connected with democratization. DHR restores emancipation to a central place within democratic thinking (thus breaking the recent monopolization of the language of nondomination by republican revivalists (Pettit 1997; Skinner 1998; cf. Gould 1988, 1993). In DHR both dependence and unwarranted interference create subjection; an adequate account of democratic emancipation must take both into account (see Wall 2001).[5] As Shapiro (1999, 30) argues, "democracy is as much about opposition to the arbitrary exercise of power as it is about collective self-govern-

    4. For a more complete elaboration and defense of DHR, see Goodhart 2005.
    5. Hereafter I shall use *subjection* to refer to a condition of being dominated and/or experiencing unwarranted interference or coercion from another or others.

ment," even though this oppositional aspect of democracy is not frequently mentioned in the academic literature. In fact, one can think about self-government in the democratic tradition as instrumental in securing emancipation. Self-government is an indispensable mechanism for reining in the power of government and defending one's rights. The commitment to *universal* emancipation simply emphasizes that DHR applies and is open to all.

DHR seeks to realize emancipation through securing fundamental human rights for everyone. Fundamental rights are all those rights needed to eliminate subjection—the set of rights that when realized together constitute emancipation. Following Shue (1996), I conceive the relationship among basic or fundamental rights as one of indivisibility and interdependence: enjoyment of each is a necessary condition for the enjoyment of all the others. Unless each fundamental right is secure, none is; unless all the fundamental rights are secure, emancipation is not achieved. DHR thus deepens the idea of fundamental rights in an important way: it reconceives a purely formal right as one *through which* emancipation is secured by the equal enjoyment of human rights for everyone. This commitment to emancipation through human rights recognizes that when people are deprived of any fundamental right they become open to the arbitrary will or actions of another person, of the state, of a corporation, or of some other actor. So fundamental rights guarantee emancipation by protecting against potential subjection. "Potential" is an important modifier here: the threat of domination or the availability of means for interfering with people's rights themselves constitute forms of subjection that democracy must not tolerate. Emancipation is thus defined by the secure enjoyment of all the fundamental human rights, linking democracy's commitment to freedom and equality for all with the specific guarantee of fundamental human rights. These rights become central to democracy's meaning on this interpretation, as they were historically for emancipatory theorists of democratization.

There are four main groups or clusters of fundamental human rights.[6] Rights relating to *liberty and security* concern the physical safety and integrity of individuals, their freedom of activity, choice, and movement, and their right to noninterference in matters of personal or intimate concern. Rights concerning *fairness* entitle people to equal treatment before the law and in politics and society. These rights include guarantees concerning legal and criminal procedure (e.g., due process), and equal access to public benefits and

---

6. I borrow the term "clusters" from Held 1995, who uses it to denote bundles of rights associated with sites of power in modern societies; for a classification similar to mine see Beitz 2001.

services. Rights essential to an *adequate standard of living* concern the satisfaction of basic needs and the conditions in which one works and lives. These rights include such things as a guarantee of subsistence (food, shelter), access to health care, a decent education, choice in family and relationship status, and rights to enjoy and participate in cultural life. Finally, *civil and political rights* encompass rights and guarantees concerning one's social and political activities. These include freedoms of assembly, conscience, and expression, a right to choose one's own lifestyle, and rights to political participation. Nothing in the theory rides on the classification of any particular right or on the names assigned to the categories, however; grouping the rights into clusters simply makes it easier to talk about them in general terms.[7]

The goal of emancipation and the interdependence of fundamental rights together constitute a test or threshold for whether any particular right should be considered fundamental. We can work out a conception of fundamental rights analytically, but the ultimate test of its adequacy is whether guaranteeing the rights it specifies actually results in emancipation. Put differently, we can check the analytic account's adequacy by seeing whether realizing the rights it specifies actually constitutes emancipation.[8] Thus the category of fundamental rights, while clearly defined and expansive, is also provisional and self-limiting. Defining fundamental rights this way points toward a possible solution to one of the thorniest problems in debates over human rights, that of differing cultural understandings of rights. Even human rights universalists (e.g., Donnelly 1999) accept that universal rights must be interpreted in varying cultures and contexts. The difficulty has been in determining what constitutes a reasonable or legitimate interpretation of a given right. DHR suggests an appropriate criterion: all fundamental rights must be defined and secured in such a way that they actually constitute emancipation. Take the right to expression: certain limits on Nazi propaganda in Germany or on incitement to ethnic violence in deeply divided societies do not seem like unreasonable limits on expression; bans on opposition political parties or on criticism of government policies that favor certain ethnic groups while disadvantaging others clearly cross the line. The distinction lies in whether the restrictions limit expression so severely that other rights are jeopardized.

---

7. I leave out so-called "group rights" because I am persuaded by Jones 1999 that in many cases these are best understood as rights held by members of groups qua individuals; rights to enjoy and participate in a culture, for example, can be conceived in this way. Rights whose subjects are groups are problematic from a democratic perspective.

8. If the account proves inadequate in practice, it might be because some rights are omitted or because recognized rights are not adequately specified.

Fundamental rights do not comprise the full range of rights people might enjoy, nor do they guarantee people a life that is substantively "good." Common objections to rights-based theories include charges of inattention to effective freedom and of excessive and destructive individualism. Charges of the first type typically associate rights with negative liberties and then show that negative liberties alone cannot ensure that we are free to become who we would like to be or really are (e.g., Taylor 1997). DHR is immune to charges of this kind; its emphasis on rights to an adequate standard of living, in particular, means that it goes well beyond the standard formulations of negative rights, as it must do to ensure emancipation. That said, DHR certainly falls short of many idealizations of the good life; one might enjoy all of one's fundamental rights and still not be happy or free in the positive sense invoked by Taylor and many others. I see this as an advantage of DHR; unlike theories that specify primary goods (Rawls 1971), essential human functions or capabilities (Nussbaum 1992), or accounts of flourishing (Brugger 1996), DHR avoids controversial claims about what constitutes the good life. Of course, the commitment to freedom and equality, as interpreted through DHR, is a substantive one that will itself be controversial. The paths and projects available to individuals and communities are limited by the obligations of reciprocal recognition of others as free and equal beings. Yet such recognition, while demanding, is still less demanding and certainly less controversial than any claims about what constitutes the good life might be globally. To take a position on such matters seems to me inappropriate for a cosmopolitan theory and unnecessary for a democratic one.

The second charge, of excessive or destructive individualism, is usually directed against liberal theories of rights and autonomy (e.g., Pollis and Schwab 1979; Barber 1984; Kausikan 1993; Sandel 1998). DHR reflects a shared commitment to emancipation, a commitment reflected in social guarantees of fundamental rights (see below). This shared democratic commitment constitutes a kind of community in itself, one in which political care is expressed through reciprocal recognition of others as free and equal, through social guarantees of rights, and through the concern those rights express for others (Gould 1993, 409). Second, because DHR privileges no substantive conception of the good life, it leaves open to people the chance to pursue, collectively or individually, those forms of it which they find most appealing. Of course, "some conceptions of rights are incompatible with some conceptions of community. . . . Likewise, some conceptions of community . . . do not recognize individuals as beings with rights. But not all conceptions of rights are at odds with all notions of community" (Jones 1994, 210–11). Democracy certainly rules out some kinds of group or community practices, but it is a mistake to create a false dichotomy between individuals and communities; neither can exist without the other. In fact, the point of rights is to provide for human interaction (Jones 1994, 211), to define in part how and on what terms community is possible. Rights themselves can form part of a broad and appealing definition of the community and its values (Habermas 2001). These two observations show the wisdom of LeFort's (1986) claim that human rights are generative of democracy and that their effectiveness is linked to our allegiance to them as a certain way of being in society.

DHR requires securing the enjoyment of all fundamental rights for everyone so that everyone will be free from subjection. Securing a right means providing social guarantees for its enjoyment. Shue (1996, 16) argues that a social guarantee implies correlative duties associated with rights: "a right is ordinarily a justified demand that some other people make some arrangements so that one will still be able to enjoy the substance of the right even if—actually *especially* if—it is not within one's own power to arrange on one's own to enjoy the substance of the right. It is not enough," he adds, "that at the moment it happens that no one is violating the right" (cf. Vincent 1986). These duties and obligations need not be assigned to particular individuals, however: they are shared responsibilities to be met through the design of proper social institutions. An institutionally grounded approach to human rights is thus required by the duties correlated with basic rights and by the need for viable and effective social guarantees of those rights (Pogge 1992; Shue 1996).

For a right to be secured its actual enjoyment must be socially guaranteed against standard threats (Shue 1996, 13). We can specify three conditions that must be part of such a social guarantee: first, the right in question must be generally recognized and understood. Second, the standard threats to the right must be identified and means of addressing those threats devised. Finally, those means must be incorporated into legal and social institutions that are adequately empowered to actually check the threats; they must be fully funded, must have the appropriate jurisdiction, and so on. Simply signing on to international conventions or placing laws on the books are not in themselves enough—though both can obviously be a great help. To secure fundamental rights three types of institution are necessary: representative political institutions; direct functional institutions like schools, police, and social welfare agencies whose work contributes directly to implementing specific rights; and indirect functional institutions, which are charged with policy, oversight, and enforcement functions.[9] DHR also requires that all of these democratic institutions adopt and implement procedures that follow fairly straightforwardly from respect for fundamental human rights (I elaborate on these procedures in Goodhart 2005).

Achieving emancipation for everyone implies a general concern with governance. Governance is a more encompassing term than government; it is sometimes referred to as "government-like" activity, especially in the supranational domain, where authority is exercised in international or transnational space in the absence of sovereign governments (Finkelstein 1995, 368). I shall use "governance" to mean any system of rule characterized by the goal-oriented exercise of control in any sphere of human activity (cf. Rosenau 1992, 15).

Focusing on governance proves particularly congenial to DHR's emancipatory project because governance encompasses systems of rule in diverse domains of human interaction. The commitment to securing emancipation means that DHR must be concerned with structures of unfreedom wherever they occur. Governance is necessary whenever and wherever common ends and interests require cooperation and interaction among groups and individuals. Because rule involves the exercise of control, power, and coercion, however, it creates conditions in which there exists a significant threat of subjection. Since governance occurs in all kinds of social activities and interactions, subjection often originates in domains outside the narrowly conceived public realm of traditional democratic theory; indeed, the fundamental interdependence of social life makes compartmentalizing different systems of rule into separate spheres or domains arbitrary and undesirable from a democratic point of view. DHR recognizes the analytic value of such conceptual boundaries but denies their political salience; it treats the fundamental interdependence of social life as a fact demanding an integrated and comprehensive democratic response.

While subjection can occur wherever governance transpires, it takes different forms within different systems of rule, each requiring appropriate responses. DHR is well suited to this complex challenge for several reasons. First, it provides a single normative framework that integrates democratic responses across many domains of governance. Democracy requires that all governance activities respect and conform with the requirements of funda-

---

9. Many of these institutions help with the vertical or supranational extension of democracy; unfortunately, space constraints prevent me from discussing these here. See Goodhart 2005.

mental human rights. Democracy thus means the same thing in the state, the family, the economy, and in civil society; one standard of democratic legitimacy applies consistently in all domains. Another advantage of DHR is that this uniformity does not dictate institutional similarity across domains. DHR is concerned with an end, emancipation, and is not wedded to a any particular institutional method or procedure for ensuring it. Of course, certain institutions are more democratic than others, precisely because they are instrumental in securing fundamental human rights; representative political institutions are a clear example. But many rights can be secured differently in different contexts. Because DHR is not defined exclusively in terms of a particular political method, it allows a great deal of flexibility in the pursuit of democratic aims.

A Democratic Justification of Basic Income

DHR makes the central role of a democratic right to subsistence clear. Economic independence is a key component in securing political freedom and equality and realizing emancipation. Without a guaranteed subsistence, other fundamental rights become insecure. The rights to education, to political participation, to personal security, freedom of expression, and personal choice or autonomy are all compromised by economic dependence. In addition, economically dependent individuals are open to potential domination by those upon whom they count for their subsistence: spouses, employers, aid workers, and governmental agencies and bureaucrats, for example.[10] DHR requires securing a right to subsistence for everyone, unconditionally, against standard threats; BI is the best way to guarantee this right.

Among the standard threats to economic independence in the more developed countries today are unemployment, underemployment, or unsafe or degrading work; changes in relationship status or the need to remain in unsafe or degrading relationships; serious illness or long term disability; and simple bad luck. From a democratic perspective, one emphasizing emancipation, BI has several distinct advantages over other social welfare schemes in addressing these threats. First, it provides maximum flexibility for individuals to change jobs, retrain, take lower-paying or part-time work, or to leave paid employment altogether. Second, it frees individuals—especially women—from the economic need to remain in unsafe, abusive, or demeaning relationships

---

10. The difficult question of children, whose dependence on their parents goes well beyond economic need, lies beyond my scope here.

(Pateman 2003, 2004). Third, it provides the most efficient scheme of social insurance against misfortune (Goodin 1992), economic or otherwise, by ensuring that no one falls below the level of subsistence. In developing countries the threats are somewhat different and arguably more severe: grinding poverty, often coupled with political and extrapolitical oppression and exploitation; health crises like AIDS; precarious access to food and water, and so on. Still, BI can provide an important part of an effective solution to these threats when used in conjunction with sensible development policies and democratic political reform, as I discuss briefly below.

BI has another important advantage over alternative means of institutionalizing guarantees for subsistence: its unconditionality. This feature of BI prevents benefits being manipulated as tools of domination. At present, means tests, lifestyle tests, assessments of "desert" or willingness to work, and other welfare requirements in developed countries create the possibility for recipients to be dominated by those who make decisions about the conditions attached to benefits (Fitzpatrick 2000, chap. 8; Handler 2004). These decision-makers might be aid or social workers, bureaucrats, politicians, or electoral coalitions who use their control over necessary resources to coerce or influence potential recipients (cf. Barry 1996). In developing countries, aid is too frequently linked to social and political connections or to support for the ruling party. In all these cases, the contingency of conditional benefits violates DHR's requirement that fundamental rights be secured against all standard threats. Precisely because such contingency can easily be and has in fact been translated into domination, DHR requires an unconditional guarantee of subsistence for everyone. BI is preferable to other schemes both because of its unconditionality and because it entails the minimum amount of interference in people's lives—it is "minimally presumptuous" (Goodin 1992) as well as minimally coercive.

BI is one pillar in the broader structure of social guarantees necessary to secure fundamental rights to an adequate standard of living. Among the other important pillars of this democratic social edifice are effective public education and public health systems (including guaranteed health care for all), effective workers' rights, and transparent, accountable, and participatory systems of governance. BI is crucial, again, because it provides a guarantee of economic independence that satisfies a long-recognized requirement of emancipation. I should emphasize again that to adequately safeguard this right BI should be set at subsistence; otherwise economic independence is not assured, other fundamental rights are endangered, and emancipation is undermined. This requirement has important implications for debates about the gradual introduction of a BI program, suggesting that a "full" BI for the most vulnerable members of society might be preferable on democratic grounds to a partial BI for everyone.

It is clear that only a BI set at subsistence level provides a satisfactory social guarantee of economic independence. Yet it might seem that certain conditions—particularly those associated with a "participation income" (Atkinson 1996; Goodin 2001) or a "reciprocal contribution" (White 2003, 131–38)—would be unobjectionable from a democratic perspective. After all, what White defines as a right to "reasonable access" to a minimum income is not equivalent to the right to be given an income without conditions. In particular, conditions designed to increase people's contributions to society through community service of some kind might appear to be beneficial to democracy. DHR certainly endorses a participatory social framework encouraging voluntarism, engagement in politics or community service, and other community contributions (see Veen 1998, 160). But to make guarantees of subsistence contingent upon such contributions would undermine the secure guarantee of this right, reintroducing conditions for potential subjection. A requirement of this kind would create a distinction between those who have to fulfill certain societal demands to realize their political freedom and those who are under no such obligation. Further, such requirements would undermine the advantages that BI provides for those who elect not to engage in paid employment, a crucial aspect of political freedom (Parijs 1992; Standing 1992; Parijs 1995; Veen 1998) especially for women (Standing 1992; Alstott 2001; Pateman 2003, 2004). Moreover, conditionality would invite domination and coercion through those measures necessary to assess and verify contributions, undermining economic independence and thus threatening other fundamental rights as well. As Pateman (2004, 93–94) has argued, a conditional BI is a privilege rather than a democratic right. Linking BI to a reciprocal contribution is like linking suffrage or free expression to a similar requirement; haggling for such rights in a democratic society is absurd.

This democratic defense of BI is, I think, broadly consistent with the arguments Pateman has offered for preferring BI to citizens' grants and other similar schemes. Rather than emphasize self-governance, as Pateman does, DHR stresses emancipation; this difference originates in my wish to avoid certain global implications of "self-government" arguments, but at the individual level self-government as Pateman uses it and emancipation as defined here seem functionally equivalent. The other significant difference between Pateman's views and my own concerns the universal application of BI, a question she has not directly addressed and to which I now turn.

Universal Basic Income

DHR is a universal theory: it seeks to achieve emancipation for everyone. This makes it necessarily a global theory, one well suited to addressing the challenges globalization poses for democracy. DHR conceives of global democracy as part of a general requirement to democratize all structures or systems of governance. Globalization occasions the reassessment of whether and how democracy meets its universal commitments, but it is those commitments that animate the theory's vertical and horizontal extensions of democracy.

Because of its universality, DHR makes no distinctions with respect to the origin of threats to rights or the physical or political location of the subjects of those threats; likewise, it makes no allowances based upon the systems of governance within which the threats arise. Democrats should be equally concerned with the activities of state and municipal governments, of international governance organizations (IGOs), clubs, families, schools, churches, local businesses, and transnational corporations (TNCs). Democratization, as it is conceived through DHR, requires extending the social guarantees of fundamental human rights beyond the boundaries of the political as it has traditionally been understood to encompass all those domains where governance occurs and where domination and unwarranted interference are therefore likely. DHR's analytic and critical focus on governance facilitates democracy's extension into the family, the workplace, and civil society as well as into the supranational domains of globalization.

In DHR the same basic logic applies to democratization within the state and beyond it: effective social guarantees for fundamental rights must be institutionalized as a means of eliminating subjection and securing emancipation for all. Standard threats to fundamental human rights, whether posed by state governments, IGOs, TNCs, or any other actors must be neutralized by effective institutions. Whether societies were ever sufficiently well contained to guarantee fundamental rights against "outside" threats is doubtful. Today, however, there is no doubt: states cannot adequately secure citizens' rights in an interdependent world. This means (in part) extending institutional guarantees for fundamental human rights into supranational domains not typically associated with democratic politics. This requirement establishes demanding criteria for the validity of borders and boundaries: no borders can justify or excuse violations of fundamental rights. No territory, no conceptual domain, no group, class, or category, can be excluded from democracy's guarantees and requirements.

Under this interpretation, familiar elements of modern democracy—states, exclusive citizenship, popular rule over a homeland—must be thoroughly reconsidered. Similarly, routine acceptance that different norms govern social activity and interaction in the home or the workplace, on this side of the river or that one, on this continent or another, must be abandoned. Among the limits DHR will have to overcome are the ethical and psychological limits that confine our conceptions of democracy to our country, to fellow citizens, to the public sphere—in short, to the familiar boundaries of the political. DHR does not require the elimination of boundaries or differences; it recognizes that boundaries sustain important aspects of community in many ways. But it also recognizes that such boundaries can sustain domination and oppression. Thus DHR requires that boundaries not interfere with human emancipation. As I indicated above, many of DHR's guarantees will be provided through indirect functional institutions, multilateral agencies working in conjunction with direct local participatory and political institutions to protect and promote fundamental human rights.

Here I want to focus on the requirement for a universal basic income (UBI).[11] Strangely, even many proponents of an otherwise unconditional BI tacitly or explicitly endorse its restriction to citizens or residents (see Jordan 1992, 165; Purdy 1994, 38; Parijs 1995; Barry 1996, 247ff.; cf. Barry 1998, 153). Yet, as Fabre (2003, 123) notes, "any proposal which regards membership as the basis for distribution . . . needs to account for the relationship between our obligations to fellow members and our obligations to foreigners." From the perspective developed here, it is uncertain how conditions of geographical location or citizenship would be any more legitimate as objections to fundamental rights than requirements to work or to adopt a bureaucratically preferred lifestyle. From the foregoing account of DHR's global implications, its requirement for a UBI follows straightforwardly. Borders and other boundaries should not affect the requirements of democracy on this account; universal emancipation requires that everyone's fundamental rights be secured. This position is similar to that taken by left-libertarian advocates of BI (Steiner 1992; Parijs 1995; cf. Purdy 1994, 37). The similarity is not surprising: classical libertarianism, like DHR, begins from an assumption of the natural (universal) freedom and equality of all people (as well as from the democratically problematic assumption of self-ownership; see Pateman 2002). UBI need not be set at a uniform level; it must uniformly be adequate to guarantee subsistence. What suffices for this purpose will vary with local conditions.[12]

11. Some commentators use UBI to refer to a basic income without conditions. In the terminology I have adopted here, that usage is redundant. I use UBI exclusively to refer to a *global* basic income scheme.
12. Barry 1996 (249) sensibly proposes setting UBI levels based on purchasing power.

In lieu of a conclusion, I want to consider briefly some likely objections to UBI and some strengths attributable to its global reach. BI proposals are quite controversial; UBI can hardly fail to be even more controversial. Perhaps counter-intuitively, however, in at least one important way a UBI might be more practical than the territorially conditional alternative. One common objection to BI schemes is that they will touch off massive immigration as people move to take advantage of the program. UBI might significantly blunt this effect, anticipated variations in levels of benefit notwithstanding. Evidence from studies of migration suggests that mobility is more sensitive to absolute levels of income and welfare in the state of origin than it is to differentials between states (Arango 2000, 286–87). So a UBI might actually help to stabilize migration by reducing the need to move to secure one's subsistence.[13] There are numerous pragmatic reasons why primary responsibility for social welfare provision lies with states; these reasons are not incompatible with global moral obligations, but they do entail that when states are unwilling or unable to fulfill these responsibilities, the obligations of the wider global community kick in (Goodin 1988). For the wealthier countries, BI can and should be funded domestically; in developing countries, there might well be an immediate need for global assistance.

Funding for a UBI is another likely objection, given the prominent cost objections raised against BI in the domestic context. Assessing the costs of BI is difficult; its effects on incomes, on economic output, and on labor force participation, for example, are difficult to anticipate in advance. Much also hinges on subtle details of the program's design. Moreover, as mentioned at the outset, our evaluation of the program's cost depends in part on our reasons for supporting it. Put differently, the question is less one of affordability than of what price we are willing to pay. An adequate treatment of these issues is impossible here; instead, I want to identify three key points central to the debates over UBI's cost. First, BI is often conceived of as a welfare or poverty-reduction program. Treating it this way centers the debate on comparisons of its costs with those of existing programs. Conceiving BI as a democratic entitlement changes this perspective, demonstrating the often-hidden political costs—the costs measured in terms of domination and unwarranted interference—incurred under existing arrangements. BI costs more and delivers more; the value of what it delivers is ultimately a measure of our political commitments. Second, the democratic, universal justification of BI reminds

---

13. DHR might further suppress politically driven migration by its extension of fundamental rights.

us that the costs of global poverty—violence, disease, migration, instability, and the resources (including military expenditures) expended to manage them—are staggering. Investing in democracy globally makes good political and, in the long run, economic sense. Third, most BI proposals rely on income taxes as sources of revenue. UBI might entail some international redistribution, but it also provides an opportunity to wed social guarantees with other policy objectives through revenue-generating mechanisms. One attractive possibility is taxation of "bads" rather than goods like income or tradable items (Robertson 1996; cf. Purdy 1994, 44; Barry 1996, 242–43). Such taxable "bads" include pollution (taxes on carbon emissions, chemicals), financial speculation (Tobin tax), and weapons sales, to name a few. Global authorities like the UN or the IMF might administer the collection of revenues and distribution of funds in coordination with states.

With respect to feasibility, it should be stressed that there might be good reasons for proponents of economic globalization to support UBI. It offers a simple, concrete, and effective response to many of the ills commonly attributed to economic globalization. It is thus consistent with calls to reform globalization, to give it a human or humane face, or, as I would prefer, to democratize it. If globalization is to truly make everyone better off, as its most ardent defenders insist it can, social institutions must be designed to ensure that the gains from trade and integration do in fact benefit everyone. A UBI is one way to deliver on that promise. One of the principal objections to IMF-backed structural adjustment programs promoting long-term economic development is their high short-term costs in terms of human welfare. The "shock therapy" administered by governments following IMF guidelines often entails reductions in social spending on education, health care, and income support schemes for the worst-off, cuts that not only harm but often alienate and radicalize already marginalized members society. Implementation of UBI would in effect "embed liberalism" globally, cushioning the blows of productive forces reshaping the global economy and contributing to human security and geopolitical stability (cf. Ruggie 1982).

In addition, UBI helps to eliminate a moral hazard for rich democracies, namely, their propensity to export social problems to developing countries. One example of this is the heavy subsidies paid to sectors like agriculture as a means of preventing job losses and consequent unemployment (and its political ramifications). Such subsidies price out competing commodities produced elsewhere, perpetuating poverty and stifling development (Oxfam International 2005). UBI would make a tremendous contribution to global development efforts more generally by providing the economic independence on the basis of which people could exercise their democratic freedoms. Effective political freedoms are a crucial component of any effective development strategy (Sen 1999), and economic independence is a crucial component of political freedom—especially for women, whose emancipation is crucial to any successful development scheme.

Finally, UBI would provide one part of an answer to the objection that supranational democracy is impossible because democracy is based upon affective ties, upon a sense of community, that is manifestly lacking globally. Critics will object that a global extension of BI—or of any version of democracy—ignores or violates the foundations of communal reciprocity on which democracy is based (e.g., Taylor 2003, 2003/4). It is true that democracy requires solidarity, but the tendentious implication of such critiques is that this solidarity must precede democracy's establishment. In fact, solidarity must be nurtured over time, called forth in part through the design of democratic social institutions emphasizing our common humanity and our common human concerns. One lesson to be learned from interdependence is that when one person suffers subjection, everyone does. Perhaps the greatest advantage of UBI is its clear affirmation that the freedom and equality of each of us is dependent upon freedom and equality for all.

Pateman's defense of BI underscores her insistence that democracy and subordination are incompatible. My emphasis on global interdependence extends her insights into how social relationships and institutions create subordination, casting her insistence on deep democratization in a new and perhaps (even more) radical and compelling light. I have argued that democracy on Pateman's terms and on mine *must* be global because the social arrangements that structure and perpetuate subordination today are manifestly global. Democratization thus requires transforming these global arrangements in ways that make emancipation possible for everyone. Universal basic income is a central element in this transformation, for the same reasons Pateman articulates in defending BI within the democratic state: so that everyone can live in equal freedom and dignity.

References

Ackerman, Bruce. 2003. "Radical Liberalism." In *The Ethics of Stakeholding*, edited by K. Dowling, J. de Wispelaere, and S. White, 170–89. New York: Palgrave.

Ackerman, Bruce, and Anne Alstott. 1999. *The Stakeholder Society.* New Haven: Yale University Press.

Alstott, Anne. 2001. "Good for Women." In *What's Wrong with a Free Lunch?* edited by J. Cohen and J. Rogers, 75–79. Boston: Beacon Press.

Arango, Joaquin. 2000. "Explaining Migration: A Critical View." *International Social Science Journal* 52, no. 165:283–96.

Atkinson, A. B. 1996. "The Case for a Participation Income." *Political Quarterly* 67, no. 1:67–70.

Baker, John. 1992. "An Egalitarian Case for Basic Income." In *Arguing for Basic Income: Ethical Foundations for a Radical Reform,* edited by P. van Parijs, 101–27. London: Verso.

Barber, Benjamin. 1984. *Strong Democracy: Participatory Politics for a New Age.* Berkeley and Los Angeles: University of California Press.

Barry, Brian. 1996. "Real Freedom and Basic Income." *Journal of Political Philosophy* 4, no. 3:242–76.

———. 1998. "International Society from a Cosmopolitan Perspective." In *International Society: Diverse Ethical Perspectives,* edited by D. R. Mapel and T. Nardin, 145–63. Princeton: Princeton University Press.

Beitz, Charles R. 2001. "Human Rights as a Common Concern." *American Political Science Review* 95, no. 2:269–82.

Bohman, James. 1997. "Deliberative Democracy and Effective Social Freedom: Capabilities, Resources, and Opportunities." In *Deliberative Democracy: Essays on Reason and Politics,* edited by J. Bohman and W. Rehg, 321–48. Cambridge, Mass.: MIT Press.

Booth, Ken. 1999. "Three Tyrannies." In *Human Rights in Global Politics,* edited by T. Dunne and N. J. Wheeler, 31–70. Cambridge: Cambridge University Press.

Brugger, Winfried. 1996. "The Image of the Person in the Human Rights Concept." *Human Rights Quarterly* 18, no. 3:594–611.

Donnelly, Jack. 1999. "Human Rights and Asian Values: A Defense of 'Western Individualism.'" In *The East Asian Challenge for Human Rights,* edited by J. R. Bauer and D. A. Bell, 60–87. Cambridge: Cambridge University Press.

———. 2003. *Universal Human Rights in Theory and Practice.* 2nd ed. Ithaca: Cornell University Press.

Dore, Ronald. 2001. "Dignity and Deprivation." In *What's Wrong with a Free Lunch?* edited by J. Cohen and J. Rogers, 80–84. Boston: Beacon Press.

Dowling, Keith, Jurgen de Wispelaere, and Stuart White. 2003. "Stakeholding—a New Paradigm in Social Policy." In *The Ethics of Stakeholding,* edited by K. Dowling, J. de Wispelaere and S. White, 1–28. New York: Palgrave.

Fabre, Cécile. 2003. "The Stake: An Egalitarian Proposal?" In *The Ethics of*

Stakeholding, edited by K. Dowling, J. de Wispelaere, and S. White, 114–29. New York: Palgrave.

Finkelstein, Lawrence S. 1995. "What Is Global Governance?" *Global Governance* 1, no. 3:367–72.

Fitzpatrick, Tony. 2000. *Freedom and Security*. New York: Palgrave.

Freeman, Michael. 2000. "The Perils of Democratization: Nationalism, Markets, and Human Rights." *Human Rights Review* 2, no. 1:33–51.

Goodhart, Michael. 2005. *Democracy as Human Rights: Freedom and Equality in the Age of Globalization*. New York: Routledge.

Goodin, Robert E. 1988. "What Is So Special about Our Fellow Countrymen?" *Ethics* 98, no. 4:663–86.

———. 1992. "Towards a Minimally Presumptuous Social Welfare Policy." In *Arguing for Basic Income: Ethical Foundations for a Radical Reform*, edited by P. van Parijs, 195–214. London: Verso.

———. 2001. "Something for Nothing?" In *What's Wrong with a Free Lunch?* edited by J. Cohen and J. Rogers, 90–97. Boston: Beacon Press.

Gould, Carol C. 1988. *Rethinking Democracy: Freedom and Social Cooperation in Politics, Economy, and Society*. Cambridge: Cambridge University Press.

———. 1993. "Feminism and Democratic Community Revisited." In *Democratic Community: NOMOS XXXV*, edited by J. W. Chapman and I. Shapiro, 396–413. New York: New York University Press.

Habermas, Jürgen. 2001. "Why Europe Needs a Constitution." *New Left Review* 11:5–26.

Handler, Joel F. 2004. *Social Citizenship and Workfare in the United States and Western Europe: The Paradox of Inclusion*. Cambridge: Cambridge University Press.

Held, David. 1995. *Democracy and the Global Order: From the Modern State to Cosmopolitan Governance*. Stanford: Stanford University Press.

Hunt, Lynn. 2000. "The Paradoxical Origins of Human Rights." In *Human Rights and Revolutions*, edited by J. N. Wasserstrom, L. Hunt, and M. B. Young, 3–18. Lanham, Md.: Rowman and Littlefield.

Jones, Peter. 1994. *Rights*. Hampshire, UK: Macmillan.

———. 1999. "Human Rights, Group Rights, and People's Rights." *Human Rights Quarterly* 21, no. 1:80–107.

Jordan, Bill. 1992. "Basic Income and the Common Good." In *Arguing for Basic Income: Ethical Foundations for a Radical Reform*, edited by P. van Parijs, 155–77. London: Verso.

Kausikan, Bilahari. 1993. "Asia's Different Standard." *Foreign Policy* 92:24–41.

Lefebvre, Georges. 1957. *The Coming of the French Revolution: 1789*. Translated by R. R. Palmer. New York: Vintage Books.

LeFort, Claude. 1986. "Politics and Human Rights." In *The Political Forms of Modern Society: Bureaucracy, Democracy, Totalitarianism*, edited by J. B. Thompson, 240–72. Cambridge: Polity.

Locke, John. [1689] 1960. *Two Treatises of Government*. Edited by P. Laslett. Cambridge: Cambridge University Press.

Nussbaum, Martha C. 1992. "Human Functioning and Social Justice: In Defense of Aristotelian Essentialism." *Political Theory* 20, no. 2:202–46.

Offe, Claus. 1992. "A Non-Productive Design for Social Policies." In *Arguing for Basic Income: Ethical Foundations for a Radical Reform*, edited by P. van Parijs, 61–78. London: Verso.

Oxfam International. 2005. "A Round for Free: How Rich Countries Are Getting a Free Ride on Agricultural Subsidies at the WTO." Edited by L. Stuart and G. Fanjul. Washington, D.C.: Oxfam International.

Parijs, Philippe van. 1992. "The Second Marriage of Justice and Efficiency." In *Arguing for Basic Income: Ethical Foundations for a Radical Reform*, edited by P. van Parijs, 215–40. London: Verso.

———. 1995. *Real Freedom for All: What (If Anything) Can Justify Capitalism?* Oxford: Oxford University Press.

———. 2004. *A Short History of Basic Income* [Web page]. 2004. Available at http://www.etes.ucl.ac.be/BIEN/BI/HistoryBI.htm (accessed August 4, 2004).

Pateman, Carole. 1988. *The Sexual Contract*. Stanford: Stanford University Press.

———. 1998. "Contributing to Democracy." *Review of Constitutional Studies* 4, no. 2:191–212.

———. 2002. "Self-Ownership and Property in the Person: Democratization and a Tale of Two Concepts." *Journal of Political Philosophy* 10, no. 1:20–53.

———. 2003. "Freedom and Democratization: Why Basic Income Is to Be Preferred to Basic Capital." In *The Ethics of Stakeholding*, edited by K. Dowling, J. de Wispelaere and S. White, 130–48. New York: Palgrave.

———. 2004. "Democratizing Citizenship: Some Advantages of a Basic Income." *Politics and Society* 32, no. 1:89–105.

Pettit, Philip. 1997. *Republicanism: A Theory of Freedom and Government*. Oxford: Oxford University Press.

Phelps, Edmund S. 2001. "Subsidize Wages." In *What's Wrong with a Free Lunch?* edited by J. Cohen and J. Rogers. Boston: Beacon Press.

Pogge, Thomas W. 1992. "Cosmopolitanism and Sovereignty." *Ethics* 103, no. 1:48–75.

———. 2000. "The International Significance of Human Rights." *Journal of Ethics* 4, no. 1:45–69.

Pollis, Adamantia, and Peter Schwab, eds. 1979. *Human Rights: Cultural and Ideological Perspectives.* New York: Praeger.

Purdy, David. 1994. "Citizenship, Basic Income, and the State." *New Left Review* 208:30–48.

Rawls, John. 1971. *A Theory of Justice.* Cambridge, Mass.: Harvard University Press.

Robertson, James. 1996. "Towards a New Social Compact: Citizen's Income and Radical Tax Reform." *Political Quarterly* 67, no. 1:54–58.

Rosenau, James N. 1992. "Governance, Order, and Change in World Politics." In *Governance without Government: Order and Change in World Politics,* edited by J. N. Rosenau and E.-O. Czempiel, 1–29. Cambridge: Cambridge University Press.

Rothschild, Emma. 2001. "Security and Laissez-Faire." In *What's Wrong with a Free Lunch?* edited by J. Cohen and J. Rogers, 43–50. Boston: Beacon Press.

Ruggie, John Gerard. 1982. "International Regimes, Transactions, and Change: Embedded Liberalism in the Postwar Economic Order." *International Organization* 36, no. 2:379–415.

Sandel, Michael J. 1998. *Liberalism and the Limits of Justice.* 2nd ed. Cambridge: Cambridge University Press.

Sen, Amartya. 1999. *Development as Freedom.* New York: Alfred A. Knopf.

Shapiro, Ian. 1999. *Democratic Justice.* New Haven: Yale University Press.

Shue, Henry. 1996. *Basic Rights: Subsistence, Affluence, and U.S. Foreign Policy.* Princeton: Princeton University Press.

Skinner, Quentin. 1998. *Liberty before Liberalism.* Cambridge: Cambridge University Press.

Soboul, Albert. 1977. *A Short History of the French Revolution: 1789–1799.* Translated by G. Symcox. Berkeley and Los Angeles: University of California Press.

Solow, Robert M. 2001. "Foreword." In *What's Wrong with a Free Lunch?* edited by J. Cohen and J. Rogers, ix–xvi. Boston: Beacon Press.

Standing, Guy. 1992. "The Need for a New Social Consensus." In *Arguing for Basic Income: Ethical Foundations for a Radical Reform,* edited by P. van Parijs, 47–60. London: Verso.

Steiner, Hillel. 1992. "Three Just Taxes." In *Arguing for Basic Income: Ethical Foundations for a Radical Reform,* edited by P. van Parijs, 81–92. London: Verso.

Taylor, Charles. 1997. "What's Wrong with Negative Freedom?" In *Contemporary Political Philosophy: An Anthology,* edited by R. E. Goodin and P. Pettit, 418–28. Oxford: Blackwell.

———. 2003. "No Community, No Democracy, Part I." *Responsive Community* 13, no. 4:17–28.

———. 2003/4. "No Community, No Democracy, Part II." *Responsive Community* 14, no. 1:15–25.

Veen, Robert J. van der. 1998. "Real Freedom versus Reciprocity: Competing Views on the Justice of Unconditional Basic Income." *Political Studies* 46, no. 1:140–63.

Vincent, R. J. 1986. *Human Rights and International Relations.* Cambridge: Cambridge University Press.

Wall, Steven. 2001. "Freedom, Interference, and Domination." *Political Studies* 49, no. 2:216–30.

White, Stuart. 2003. *The Civic Minimum.* Oxford: Oxford University Press.

SECTION III
Democracy, Political Participation, and Welfare

Participation Revisited: Carole Pateman vs. Joseph Schumpeter

Alan Ryan

This essay pays tribute to Carole Pateman only indirectly. It reflects on themes that she has made her own, but my reflections take her work as an inspiration, not a target of praise or criticism. This and the following paragraph are the only direct acknowledgment of her influence on what follows. Professor Pateman's first book was a wonderful example of what one would wish all young scholars to launch their careers with: a short, crisp, engaged, and imaginative essay on a theme of central importance (Pateman 1970). Reread thirty years later, it bears the marks of its own provenance; it was a distinguished product of the reaction by the rising generation of political theorists against the *bienpensant* political science of the 1950s and 1960s, and I mention below one way in which its author was more innocent than one would be now. Nonetheless, it has over more than three decades earned a permanent place in the history of our discipline while retaining the youthful freshness that marked its first appearance.

What follows pays tribute to Professor Pateman's energy and intellectual ambition by offering a slightly chastened defense of those youthful enthusiasms from a different perspective. Professor Pateman's subsequent career has focused on issues of a broadly feminist kind, to which I add nothing here; but her work has everywhere been distinguished by the same crispness and sharpness.[1] Her talent has been to make political issues personal, turning the old cliché that "the personal is political" inside out, without losing the truth the cliché contains. She writes with the jargon-free attention to the concrete

---

1. I think especially of Pateman 1988.

reality of individual lives and their vulnerability to misfortune that should be a condition of being allowed into print on these matters. It is a pleasure to pay tribute to her work, though I shall not match her standards.

The structure of what follows is simple. The second half of the paper takes up two topics: the fate of participatory democracy over the past forty years, and whether there are arenas other than the national political stage in which participatory self-government is possible and desirable. I allow myself a coda to ask "participation or plebiscite?" and offer an answer; it is there that I make good on my subtitle. Carole Pateman defended a conception of democracy as something that involved continuous engagement by citizens; Joseph Schumpeter had argued some thirty years earlier that it was unrealistic to expect so much of ordinary people, and that their role in the political system was to answer one simple question: "Do you wish Team A or Team B to constitute the government for the next four or five years?" This is what I describe as democracy by plebiscite, an electorate confronting a question to which a simple Yes or No is appropriate. I argue that politics must in the nature of the case simplify issues, and therefore that a plebiscitory element is inescapable, but that a highly participatory civil society is both possible and frequently actualized.

On my first topic, I argue that the defense of participatory democracy was in part provoked by the excesses of the "end of ideology" movement of the 1950s and 1960s and lost energy when it won that argument. I argue further that the revelation of the nastiness of the socialist regimes on which enthusiasts for participatory democracy had pinned their hopes undermined the arguments for a more participatory politics in the capitalist West. I argue, thirdly, that the end of the great post-1945 economic boom at the end of the 1960s made many supporters of participatory democracy less optimistic about the prospects of any form of democracy, whether in the workplace or elsewhere. As to the second topic of democracy outside the conventionally defined political sphere, I argue that there is much room for participation in a great many contexts, but that there is no reason to think that participation in those contexts will lead very directly to a more participatory politics. The first part of this paper is prefatory to the second, though longer than the discussion it prefaces. The last introductory remark that I ought to make is that as an exact contemporary of Carole Pateman's, I have shared her hopes and disappointments for thirty-five years, and that this fact colors what follows.

I

To describe contemporary western polities such as the United States or Great Britain as "liberal democracies" is inescapable because the linguistic habits of the day are not to be overturned in a moment. Nonetheless, it does no harm to remember that they are *not* democracies. What they are best called is not obvious: *plutocratic mixed republics with a substantial populist component* is stronger on descriptive accuracy than on elegance, though Polybius or his disciple Cicero might have described them thus (Polybius 1971, Book VI, "On the Form of States"; Cicero 1999, 59–78). Unlike any republic they had encountered or could imagine, modern polities are *liberal* in matters of religion and sexual morality, if less so in matters such as the state's surveillance of its citizens and its control over their physical movements and their economic activities. What they are not, sensu stricto, is democratic. They are government by the rich, though the rich have to compete for the favor of the ordinary person to secure office.

Intellectual tidiness and a decent respect for the opinions of our forbears suggest that we should from time to time consider whether we are, could be, or would rationally wish to be, citizens of a twenty-first century democracy in the strict sense of the term. We should take seriously the view that was a cliché for two millennia, that democracy is undesirable; the friends of aristocracy, mixed republics, moderate constitutional monarchies, and similar political systems were neither malign nor deluded. It is neither wicked nor incoherent to think that the short way with my two themes is to say that we have stopped thinking about participatory democracy because it was a dead end, and that there is no point asking whether we might usefully try to extend participatory democracy to more areas of life. Accountability, honesty, accessibility, and a meticulous concern for civil and human rights are good topics for discussion; democratization strictly speaking is not. Because I am interested in the question of whether we might rebuild our political and administrative systems in such a way that the pleasures and burdens of self-government are more widely available to more people, and because I think that democracy in the strict sense is one answer to the question, I do not propose to accept that response without a struggle; but I do not pretend that no rational person could offer it. This stance does not put me at odds with the Carole Pateman who wrote *Participation and Democratic Theory* (Pateman 1970), but there is some danger of terminological cross-purposes. Her book pursued a critical agenda that nothing in what follows casts doubt on, and a constructive agenda about which I am more skeptical, though for reasons that do not impugn what she and others have said about citizen competence and related subjects. She does not, however, challenge the ordinary view of what democracy amounts to as I do. She is readier to describe Rousseau as a democrat than I—or he; and she quibbles less than I about the extent to which Mill's defense of "representative government" was a defense of democracy. *Participation and Democratic Theory* was written at a time when Joseph Schumpeter's "realistic" theory of democracy was the conventional wisdom, and his criticisms of the so-called "classical" theory of democracy were widely accepted (Schumpeter 1942). Pateman's first achievement was to point out that Schumpeter's account of the "classical" theory was mostly hand-waving; Schumpeter had claimed that the "classical" theorists had believed that democracy was justified because ordinary people would, by a majority, see and vote for the common good when they were asked to decide what governments should do. Carole Pateman pointed out that Rousseau, Mill, and G. D. H. Cole were enthusiasts for participation but held none of the views by which Schumpeter defined the "classical" theory. This task of demolition was negative, but it achieved something positive: it saved enthusiasts for greater participation from feeling obliged to defend the more implausible ideas with which Schumpeter had tried to saddle the tradition.

Her positive program was to defend the possibility of a participatory democratic politics at the opposite pole from Schumpeter's jaundiced recommendation that the electorate should vote every so often to install a government and should thereafter leave decisions and their implementation to a political elite and their civil servant helpers (Schumpeter 1942, 289–95). Her case rested not only on showing that Mill and Cole in particular were realistic about the extent of the training in the skills of participation required to make participatory democracy work, but on showing on her own account that there was room for a much more participatory regime in the workplace. Workplace democracy was a deep passion shared by Mill and Cole as well, though not, in the nature of the case, by Rousseau; Mill, indeed, was a more unequivocal enthusiast for socialist self-management than for political democracy. The empirical evidence for the possibility of workplace democracy that Carole Pateman cited included the system of workers' control that the Yugoslav government was experimenting with in the 1960s, as well as a good deal of justly famous industrial sociology from the United States and Britain (Pateman 1970, 67–111).

Defenders of democracy have usually started, as Aristotle said, from a desire to achieve political equality.[2] The simplest way to achieve that is to choose members of Congress and Parliament by lot—as Aristotle also pointed out. Today, this thought enters discussion by way of George Will's observation that we would do better to choose members of Congress from the first several hundred names in the Boston phone book than from the faculty of Harvard. The plausibility of that claim depends on what tasks we think that members of Congress should perform; but it is at least an open question whether we would do better to select members of Congress at random than by the electoral processes currently fashionable. A random sample of the Boston phone book might well produce not only a better Congress than the faculty of Harvard, but a better Congress than one made up of professional politicians in hock to their financial backers as we have at present. However that might be, everyone whose name was in the lottery would have what they do not have now: an equal, though very small, chance of serving in Congress.

Let us elaborate on that thought. A democracy is one of two things: a political system in which influence over the binding decisions of government is exercised equally by all citizens, or a political system in which the holders of power are continuously and directly accountable to "the people," which is to say, to *all* the people. *Pace* Lincoln's Gettysburg Address, government *for* and *of* the people are readily attainable; government *of* the people is just government tout court. Government *for* the people is attainable under favorable conditions in many different ways; one is benevolent despotism, administration by a dispassionately benevolent and well-informed ruler who is not elected by, nor formally answerable to, the people whose welfare he or she pursues; another is benevolent oligarchy, perhaps in the form of management by anxious, efficient, and well-informed bureaucrats whose positions depend on the support of an elite who vote as "the people" *would* vote if they were rational and well-informed about their interests. We do not need to believe that John Stuart Mill was right in thinking that the East India Company provided such a government for India in order to see that it was not wholly implausible to think so (Mill 1969, chap. 18, 562–77). The difficulty lies with government *by* the people, since the one thing that is very unlikely in modern societies is that more than a very small proportion of "the people" will do much governing at the national level. This is not to say that the numbers involved will be small absolutely; given the size of modern states, their numbers will be large; but they will form only a small proportion of "the people."

---

2. Aristotle 1994, 120; though he also says that liberty is the basis of democracy, he treats the demand for democratic liberty as an aspect of the demand for political equality.

No contemporary political system attempts to achieve political equality in the sense of ensuring that everyone has the same chance of exercising real power over decisions affecting the whole country. More importantly, it is only in a remote sense that "the people" control the actions of government by holding political actors accountable. At best, they control the actions of government in much the same way that car buyers control the activities of the designers at the Ford Motor Company; politicians hope to secure the continued support of the public so as to continue holding their seats in Parliament or Congress, but it is politicians and their professional helpers who design the policies that the populace approves or rejects. Consumers do not design the cars they purchase, and voters do not design the policies they approve or reject. This is not to say that contemporary governments function badly, nor is it to say that they are staffed by persons who have no concern for the welfare of the populations they govern. By the standards prevailing in most of human history, the governments of modern, western, industrialized societies function well, and they behave much less brutally and corruptly than governments earlier or elsewhere. In time of war, they employ modern technology to commit mass murder on a scale hitherto unimaginable; but in times of peace they secure long life, prosperity, and tranquility to a degree equally unimaginable by earlier ages. The point is not that they work badly, but that they are not *democracies*. This is not an original observation; the Yale political scientist Robert Dahl coined the term "polyarchy" in 1953 to characterize political systems in which "a lot of people" governed, even if "the people" did not. Dahl's *Preface to Democratic Theory* discussed definitions of democracy and discussed at some length the anxieties of James Madison about what rule by uneducated and hard-up people might threaten; what most readers remember was Dahl's argument that democracy in the modern United States was not government by those Aristotle called "the many," it was government by "many" (Dahl 1953, chap. 3, esp. 63–71).

The obvious problem with Dahl's account is that in any political system "many people" will be involved in governing. David Hume argued that all regimes, including the most despotic, rested on consent; and in much the same way one could argue that all regimes are polyarchic. What was needed, and what Dahl supplied in a slightly roundabout way, is an account of how the "polyarchs" are recruited, and how their performance is checked. The essence of the systems that we describe as liberal democracies is that *in principle* anyone can put herself or himself forward, and that election or appointment depends directly or indirectly on an electoral process. Party politicians stand for election directly; administrators are appointed by those who have been elected. In aristocracies, only persons eligible by virtue of birth and the possession of the right sort of wealth can put themselves forward; in family-based kleptocracies only the dictator's family and friends can join in the looting. Where voting is restricted by age or sex, only the middle-aged or only men may vote or put themselves forward for election.

Dahl argued that in a democracy elections must be "in some sense controlling"; the condition is met where achieving political office is the result of election or of appointment by those whose entitlement to make the appointment is itself directly or indirectly acquired by election. The person appointed to be permanent secretary in the Home Office in the British political system is appointed by the prime minister with the aid of an appointment committee appropriately constituted according to civil service rules. His immediate boss is the home secretary, who is appointed by the prime minister from among senior politicians in the governing party of the day who are also members of the House of Commons. In this sense, elections are "controlling." Nonetheless, from the point of view of democratic theory, controlling is not ruling; the tastes of consumers control the activities of the Ford Motor Company, but consumers do not run the company. The managers run Ford. One might ask whether this means that the managers of Ford "rule," and the answer is surely that they do. They rule only in a particular area and subject to many constraints; but politicians and administrators govern whole countries subject to many constraints and it is not an accident that "running a country" and "running a business" are thought of as similar activities.

How might we make the modern political system more democratic? The most obvious way is to rethink our obsession with representation. If elected members of Parliament or Congress were replaced by persons chosen by lot for a period of three years or so, while these institutions retained the ability to legislate and to hold the executive to account, we would advance a long way toward political equality. Each citizen would have an equal (very small) chance of really ruling. The question is how such a scheme would work; the answer is in something of the way that a jury works. There would have to be a two-stage process in which persons selected for the purpose—a legislative committee chosen by lot from among the members of the assembly would be one device—would propose to the assembly that there should be legislation on such and such a basis, and if the proposal was agreed, bring back for approval or rejection the legislation itself. It would be essential to have a skilled civil service to draft intelligent legislation, and tight rules to restrict ad hoc amendments moved from the floor. The relationship of this body to the executive is a topic on which I shall say nothing other than that the Athenians organized the process in ways we could emulate, as for a much shorter period did the Florentine republic that Machiavelli served.

There would be "representativeness," because a random sample is a random sample and successive samples produce over the long run a representative cross-section of whatever they are samples of. It would not be "representative government." Modern representative government is the end stage of a long process that began with persons chosen by entities such as boroughs and shires putting to a monarch and his servants the case for whatever they had in mind—maintaining their legal privileges, a reduction of taxation or alterations in its basis, "the redress of grievances" generally. The purpose of increasing the range of interests represented was to improve the ability of the population at large to police the conduct of a government that everyone expected to be headed by kings and managed by the king's servants. It was not the expression of a desire for self-government, let alone a desire for democracy.

Political representation historically rested on rights attached to geographically and historically grounded roles and statuses, not on a "natural" or "subjective" conception of individual rights. The modern conception of natural or subjective rights emphasizes the individual and his or her choices; the older notion emphasizes status rather than choice. Members represented places and interests. The modernization of representative government was the process well described by Gladstone as that of bringing excluded classes "within the pale of the constitution." It was not intended as democratization either by Gladstone or by most of his contemporaries; they had had a classical education and remained cautious about what they and classical writers thought of as democracy. Nevertheless, it certainly represented *social* democratization, in the sense of a step on the road to establishing that citizenship was a universal entitlement and not acquired by being born into a particular social class, occupation, or sex (Marshall 1987). It was a condition of genuine political equality without regard to race, class, or gender; but it was not itself part of a drive toward that goal.

There are many things to be said against the lottery-based scheme I have sketched. Consider three. Would persons selected by lot wish to serve? Politicians in our world devote what a dispassionate observer might think is a crazy amount of time and emotional commitment to securing election. But politicians are the product of a particular kind of political system, where a mass electorate has to be organized, persuaded, or induced by fair means and foul to vote the right way, and kept on side thereafter. This was part of what Weber meant when he described modern democracy as rule by professional politicians; it is the management of a mass electorate. No such career would be available in the purest version of the system I have just described.

It is not only people who are temperamentally attracted to the life of the professional politician who would find that system unattractive. Given the similarities between the process envisaged here and serving on a jury—listening to arguments pro and con and coming to a decision on which side is to be preferred—there seems no reason why anyone would be more willing to serve in such an assembly than most people presently are to do jury service. The Athenians had to pay the poor to turn up; in the modern world, we would have to pay people a salary to compensate them for doing their duty, and in the case of prosperous people we would have to pay them a lot. It would be a powerful argument against such a scheme that it required either constant compulsion or enormous salaries.

The second large question is whether there would not inevitably be the reappearance of something very like the modern politician, but in this instance half in and half outside such an assembly. It would not be exactly like Athens during the Peloponnesian War, since the assembly would not be open to all the citizenry, only to those selected by lot to be members of it. Alcibiades would have to pull the strings from outside; but American history is full of figures who had no trouble manipulating the members of legislatures in their own business interests, and even though a rapid turnover of the membership would make bribery less effective, it is hard to imagine that innocent citizens would be much harder to bribe and manipulate than the venal politicians of the Gilded Age.

The third question is whether an assembly chosen by lot would become factional. Factionalism is a topic that any admirer of Madison is irresistibly drawn to (Madison, Jay, and Hamilton 1987, Paper X). Madison would surely have thought that an assembly chosen at random would present to the worst-off members of societies such as the United States and Great Britain a tempting chance to rewrite the rules of property ownership, contract, and employment in ways that favored themselves. It would import the class war that it was the task of politics to control into the mechanism that was supposed to control it. It would be a golden opportunity for the worse off to engage in what Madison regarded as a wicked and improper attempt to equalize property in violation of the natural rights of owners. Not everyone shared Madison's fears, even at the time, and perhaps we need not do so now. Hume thought the lower classes were easily seduced by the glamour of wealth and status—celebrity culture in the modern idiom—though he was hostile to democracy for all the familiar anti-Athenian reasons. Still, it is reasonable to fear both that an assembly selected at random will import unfiltered into the legislative assembly the economic and ideological tensions of the society outside, and that these will provide plenty of raw material for a modern Alcibiades or a Huey Long. Hume's cheerfulness presupposes more moderation in the elite than we should rely on.

II

How Participatory Democracy Became Unfashionable

Given that we *could* institutionalize something closer to "true" democracy, but might for good reasons flinch from doing so, let us turn to the two issues I began with: first, the diminishing attractiveness of participatory democracy over the past three decades, and second, its attractions in realms other than the narrowly political. Participatory democracy has fallen out of fashion for several reasons. One is that the theories of democracy that praised the apathy and ignorance of the modern electorate as a stabilizing force have been so discredited that they do not provide a stimulus to combat. The complacency of 1950s political science has given way to a more chastened discipline, whose practitioners are more varied in their political allegiances than those of the 1950s; nobody would today write articles in defense of apathy, nor write about the virtues of "elite" democracy on the assumption that the wildness of the lower classes needed to be tamed and filtered by the calm conservatism of their betters (Fiorina 2004).

The political scientists of the 1950s were deeply affected by the 1930s. They inherited a profound fear of the populist violence associated with Fascism in all its forms, and with the connected anxieties found in the work of critics of mass society such as José Ortega y Gasset ([1930] 1994). Not everyone has freed themselves of those anxieties, but recent writers have emphasized the commonsensical and centrist attitudes of the public at large and contrasted them with the real or factitious passions that politicians bring to the electoral and administrative battle. On this view, the wider public looks for compromise on such passion-arousing issues as abortion and euthanasia or relations between church and state, and politicians look for partisan advantage in stirring up trouble. On the other hand, nobody suggests that ordinary people can make a lot of difference to the acrimony of contemporary politics without the leadership of the political elites it is hoped they might tame. Communitarians in particular bemoan the decay of the interstitial forms of association that

Tocqueville praised as the basis of American democracy, and with their decay the decay of the ordinary person's political capacities; so, even if ordinary citizens are acquitted of wildness, so that old anxieties about their participation have died down, there is no demand that they should participate in greater numbers and in other contexts to increase the civility of contemporary politics.[3]

Although apathy and elitism are not held in high regard, enthusiasm for the participatory alternative is invisible other than in the form of discussions of social capital, where it is participation in social institutions such as the Boy Scouts or Rotary that is of interest. Part of the explanation is that the versions of participatory democracy that were popular turned out on closer inspection to be less attractive than they had looked. The discovery of how deeply the "third way" models were flawed came in installments. Cuba's support for the Soviet invasion of Czechoslovakia in 1968 was perhaps the first blow; how could Castro be a "Tankie"? The tyrannical quality of Cuban communism became increasingly difficult to ignore, no matter what excuses we made in terms of the continuous threat from the United States; the same, less obtrusively, was true of Yugoslavia, our other hope. The fact that a few philosophers could talk about humanist Marxism did not mean that Marshal Tito and the Yugoslav Communist Party operated anything other than a police state. A degree of workers' control within individual enterprises certainly existed; it did little for either political democracy or economic growth. Between 1975 and 1985, Eastern European sociologists began to explain in painful detail the ways in which "actually existing socialism" had destroyed civil society everywhere it was instituted; the moral, associational, and ideological bases of democracy of any sort were lacking, let alone the social and moral resources for participatory democracy as we imagined it.

Conversely, it emerged that there was little desire for self-government in the western countries where governments could have been trusted not to produce a fraudulent version of it, and not to stamp it out. What the public wanted was competent government, and the unpopularity of politicians owed more to the ending of twenty-five years of postwar economic growth than anything else. Voters turned out to hold the old-fashioned view that one doesn't keep a dog and bark oneself; if the dog fails to do its stuff, it has to be replaced by one that will, but otherwise, should be left to do its job. Occasional experiments in reforming local government to encourage more participation

3. Perhaps an exception should be made for James Fishkin's campaign to promote forms of local deliberative assembly modeled on the pattern of citizens' juries. See Ackerman and Fishkin 2004.

were tried, but in the mass they confirmed the findings of the prewar "Hawthorne experiments" that Elton Mayo and his collaborators had conducted at a Western Electric plant in Chicago. People responded with enthusiasm to interesting changes in their environments, especially if they seemed to promise improvements of one sort and another, but the effect died out as the novelty wore off. The political scene also saw the rise of underclass political entrepreneurs so engagingly described by Tom Wolfe, whose entitlement to speak for the ordinary person was decidedly limited (Wolfe 1970). If they were a sample of what participation would generate, so much the worse for participation.

The attractions of political pragmatism grew stronger. Both in Europe and in the United States, "stagflation"—a long period of high inflation and low economic growth—changed the political agenda. The task was not that of trying to make a securely affluent, and purportedly liberal-democratic society become the democracy it aspired to be, but trying to rewrite the terms of the socioeconomic contract in order to keep the economy on track at all and to sustain the fragile legitimacy of the state that protected it. Almost everywhere, the effect of this was sooner or later to give conservative governments long periods in power, as the electorate expressed its preference for economic competence over redistribution, multicultural liberalism, and whatever it feared from the local left. Economically, mainland Europe survived the period better than Britain, but throughout Europe it was a time of diminished confidence in the capacities of government.

It did not help that from 1969 onwards there was a continuous terrorist campaign in Northern Ireland and sporadic terrorist violence in mainland Europe; no group, whether substantial and well-organized like the IRA or fragmented and barely sane like the Red Army Fraktion in Germany, had the least chance of realizing its positive aims, but their ability to make the public more "small-c" conservative was impressive. Some members of the left remained impressively untouched by all this, and concentrated on the disputes that separated one Trotskyite sect from another. The audience for the worldview of movements for workers' control from anarcho-syndicalist to very late Trotskyite had always been limited, and it now diminished to nothing; workers occupied their workplaces and tried to take over the management of enterprises from their employers only as a desperate last resort in the face of bankruptcy and closure. The one place where workers' occupations had a real political purpose and achieved a real political goal was Gdansk, where Lech Walesa's ship workers opened the first crack in the Polish communist party's dictatorship. But Polish Catholicism was more of an inspiration and more of a beneficiary than participatory democracy.

The sting in the question mark in the title of Robert Dahl's *After the Revolution?* became impossible to ignore; as Dahl had good-naturedly pointed out, simple arithmetic is against continuous or widespread involvement in politics at anything above the level of a city block. In a city the size of New York, with perhaps five million adult inhabitants out of the total of eight million, the mayor could each year give six seconds' attention to each citizen—so long as he never ate, slept, or performed any other of the usual bodily functions. This is not in the least decisive as an argument against greater involvement by the citizenry in feasible ways. The classical model of a pyramid of institutions in which there is universal involvement at the most local level, and delegates (who might themselves be chosen by lot) to connect the base to higher levels, is perfectly feasible. We select citizens by lot to serve on juries, and we could empanel them to serve on planning committees, budget committees, and much else. This resembles Jefferson's model of "ward republics," and none the worse for it. Not everyone can participate in everything, but participation in enough areas to learn the arts of nonpolitical, semipolitical, and thoroughly political association is an achievable goal (Putnam 2000). Unlike a Congress selected by lot, it has few predictable negative side effects; but it is not popular.

Nonpolitical Participatory Democracy

Some of the seeds planted in the 1960s continued to grow throughout the period of the conservative reaction. They bore unexpected fruit, as did the movement for workers' control that turned out to be a dead end at the time we invested so much hope in it.[4] In the late 1960s, readers of *The Affluent Worker* were frequently depressed by the authors' findings that affluent workers (the people studied were assembly-line workers in a General Motors plant in Luton, England) were not interested in exercising more control over either their working conditions or their company's policies (Goldthorpe et al. 1968a, 1968b, 1969) Unionized British labor was notorious for shop-floor militancy; but however militant, British unionism was by tradition defensive. Management would be resisted if it attempted to extend its control over exactly who did what, when, how, and for how long, but the idea that the workforce might

---

4. I do not mean this dismissively; my own allegiances would be to some version of Guild Socialism if it could secure enough support to be a live option.

share responsibility in exchange for a share in power was of no interest. Some members of the "hard" left hoped to launch a revolution on the basis of workplace militancy, but they were Communists or Trotskyites with no time for outdated anarcho-syndicalist ideas about worker democracy. The rank and file understood this well enough and had a strictly instrumental attitude toward their hard-line leaders; so long as they kept their members' wages growing ahead of inflation, they would follow them. As soon as it became clear that the game was up, they deserted them.

The combination of a readiness to follow militant leaders but a rejection of responsibility for managing the enterprise against which the militancy was directed was not foolish; if British management had been better, and the workforce had understood the philosophy of Samuel Gompers, it could have sustained a successful, if pretty conflictual, relationship such as some American industries developed after the Wagner Act put an end to more violent conflict. British firms with U.S. managers are a quarter more productive than British firms with U.K. managers even now; they are better but not more democratically run. However, the idea that a successful firm could be run by tough and efficient managers whose (equally tough) workforce would exact the full price for their own (efficient) efforts was one thought too many for a trade union movement that had always been reactive.

A surprising descendant of the movements for workers' control is a by-product of the growth of the microcomputer. The important changes for our purposes are not the obvious ones such as the near-abolition of secretarial work as computer-literate managers learn to type their own letters, nor the exponential growth of targeted advertising as we all feature on ever-more refined databases; they are the impact on company formation and organization. The proliferation of start-ups, though primarily a testimony to the way in which the "animal spirits" of entrepreneurs get the better of their prudence, has also demonstrated the possibilities of self-governing cooperative forms of organization. Characteristically, the founding members of such entities have paid themselves in equity—in part because they generate little net income for a long time, but more because the participants wish for a stake in possible success and a say in the direction of the company. Like socialism more broadly, workers' control appears to be attractive to well-educated middle-class people.

This casts a curious light on the old question of whether a capitalist economy is the only possible basis of democratic government. The literature is replete with assertions that it is; they commonly boil down to the claim that prosperity brings in its wake a desire for accountable government, or, the other way about, that in the absence of accountable government, corruption and illegality undermine the search for prosperity. The hinge is prosperity, not any particular kind of capitalism. Still, there is no reason to disbelieve in the existence of a virtuous circle, whereby a democracy that rests on an economically efficient basis secures support for democracy while the prosperous economic basis provides the resources for running a transparent and law-abiding political system that in turn promotes economic success. Conversely, one can all too easily visualize the circle turning vicious if the commitment to democratic institutions was no more than instrumental. Then, the somewhat optimistic suggestion is that because capitalism disperses economic power very widely, and individuals learn to be economically self-reliant in a capitalist context, they will be natural democrats, so that their attachment to democracy will be more than merely instrumental.

How far democracy as distinct from any tolerably stable and uncorrupt form of government is a natural beneficiary of the virtuous circle, within which success reinforces legitimacy, which in turn reinforces success, is an underexplored question; one might think that any form of government consistent with a reliable legal order would benefit from it. The more difficult issue is the one flagged at the end of the previous paragraph: the suggestion that there is an affinity between the ethos of a capitalist economy and that of a liberal democracy. This takes us back to Schumpeter and Weber and the claim that liberal democracy is a political system where much like an economic entrepreneur the political entrepreneur imagines new futures, new policies, new ways of conducting political life, packages them attractively and tries them on the public. When one thinks of the "professional politician," it is easy to think of party organizers, bureaucrats rather than leaders, or low-ranking elected figures. But Schumpeter's famous account of the way capitalism is driven by "gales of creative destruction" places entrepreneurs rather than managers at the heart of the story. When he quotes an American politician saying that he dealt in votes like other people dealt in oil, it strikes us as a piece of atheoretical cynicism; but read less cynically, it might invite us to consider the political leader as a man who markets visions of the future and sees whether there are takers for them (Schumpeter 1942).

On that reading, the politician as "demagogue"—understood as a leader and teacher of the people, not as a rabble-rouser—occupies center stage. Schumpeter seems to have thought that entrepreneurs were unusual people; but one view of modern, or perhaps "postmodern" capitalism is that it has democratized the entrepreneurial spirit. Organizations with a flat or almost nonexistent managerial structure that operate in a continuous brainstorming mode do so because they understand the benefits of drawing on the insights of everyone working in the organization, and they want the loyalty to the organization that this way of working achieves. Schools sometimes operate in this fashion, as do small liberal arts colleges. The thought that they thereby encourage their staff to "take ownership" of the decisions that will affect their lives is an obvious one, and in some business contexts, it is literally the case that the staff have ownership of the enterprise in a literal fashion; they are both employees and owners and have staked their futures on the success of the enterprise.

As to the question whether these phenomena are likely to have an impact on the wider political scene, the answer is no. There is no reason to suppose that the way in which a few cutting-edge enterprises conduct their affairs will generate a demand for analogous ways of working in the wider political arena. Indeed, it is not clear what would generate such a demand. Recent small-scale experiments with deliberative juries and the like, as reported by James Fishkin and his collaborators, suggest the educative potential of forums very different from the focus groups beloved of political operatives in Britain and the United States; but they do not suggest that even the participants in such experiments have been clamoring to extend them more widely and into other arenas of policy making.[5] What the evidence of the business world and the world of experimental political science suggests is that in the right circumstances individuals are capable of participation with very high degrees of energy, commitment, and ability. This is all we need to know if what we are interested in is the possibility of designing political institutions to harness more of those qualities; but it offers no grounds for thinking that it will of itself generate a transformation of existing institutions or of the way people use those institutions.

Coda: Radicalized Schumpeterian Democracy

I end by making good on the promise to set Professor Pateman's—and my—ambitions for democracy in the framework of Joseph Schumpeter's "realist" theory of democracy. I shall argue that even if we accepted Schumpeter's deflationary expectations about the extent of the interest in and knowledge of national politics to be expected of the ordinary person, we should still entertain more radical ambitions than he. The "realist" view of democracy owes almost everything to his account of what he self-praisingly described as a

---

5. James Fishkin argues for the wider use of deliberative mechanisms in Ackerman and Fishkin 2004.

"realistic" theory in *Capitalism, Socialism and Democracy*. His own attachment to democracy was limited; he was much more frightened of the wickedness of the mob than of the wickedness of the elites who were to blame for the horrors of the first fifty years of the last century.[6] Nonetheless, Schumpeter's picture of modern democracy—understood in the ordinary way and not in my exigent fashion—offers material for reflection. If we are skeptical of the possibility of making politics on a national scale significantly more participatory than they presently are, or if we are anxious about the consequences of doing so, we may still think that we can be democratic realists while wanting much more radical results from democratic politics than Schumpeter.

The argument is brief. We have not asked why the Athenians established what they termed democracy because the reasons are too obvious. Taking it for granted that families picked out by descent and wealth—the Alkmaeonids and Pissistratids, for instance—would be likely to hold high judicial and military office, to be richer, more highly regarded, and more favored than everyone else, they understood that they needed ways of holding in check the natural tendency of the advantaged to exploit and oppress their fellows. This thought is as relevant today as it ever was; we may readily believe that the clever, the well-educated, the well-connected, and the well-off are almost certain to hold high office, but we still want democratic institutions to ensure that they hold office for the benefit of "the many" rather than "the few." The Athenian "many" seem to have shared the commentators' view of themselves as a cohesive group, whose economic and political interests united them behind particular policies and the leaders who might realize them.

The political entrepreneurs who are the heroes of Schumpeter's account of modern democracy were not absent from the Athenian scene; Pericles was one, and so, less fortunately, was Alcibiades. They faced a more responsive audience than their modern successors, and they knew that their interests and values must be reckoned with. The Athenian example is not wholly reassuring: the deal they struck relied on the success of an exploitative foreign policy between the close of the Persian Wars and the outbreak of the Peloponnesian War that amounted to siphoning off whatever they could from Athens's notional allies in the Delian League. The policy alienated the two most powerful mainland states, Corinth and Sparta, and eventually cost the Athenians almost everything they had gambled for. Nor did they learn from experience; they had no sooner recovered from defeat at the end of the Peloponnesian

---

6. Medearis 1999 paints a very alarming picture of Schumpeter's elitism and of his contempt for Jewish colleagues.

War than they embarked on an attempt to repeat their imperial exploits of the mid-fifth century; and when the intercity strife of the mid-fourth century had brought the Greek states to their knees, the Athenians were no more able than anyone else to subordinate their rivalries with other Greek states to the need to form a defensive and aggressive alliance to fend off Macedon. We may admire their verve without thinking much of their foresight.

Nonetheless, the example is not wholly dispiriting. In terms of the reciprocal interaction of competent leaders and competent interlocutors, it provides a model. Could it coexist with political parties, representative government, and elaborate constitutional rules designed to prevent snap judgments such as the decision to execute the admirals who were defeated at Argunisae? The answer is yes, but not easily. Schumpeter's account of democracy is not an "economic" theory of democracy so much as a theory of democratic legitimacy. Schumpeter's insistence that once the voters have elected a government, their job is done and they should put no further pressure on their rulers gives the game away. The divine right of kings claimed that it was divine appointment that gave the king his authority; Schumpeter's account substitutes *vox populi* for *vox dei* but that is the conceptual space in which the argument moves. It is the task of the people to put the crown on the rulers' brow and then to obey.

Because Schumpeter wrote from a very fearful perspective, he vastly overestimated the capacities of political elites and underestimated the good sense of the ordinary person. His account of the conditions under which democracy can be expected to produce good government, which follows the two chapters of *Capitalism, Socialism and Democracy* and largely goes unread, is not in fact an account of *democracy* in action, but an account of the conditions under which a self-restrained, public-spirited elite can be expected to provide liberal, economical, and sensible government; it is quite explicitly a wistful account of Gladstonian liberalism. Injecting some Athenian high spirits into the picture to offset Schumpeter's own injection of American cynicism might yield something as follows.

Democratic election is a mode of legitimation, as Schumpeter said. The ruling class will not much resemble the rank and file who legitimate its hold on authority and power. An open elite is, for all the traditional reasons, likely to be more efficient and more ready to promote the best interests of the rank and file than is an ossified elite, whether it is ossified by birth or ideological persuasion or economic interest; above all, however, the elite needs a strong sense that its legitimacy is conditional on promoting the interests of the rank and file. This is not a theory of the mandate; if the rank and file were capable of issuing mandates, there'd be no need for a political elite at all. It is a theory of dialogical interaction between leaders and led that attempts to do justice to the double dependency in which they are placed.

An adequate public must be able to act *as* a public and hold its rulers to account. This is not an invitation to engage in continuous harassment of the sort Schumpeter feared; it demands that the citizenry have a strong sense of their rights, but also that this should be tempered by a sense of mutuality so that an emphasis on rights does not sustain a beggar-my-neighbor politics rather than a democratic politics. Does it demand a participatory politics? That question might seem to invite a rerunning of the arguments of the last several pages. It does not, because we can now end where we ought. Democratic realism can only advance social justice and the general well-being of the nation if it rests on a participatory society; this is the truth in Tocqueville's emphasis on the role of interstitial forms of association in sustaining American democracy. Pateman's work has always quite rightly invited us to look outside the conventional political arena; but so did Dewey's work a century ago and so does Habermas's today. Nations of even ten million, let alone three hundred million cannot conduct their national decision making around the parish pump. National leaders constantly pretend that they are doing so, but fake immediacy is just that—fake. What they can do is operate distant but accountable forms of government in which the lines of communication are trustworthy no matter how long. Whence the need for what we might call dialogical competence on all sides, the ability to ask questions, challenge the answers, and respond to questions in turn. In that sense, no matter what the institutional embodiment of modern democracy, its institutions must have a substantial participatory component—otherwise, there are no citizens, only acquiescent or disaffected consumers.

References

Ackerman, Bruce, and James Fishkin. 2004. *Deliberation Day.* New Haven: Yale University Press.

Aristotle. [384–322 B.C.] 1994. *Politics* and *The Constitution of Athens.* Cambridge: Cambridge University Press.

Cicero. [54–51 BCE] 1999. *On The Commonwealth* and *On the Laws.* Cambridge: Cambridge University Press.

Dahl, Robert. 1953. *A Preface to Democratic Theory.* Chicago: University of Chicago Press.

Fiorina, Morris. 2004. *Culture War? The Myth of a Polarized America.* New York: Longman.

Goldthorpe, J. H., D. Lockwood, F. Bechhofer, and J. Platt. 1968a. *The Affluent Worker: Industrial Attitudes and Behaviour.* Cambridge: Cambridge University Press.

———. 1968b. *The Affluent Worker: Political Attitudes and Behaviour.* Cambridge: Cambridge University Press.

———. 1969. *The Affluent Worker in the Class Structure.* Cambridge: Cambridge University Press.

Madison, James, John Jay, and Alexander Hamilton. [1787–88]. 1987. *The Federalist Papers.* Harmondsworth, Middelsex: Penguin Books.

Marshall, T. H. 1987. *Citizenship and Social Class.* Reissued with an introduction by T. B. Bottomore. London: Pluto Press.

Medearis, John. 1999. *Schumpeter's Two Theories of Democracy.* Cambridge, Mass.: Harvard University Press.

Mill, J. S. [1861]. 1969. *Considerations on Representative Government.* Vol. 18 of *Collected Works.* Toronto: University of Toronto Press.

Ortega y Gasset, José. [1930] 1994. *The Revolt of the Masses.* New York: W. W. Norton.

Pateman, Carole. 1970. *Participation and Democratic Theory.* Cambridge: Cambridge University Press.

———. 1988. *The Sexual Contract.* Cambridge: Polity Press.

Polybius. 1971. *The Rise of the Roman Empire.* Harmondsworth, Middlesex: Penguin.

Putnam, Robert. 2000. *Bowling Alone.* New York: Simon and Schuster.

Schumpeter, Joseph. 1942. *Capitalism, Socialism, and Democracy.* New York: Harper.

Wolfe, Tom. 1970. "Mau-Mauing the Flak-Catchers." In *Radical Chic and Mau-Mauing the Flak-Catchers.* New York: Farrar, Straus and Giroux.

Participation, Deliberation, and We-thinking
Philip Pettit

One of the most influential arguments for the value of political participation is Carole Pateman's early book *Participation and Democratic Theory* (Pateman 1970). In this essay I explore the ideal with which she was concerned, identify a problem for its implementation, and then describe a strategy under which the problem can be overcome. The strategy makes a connection between the participatory ideal of democracy and what has come to be known as the deliberative ideal of democracy; specifically, it connects with the sort of deliberation that involves what I describe, for want of a better term, as we-thinking.

My focus will not be on democratic process in the large-scale context of an electorate; participatory democracy is very hard to achieve in that context. Following Pateman's lead, I will be exploring the prospects for participatory democratic processes in smaller scale contexts. Where she concentrated in particular on industrial democracy, however, I shall be concerned more generally with the possibility of democratizing a variety of decision-making units, ranging from workplaces to boardrooms, from civic associations to formal committees, from government departments to religious groupings.

In the first section of this paper I look at the content of the ideal of participatory democracy and, in the second, at the context of group behavior for which it is an ideal. In the third section I identify the problem that arises for the ideal; in the fourth section I show how a certain sort of decision-making process can solve this problem; and in the fifth and final section I comment on the deliberative we-thinking that this inevitably involves. Such we-thinking is not much discussed in the literature on deliberative democracy but assumes the first importance in any genuinely participatory theory.

The Content of the Participatory Ideal

What does it mean to make a decision-making process participatory? At the least, it means that the process should give everyone a say, and ideally an equal say. This argues at a first level that whatever form the decision-making process takes over different issues, it ought to be one that has everyone's approval. It ought to be unanimously endorsed as a way to make decisions in the relevant context, local or global; it ought to be a process that could be vetoed by anyone but is actually vetoed by none.

This unanimitarian requirement might be extended from approval of the decision-making process itself to approval of each decision made. The requirement might be not just that the procedure for making decisions is one that all approve, but that it is a procedure under which everyone must approve of each decision made. By all accounts, however, this is not going to be a feasible arrangement. The circumstances of politics, even in relatively nonpluralistic environments, are such as to make disagreement inevitable (Waldron 1999). And that means that a decision-making group that is committed to unanimity is unlikely to be able to get its business done.

The absolutely standard line, in view of this consideration, is that the way forward for participatory democracy is to require unanimous approval for a non-unanimitarian mode of decision making: usually, for a majoritarian mode, or for a majoritarian mode that puts in certain protections against majority abuse. This line is already to be found in thinkers as different as Thomas Hobbes ([1651] 1994) and Jean Jacques Rousseau ([1750, 1755, 1762] 1973).

Hobbes's name is not naturally associated with the ideal of democracy, but there are at least two respects in which he displays democratic credentials. First of all, he insists that the establishment of a sovereign who can speak for the people should be unanimously accepted among the members. "A multitude of men are made one person, when they are by one man, or one person, represented so that it be done with the consent of every one of that multitude in particular" (Hobbes [1651] 1994, 104). And second, he allows that the sovereign might in principle consist of a committee, in particular a committee-of-the-whole, and that such a committee ought to make its decisions by majority voting. "And if the representative consist of many men, the voice of the greater number must be considered the voice of them all" (104).

If Hobbes is unusual, that is mainly because he puts few if any effective limits on the power of the sovereign, including the sovereign people. Rousseau argues, first, that the committee-of-the-whole is the only legitimate sovereign, not just one possible sovereign among many; and second, that as the sovereign it is limited to legislating for the people in accord with rule-of-law constraints and cannot take on executive or other governmental duties. He follows Hobbes, however, in thinking that everyone in a society ought to approve of establishing the assembled people as this sort of legislative sovereign and that that assembled body ought to make its decisions by majority vote. He writes: "one law . . . needs unanimous consent . . . the social compact. . . . Apart from this primitive contract, the vote of the majority always binds all the rest" (Rousseau [1750, 1755, 1762] 1973, bk. 4, chap. 2).

The Hobbes-Rousseau template for participatory democracy might be applied, not just to the society as a whole, but to any decision-making site. Generalized in this way, it involves two steps. First, members are to endorse unanimously the decision-making procedure proposed for the site. And, second, that procedure is to give pride of place to majority voting, even if it is constrained to protect individual members against what would count, by unanimous agreement, as majority abuse. We may take the need for constraint as granted and describe the ideal, in a phrase, as unanimously accepted majority rule. There are different things that majority rule can mean, but I ignore that ambiguity here; as things turn out, it won't matter for our purposes.

If this model of participatory democracy is to have any chance of commanding allegiance, at least two stipulations should be explicitly added; they normally go without saying, and will do so in the remainder of this paper. The first is that those who make the decisions at any site should include everyone who lives or operates there as a member; what it means to live or operate at a site, of course, will vary between different cases. And the second is that those decision makers at any time should not be irreversibly constrained by the decisions of previous generations.

At each time, then, the voting members should include all the members there are. And at each time the members should be able to reconsider and, if this is thought sensible, reverse the decisions of the past membership. The first provision guards against synchronic control of some members by others, the second against diachronic control of the members at one time by the members at earlier times. This second provision need not mean that every decision should be regularly renewed, as in Jefferson's idea of having each generation make its own constitution (Rubenfeld 2001, 18–19). Rousseau ([1750, 1755, 1762] 1973, bk. 3, chap. 9) takes a more sensible line. "Yesterday's law is not binding today; but silence is taken for tacit consent, and the

Sovereign is held to confirm incessantly the laws it does not abrogate as it might."

The Context in Which the Ideal Applies

What sort of enterprise is meant to be governed by the ideal of participatory democracy? There are two starkly contrasting answers in the literature. According to one account, the enterprise is that of determining for a range of choices the option that answers best in each case to the preexisting preferences of the parties in the group. According to the other, the enterprise is that of determining how best some goals can be advanced by the members of the group or by their representatives.

Under the first account, participatory democracy is cast as a method for aggregating the preference orderings of members, now on the options in this choice, now on the options in that. Under the second account, it is taken as a method for aggregating the judgments of the members on issues to do with the specification, ordering, and urgency of the goals; on the opportunities available for pursuit of those goals and the problems arising from tensions between their demands; and on the best means to adopt, or the best agents to recruit, in advancing the goals. Under the first account, the group is cast as a passive beneficiary of whatever choices will be made, and the aim is to make sure that the benefit maximizes preference satisfaction overall; the idea is that that aim will be best advanced by polling members on what they each most want. Under the second account, the group is cast as an active choice-making agency, and the aim is to get members to form a common mind on the judgments required; the idea is that members can best do this by pooling their views on the matters the group has to address.

Given that participatory democracy is taken here as a method that can be used at many sites, not just in an electoral context, we have to conceive of it as a way for members of the relevant group to pool their views, not just as a way of polling them for their preferences. Think of those on the shop floor who participate, as under Pateman's model of industrial democracy, in determining the priorities of the firm. Think of those in a department of state who participate in deciding on how to implement a set of policy goals. Or think of the members of a voluntary association who participate in organizing the annual activities of the group. In none of these cases can participatory democracy be cast as a means for maximizing preference satisfaction. Its primary function will be to ensure that the requisite pattern of decision making will be implemented in a way that gives each member a say, ideally an equal say, in forming the judgments that guide decision.

There is a sense, of course, in which any pattern of choices on which the members converge in such a case will show what in some sense they most prefer. But this should not distract us from the distinctive character of the exercise. If as an individual agent one adopts a means for advancing some goal on the grounds that it is the most efficient way of doing so, then there is a sense in which this will show what one most wants. But whatever the choice shows about what one most wants, the grounds for making it will not be that it produces the most satisfaction of want; one will not have decided upon it under that aspect. There will still be an intuitive contrast between the case envisaged, then, and a case where one does look as such for the way to best satisfy certain antecedent wants (Pettit 2006). A similar contrast obtains between the exercise in which people try to come to a common mind on how best to specify or promote certain goals and the exercise in which they try to determine which of various options answers best to their antecedent desires. If they form the judgment that such and such an option is the thing to do, and then enact it, we can say that that was the action that appealed to them most, or that they wanted most. But the appeal of the action will have been that it was the best means to their ends, not that it answered best to their antecedent desires.

One way of emphasizing the contrast between the two sorts of cases mentioned has a particular prominence in the discussion of deliberative democracy (Sunstein 1993). This is to point out that while there is a sense in which preference satisfaction may be achieved under both procedures, the relationship between the preferences and the procedure is quite different in each case. In one, the preferences are brought to the table and the question raised is how best to satisfy them. In the other, the question of what judgments to form is brought to the table and preferences materialize in the course of resolving that issue. The preferences are the input to the procedure in the first case and the output of the procedure in the second.

In view of the various sites at which it is supposed to apply, I shall assume that participatory democracy is meant to be an ideal for the second sort of case, not the first. It is an ideal for how the members of a decision-making group should pool their judgments, not an ideal for how members should be polled on antecedent preferences. This makes good independent sense anyhow, as it sharpens the contrast between participatory, policy-making democracy and the indirect, electoral form of democracy in which personnel are selected to make policies elsewhere.

A Problem for the Ideal

When democracy is cast as a matter of aggregating preference orderings, then, notoriously, it runs into conflict with Kenneth Arrow's famous impossibility theorem (Arrow 1963). This shows that there is no satisfactory voting procedure that can guarantee it will produce a rational preference ordering over the options in a group choice, on the basis of the rational preference orderings of members. Take transitivity of preference, which consists in the fact that if A is preferred to B, and B to C, then A is preferred to C. Arrow shows that transitive input orderings are liable to generate an intransitive group ordering, if the voting procedure has to satisfy certain intuitively attractive constraints: if it has to work for all inputs, treat no one as a dictator, select any option that is universally preferred to alternatives, and remain constant even as irrelevant alternatives are introduced.

Do we escape this sort of aggregation problem in insisting that participatory democracy is not about the aggregation of preference orderings but about group decision making? I want to argue that even if we do escape this and related problems (Coleman and Ferejohn 1986), we have to face a distinct issue of aggregation, indeed an issue that is arguably more general in character (List and Pettit 2004). This is a problem, not in the aggregation of preference, but in the aggregation of judgment. It does not focus on the difficulty in putting together our individual orderings of the options in a given choice. Rather, it turns on the difficulty of putting together the different sets of judgments that we will each have to form in the course of considering a series of choices that we face as a group.

Take any range of choices that we may confront as a group, whether at the same time or over a stretch of time. Selecting an option in any one choice will require a number of judgments. In each case there will be a question as to the various options available as alternatives, the relevance and urgency of different goals, the extent to which those goals can be simultaneously serviced by different options, and the relative merits of the different options as means of realizing the goals; and this latter issue will usually ramify into a variety of subordinate issues about causal connections, likely consequences of the different options, and so on. Assuming that we are each to have a say on what the group decides in any such choice, and in the range of choices overall, we will each need to form a personal judgment on every question raised, and so we will each have to develop quite a complex body of judgments.

The bodies of judgment we form will inevitably be quite different, however, even if we consult one another in the course of forming them; the burdens of judgment, as John Rawls (1993) calls them, will ensure that we go different ways. And so there will be a problem as to how our different bodies of judgment are to be aggregated into a single body of judgment: one that the group can act on when it acts as a whole—if it ever does this—and one that those authorized to speak or act in its name can be required to follow.

It may seem that we can wheel in the participatory ideal of unanimously endorsed majority voting to solve this problem of aggregation. After all, the obvious thing to do in determining the group view on any issue, say whether or not it is the case that p, is to take a vote among the members and to let the group view be determined by the majority view among the membership. But this, it turns out, we cannot do—at least not with any assurance that the group will be able to perform as a rational decision-making center.

The problem is one that I have described elsewhere as the discursive dilemma (Pettit 2001, chap. 5; 2003c). Assume that if a group is to be able to perform as a decision-making center, then it must be able to ensure consistency in its judgments; it must be sensitive to the recognition of inconsistencies, even if it occasionally slips on this front. This is a reasonable assumption since the group that is insensitive to the inconsistency of its judgments on issues related to action will be unable to make a rational decision on what to do. The problem that arises with the majoritarian aggregation of judgments on a range of issues, in particular a range of issues that are logically connected with one another, is that individuals with perfectly consistent sets of judgments on those issues can vote for a set of group judgments that is quite inconsistent.

Let me illustrate the problem schematically, to begin with. Consider a group of three agents, A, B, and C. Imagine that under the pressure of decision and action, they have to form judgments, now on whether p, now on whether q, now on whether r, and yet again on whether p&q&r. All but A might vote for p; all but B for q; all but C for r; and, consequently, none for p&q&r: each would reject it because of rejecting one conjunct. These votes would have the group holding that p, that q, that r, but that not-p&q&r. The position would be as represented in the following matrix:

	p?	*q?*	*r?*	*p&q&r?*
A	No	Yes	Yes	No
B	Yes	No	Yes	No
C	Yes	yes	No	No
Majority	Yes	Yes	Yes	No

This problem can be readily illustrated with real-life examples. Consider an issue that might arise in a workplace, among the employees of a company: say, for simplicity, a company owned by the employees (Pettit 2001, chap. 5). The issue is whether to forego a pay rise in order to spend the money thereby saved on introducing a workplace safety measure: perhaps a guard against electrocution. Let us suppose for convenience that the employees are to make the decision—perhaps because of prior resolution—on the basis of considering three separable issues: first, whether there is a serious danger of electrocution, by some agreed benchmark; second, whether the safety measure that a pay sacrifice would buy is likely to be effective, by an agreed benchmark; and third, whether the pay sacrifice involves an intuitively bearable loss for individual members. If an employee thinks that the danger is sufficiently serious, the safety measure sufficiently effective, and the pay sacrifice sufficiently bearable, he or she will vote for the sacrifice; otherwise they will vote against. And so each will have to consider the three issues and then look to what should be concluded about the pay sacrifice.

The pattern here is exactly as in the case with p, q, r, and p&q&r. And as in that case, the employees may have views such that if the majority view on each issue is to fix the group view, then the group will end up with an inconsistent set of views. Let A, B, and C represent the employees; if there are more than three employees, the problem can still arise. A, B, and C may hold the views ascribed in the following matrix, generating the inconsistent majority set of views represented in the bottom row.

	Serious danger?	*Effective measure?*	*Bearable loss?*	*Pay sacrifice?*
A.	No	Yes	Yes	No
B.	Yes	No	Yes	No
C.	Yes	Yes	No	No
Majority	Yes	Yes	Yes	No

It may seem that the participatory ideal might be altered, so that what is required is not a procedure of majority voting but a procedure of some other kind. But this avenue does not hold out much promise. The problem is that, even with wholly consistent individual voters, no voting procedure can be guaranteed to generate a consistent set of judgments on a logically connected set of issues if it is to satisfy three conditions. These are, first, that it work under any variation in the input bodies of judgment; second, that it treat every individual as an equal in the voting procedure, giving no one a casting vote and allowing no one a dictatorial position; and, third, that it treat every issue in its own right as an issue to be determined by the members' views on that question, not by what their views on other issues imply. We may refer to those conditions as universal domain, voter anonymity, and voting systematicity. There is now a formal theorem to the effect that no procedure satisfying those conditions can guard against the sort of inconsistency illustrated by the discursive dilemma (List and Pettit 2002; for references to later theorems see List and Pettit 2005). This theorem shows that it is impossible for a voting procedure to guarantee to deliver a complete, consistent set of judgments as the output from complete, consistent input sets, and at the same time conform to universal domain, voter anonymity, and voting systematicity.

This impossibility is threatening—perhaps more threatening than the Arrovian impossibility—so far as it hangs over any group, as the group continues to make decisions through time and builds up a record of judgments. For as the group commits itself to more and more propositions, say by majority voting, the probability increases that it will have to make up its mind on a proposition such that existing commitments imply that it should be resolved in one way (as commitments on p, q, and r imply that the group should endorse p&q&r) but the majority vote goes in the opposite direction. This would not be a problem if the group could just ignore past judgments, treating them like the judgments of a different subject. But of course the normal, democratically organized body won't be able to do this. It will be subject to expectations of diachronic as well as synchronic consistency, both by its own members and by other groups and individuals. Unless it sustains such expectations it won't be able to display the scrutable profile of an agent; it won't be able to commit itself to others in promises, contracts, and the like; and it won't be capable of being subjected to a discipline of non-arbitrary decision making: for those over whom it exercises authority it will have the aspect of a wayward force in their lives.

Solving the Problem

The problem posed by the impossibility theorem is not insurmountable, however. What the theorem shows, in effect, is that there may be ways in which a group can form judgments that are reliably consistent, but they must breach one or another of the presuppositions of the theorem. The group might avoid the problem raised, for example, by renouncing the ideal of forming complete judgments over all the issues it faces. It might decide to suspend judgment on one of any set of issues where majority voting would lead it into inconsistency. This, however, won't be a very satisfactory way of dealing with the difficulty. The group will only be disposed to form judgments on issues related to the choices or decisions it has to make, and any suspension of judgment is liable to constrain its capacity for decision and action. A more promising line would be for the group to avoid the problem raised, by taking steps that reduce its commitment to universal domain, voter anonymity, or voting systematicity.

The group might try to reduce its commitment to universal domain by imposing a discipline of deliberation designed to push individuals toward an unproblematic configuration of views: a configuration that is unlikely to generate inconsistency on the basis of majority voting (List 2002). There is no guarantee, however, that such a discipline can be identified and reliably implemented. The more promising ways for a group to escape the problem would be to reduce its commitment to either voter anonymity or voting systematicity: either to the principle that every voter should be treated equally or to the principle that every issue should be treated on its own merits.

The way in which most groups manage to conduct the formation of judgment and the making of decisions is by breaching voter anonymity, giving some individuals a special role. A common but extreme form of this is represented by how the shareholders in a company invest the board with the power of making judgments in the company's name, when the exercise of this power can only be challenged with difficulty. The situation approximates the way in which, according to Hobbes, the people in a commonwealth invest the sovereign with a more or less unconstrained power of judgment and decision making. The alienation of such power may also take less extreme forms, of course. It might consist, for example, in an arrangement whereby the members of a group give one individual authority to decide the group's judgments, should inconsistencies arise from majority voting. The position of the courts in relation to a legislature can resemble that sort of regime, with the courts reinterpreting what the legislature declares in order to ensure that its dictates come out as consistent.

But while many groups maintain consistency in judgment by giving certain parties special privileges in this way, the strategy cannot represent a natural path for a group that is committed to participatory democracy, being disposed to decide everything by majority vote. To give over authority to an individual or subset of individuals, in however small a measure, is inevitably to diminish the ideal of participatory democracy. It is to reduce the participation that people enjoy in the decisions faced by the group.

This leaves only one strategy whereby a group might hope to ensure collective consistency and yet remain true to the ideal of participatory democracy. The strategy would consist in reducing the commitment to systematicity, and allowing that on some issues the view of the group need not be decided by the members' views on that issue; it is to be decided, rather, by their views on related issues. Think about the schematic case where A, B, and C vote in such a way that the group is forced by majority voting to claim that p, that q, that r, but that not-p&q&r. Were systematicity not enforced, then it would be possible to have the group's judgment on, say, p&q&r determined by member votes on p, q, and r, rather than by member votes on the compound proposition itself; and it would be possible to ensure consistency thereby in the group's judgments as a whole. Indeed the same holds for each proposition. Absent the requirement of systematicity, it would be possible to have the group's judgment on any of the four propositions determined by member votes on the other three, thereby ensuring consistency. If the members vote "yes" for p, for q, and for p&q&r, for example, then those votes will dictate a vote for not-q; and if systematicity is not enforced, then this will be permissible.

What form, more positively, might the rejection of systematicity take? It is one thing to say that inconsistency ceases to be inevitable if systematicity is not enforced. It is quite another to identify tactics for determining where systematicity should be breached and breached in a way that saves consistency. There are two families of approaches. One would enforce a static procedure, fixed in advance for all cases. The other would invoke a more dynamic, open-ended process.

Just to illustrate the static procedure, the group might decide to authorize past judgments over present judgments in the case of any inconsistency arising from majority voting, and to let past judgments trump the present judgment, regardless of the majority support it enjoys. Suppose that our group of workers had committed to the first three propositions in the matrix given, prior to considering the issue of the pay sacrifice. This strategy would deny them the possibility of reconsidering any of those past judgments in the light of where, as it turns out, they lead: to acceptance of the pay sacrifice. It would force the group to impose on itself procrustean, potentially irrational constraint. It would forbid any change of mind.

Still illustrating the static procedure, the group might decide to prioritize more general issues over more specific ones, rather than issues addressed previously over issues under current consideration. It might decide that its judgments on more general issues should determine its judgments on more specific ones, whenever systematicity would lead to inconsistency. But this again would be a costly approach to take. It would deny the group any possibility of following the method of reflective equilibrium described by John Rawls (1971), since such equilibration consists in going back and forth between more general and more specific judgments, seeking out the best place at which to make revisions and ensure coherence.

The basic problem with reducing the commitment to systematicity in any such static manner is that it will require a group to prioritize certain judgment types once for all time—more general judgments, for example, or judgments addressed earlier—and to let them dictate what other judgments should be endorsed. But this will often lead the group, intuitively, toward the wrong views. Propositions do not come prepackaged into the more privileged issues that ought to be decided first and the less privileged issues that ought to be decided by reference to the pattern of judgment in the privileged category. In reasoning sensibly about what to believe we are often led as individuals to revise past beliefs in the light of current inclinations (Harman 1986). It would be crazy to deny ourselves in groups an exercise of intelligence that we prize as individuals.

This takes us, finally, to the dynamic version of the strategy of rejecting systematicity. The best way of summing this up may be to describe a set of instructions whereby a group could be enabled to implement it. The instructions to the group might go as follows.

I. With every issue that comes up for judgment take a majority vote on that issue and, as issues get progressively settled in this way, keep a record of the accumulating body of judgments.

II. If majority voting on some issue generates inconsistency, treat the judgment supported, and any judgments with which it is inconsistent in the record, as candidates for reversal.

III. Identify those candidate judgments—say, the judgments that p, that q, that r, and that not-p&q&r—and address the question of how to resolve the inconsistency between them.

IV. If it turns out that some members have independently changed their original opinion on some issue, ask whether this will resolve the inconsistency, and if it does, go with the resulting set of judgments.

V. If the inconsistency is not resolved thereby, take a vote on where it would be best to revise the judgments: whether, for example, to revise the judgment that p, that q, that r, or that not-p&q&r.

VI. Take the proposition identified in this way, and hold another vote on how the group should judge that proposition.

VII. If the group reverses its previous judgment, treat the new verdict on that proposition as the one to be endorsed by the group.
VIII. If the previous judgment is not reversed in that vote, go back to stage III and try again.
IX. If it appears that there is no prospect of success in this process, try to quarantine the inconsistency, and the area of decision it would affect, so that it does not generate problems elsewhere.
X. If this quarantining is not possible, perhaps because the area of action affected is important to the group's aims, there is no alternative but to disband; go your separate ways.

The approach prescribed in these instructions would escape the impossibility theorem because it breaches the systematicity condition in the same way as its static counterparts. So far as the approach is implemented—or at least implemented beyond stage IV—there will be some issues decided on a basis other than that of the majority position of members. If the members of our working group were to follow this procedure, for example, and were to decide that they ought to reverse the majority view on whether to have a pay sacrifice, then the judgment on that issue would not be decided by reference to the majority procedure followed with other issues. The issue about the pay sacrifice would be determined, not in its own right, but on the basis of the views of the group on the other three issues discussed.

This approach, or an approach in the same general family, is the only way I see in which a group might realize the ideal of participatory democracy—the ideal of conducting its business on the basis of a unanimously accepted pattern of majority voting—and yet not fall afoul of the problem illustrated in the discursive dilemma. That is its great merit. The problem with the approach, of course, is that it cannot be relied upon to produce a surefire resolution. It may lead the group to try to live with inconsistency, as in the quarantining option, or it may lead the group to disband. And whether it is to lead in a negative direction of that kind or along a more positive route may turn on nothing more reliable than fortune. The chemistry between members, the resources of rhetoric and persuasion available to them, or just the pressures under which they operate may determine the extent to which the exercise succeeds. The approach falls well short of an algorithm for participatory democracy.

The process may be deficient in other respects too. It may be subject to influence from the order in which issues happen to be taken, it may be vulnerable to insincere voting on the part of more strategic members, it may represent only a fallible way of tracking the truth on the questions addressed. In short, it may be hostage to all the usual slings and arrows. But did we have reason to expect anything else? This may still be as good as it gets.

We-thinking

The most striking way in which the process described falls short of being an algorithmic decision procedure is in the room it makes for deliberation and in the reliance that it is bound to place on deliberation at various points. It makes room for deliberation not only at the point where each thinks about how to judge and vote but also when a range of other issues come up. These are issues to do with whether to revise that original judgment in light of the opinions of others; what the best issue is on which to revise the group judgment; how to vote personally on a proposition that is put up for revision; and whether it may be possible to quarantine any inconsistencies that the group cannot eliminate.

The deliberation accommodated at these loci may be more personal or more communal; it may involve thinking to oneself or also, as in the normal case, exchanging with others. But whatever form it takes, it must induce people to think in terms of "we, the group" rather than "I, this member." I conclude the paper with a discussion of that claim.

Any decision-making group that resolves issues of inconsistency along the participatory line sketched in the last section—or indeed on many of the alternative lines—will constitute itself as a more or less autonomous group agent. My claim about we-thinking is that in order to give life to that agent, the members of the group will have to begin thinking, not just as executors of their own personal attitudes, but also as executors of this distinct entity. They will have to think in terms of a plural as well as a personal identity (Rovane 1997).

Let it be agreed that a group will constitute an agent or subject that is distinct from its members so far as its intentional states get set up in a way that makes them more or less independent from the intentional states of a majority of members. Were the goals and judgments of the group just whatever goals and judgments happened to be espoused by a majority of the members, then we might well think that talking of the group and its attitudes was just a fancy way of talking about the majority attitudes among its members. That is the sort of position adopted by many thinkers who have wanted to say that the only true agents are individuals; that, in the words of John Austin, the nineteenth-century utilitarian, groups can be described as subjects "only by figment, and for the sake of brevity of discussion" (Austin 1869, 364).

In a well-known discussion, Anthony Quinton (1975, 17) argues for precisely this point of view. He maintains that to ascribe judgments, intentions, and the like to social groups is just a way of ascribing them, in a summative manner, to individuals in those groups. And he denies, for that reason, that there ever are group agents.

> We do, of course, speak freely of the mental properties and acts of a group in the way we do of individual people. Groups are said to have beliefs, emotions, and attitudes and to take decisions and make promises. But these ways of speaking are plainly metaphorical. To ascribe mental predicates to a group is always an indirect way of ascribing such predicates to its members. With such mental states as beliefs and attitudes, the ascriptions are of what I have called a summative kind. To say that the industrial working class is determined to resist anti–trade union laws is to say that all or most industrial workers are so minded.

Our discussion of how a participatory decision-making body might come to form and develop its goals and judgments gives the lie to this "singularist" view that there are no group agents; this view is criticized under that name by Margaret Gilbert (1989, 12). For if we consider a group that has followed the dynamic process of judgment formation described, we recognize that on pain of having to live with inconsistency, it will almost inevitably have come to form some judgments that do not correspond to the majority judgments of its members; indeed it may even have come to form judgments that none of its members endorses. Imagine for example that the workers in our example come to accept that they as a group should give up the pay sacrifice. In that case, they will endorse as a group a judgment that they all reject as individuals. They will do so as a result of recognizing that if they are to hold together as a group that does its business in an effective and rational manner, they will have to make that sort of individual accommodation. They will have to be prepared to condone the idea of the group's holding by commitments that are rejected at the personal level: rejected, not just by a minority of the members, but also by a majority among the membership, even perhaps by every single individual.

Let it be granted, then, that the participatory democratic group is more or less bound to develop this sort of autonomy, becoming a subject with distinct attitudes and actions: a group with a mind of its own (Pettit 2003b). The thing to notice now is that if the members are to sustain those attitudes and actions, enacting their shared mind, then they must put their individual identities aside, and must begin to think as a group. This is one sort of deliberative thinking that they cannot avoid, whether or not they conduct the deliberation in their own heads or—surely the natural course—in dialogue with others.

In order to emphasize the sort of identification with the group that members must develop, it may be useful to mark the way in which groups may fail or falter on this front. I have discussed the topic elsewhere, under the title of group *akrasia:* collective weakness of will (Pettit 2003a).

Imagine a noncommercial academic journal with an editorial committee of three members that resolves all the issues it faces by majority vote. Suppose that the committee votes in January for promising subscribers that there will be no price rise within five years. Suppose that it votes in midyear that it will send papers to external reviewers and be bound by their decision as to whether or not to publish any individual piece. And suppose that in December the committee faces the issue as to whether it should be just as prepared to publish technical papers that involve costly typesetting as it is to publish other papers. The earlier votes will argue against its being prepared to do this, since a rise in the number of technical papers submitted and endorsed by reviewers—endorsed, without any eye to overall production costs—might force it to renege on one or other of those commitments. But nonetheless a majority may support the acceptance of technical papers, without any individual being in any way irrational. The members of the committee might vote as follows.

	Price freeze?	*External review?*	*Technical papers?*
A.	Yes	No	Yes
B.	No	Yes	Yes
C.	Yes	Yes	No

The group now faces a hard choice of precisely the kind we have been discussing. Suppose that they implement the participatory democratic process that we characterized in the previous section. And suppose that they agree that the issue on which the group should revise its view is that of whether to treat technical papers on a par with other papers; they may vote unanimously that it is impossible to revise its position on either of the other issues, perhaps because the editorial position on those questions has already been made public. How, then, may we expect the consequent vote to go?

If members are individually devoted in a consuming, wholehearted way to the group and are in no way tempted to defect from what it requires of them, then of course they will each vote for offering less than equal treatment to technical papers; they will reverse the previous group position. A group whose members were dedicated in this way would operate like a perfectly virtuous agent, always spontaneously supporting what the balance of available reasons requires of the group. But not all members need be so devoted to the group in which they figure; and when something less than full collective devotion is on offer, then it may prove very difficult for members to get their act together and ensure that the group lives up to the considerations that it endorses.

Take the majority who originally supported an open policy on technical papers. That majority may remain individually and stubbornly inclined to support the acceptance of technical papers. We can imagine them turning their eyes from the group as a whole, and sticking to their votes when the issue is raised again. We can imagine them refusing to hear the call of the group and acting like encapsulated centers of voting who are responsive only to their own modular prompts. As we imagine this, we envisage the group failing to reverse its judgment on the only issue where every member of the group thinks it is possible to reverse judgment.

The recalcitrant majority in this sort of case might be moved by a more or less selfish inclination or identification, being technically minded themselves, or they might be moved by a sense of fairness toward those who would be disadvantaged; personal virtue is as likely as personal vice to source recalcitrance towards the collectivity. But could it really be rational for the recalcitrant members to stick to a deviant pattern of voting, whether out of individual bias or virtue? I don't see why not. They would satisfy their private motives, partial or impartial, by doing so. And they might individually expect to get away with such voting, being outvoted by others; they might each expect a free ride. Or they might hope that even if a majority remains recalcitrant, this will not cause problems: there will not be a deluge in the number of technical papers submitted and accepted, and the committee can get away with holding by all of the three commitments involved.

The possibility of people remaining encapsulated in their personal identities in this way, and the danger that that holds out for the survival of the group, shows why it is essential in general that the members should break out of their capsules. If the group is to evolve as a center of agency, with a capacity to be responsive to the demands of consistency, then it must be able to discipline itself into holding only by certain patterns of judgment; it must be able to regulate itself for the formation or maintenance only of judgments that cohere with one another. And if a group is to have that capacity, then its members must be able to put their own views aside, identify with the group as an independent center of intentionality, and then reason and act from the perspective of that common center. They must be able to depart from normal, I-centered patterns of thought and begin to think in terms the "we."

This brings our considerations to a close. We have seen that the ideal of participatory democracy, as an ideal for a decision-making body, runs into trouble with the discursive dilemma, and with the more general problem of aggregating individual sets of judgments into a consistent, group-level set of judgments. There is a way of overcoming that problem, as we saw in the last section, that preserves the ideal of participatory democracy. But this, so we have just seen, requires people to deliberate with themselves or one another from the perspective of how we, the members of the group, see the world, not from the perspective that is proper to each in their individual person.

With perhaps a different view in his sights, G. A. Cohen (1976, 66) inveighs against the suggestion that one might be reasonably engulfed in a role to the point of holding by certain judgments as an occupant of that role, but not in one's own right. "The propensity to engulfment should be resisted in theory and in practice, for it poses a threat to the exercise of our freedom, and, ultimately, some threat to freedom itself." If the line of argument in this paper is correct, then that is dead wrong. Few will deny the connection, however complex, between the ideal of participatory democracy and the ideal of freedom. And if my argument is right, then the only way to achieve participatory democracy in decision-making forums is precisely to persuade people that they should lend their minds to the service of a group mind; they should learn to think, not just in their own personal name, but in the name of any group in which they democratically participate.

None of this should come as a surprise to those like Carole Pateman who have emphasized the participatory point of view in politics. Participatory democracy requires people to cooperate, not just in the pursuit of common goals, but in the pursuit of common goals according to common judgments. And that sort of enterprise is more or less inevitably going to require members to adopt the group point of view and to be prepared, at least in certain contexts, to prioritize their group identity. Participatory democracy is not just a way in which individuals combine to satisfy their existing goals, according to their existing judgments; it is a way in which they combine to determine the goals and judgments that they will enact together.

References

Arrow, K. 1963. *Social Choice and Individual Values.* New York: John Wiley and Sons.

Austin, J. 1869. *Lectures on Jurisprudence, or the Philosophy of Positive Law.* London.

Cohen, G. A. 1976. "Beliefs and Roles." In *The Philosophy of Mind*, edited by J. Glover, 53–66. Oxford: Oxford University Press.

Coleman, J., and J. Ferejohn. 1986. "Democracy and Social Choice." *Ethics* 97:6–25.

Gilbert, M. 1989. *On Social Facts.* Princeton: Princeton University Press.

Harman, G. 1986. *Change in View.* Cambridge, Mass.: MIT Press.

Hobbes, T. [1651] 1994. *Leviathan.* Indianapolis: Hackett.

List, C. 2002. "Two Concepts of Agreement." *The Good Society* 11:72–79.

List, C., and P. Pettit. 2002. "The Aggregation of Sets of Judgments: An Impossibility Result." *Economics and Philosophy* 18:89–110.

———. 2004. "Aggregating Sets of Judgments: Two Impossibility Results Compared." *Synthese* 140:207–35.

———. 2005. "On the Many as One." *Philosophy and Public Affairs* 33:377–90.

Pateman, C. 1970. *Participation and Democratic Theory.* Cambridge, Cambridge University Press.

Pettit, P. 2001. *A Theory of Freedom: From the Psychology to the Politics of Agency.* Cambridge: Polity; and New York: Oxford University Press.

———. 2003a. "Akrasia, Collective and Individual." In *Weakness of Will and Practical Irrationality*, edited by S. Stroud and C. Tappolet, 68–96. Oxford: Oxford University Press.

———. 2003b. "Groups with Minds of Their Own." In *Socializing Metaphysics*, edited by F. Schmitt, 167–93. New York: Rowman and Littlefield.

———. 2006. "Preference, Deliberation, and Satisfaction." In *Preferences and Well-being*, edited by S. Olsaretti, 131–53. Cambridge: Cambridge University Press.

Quinton, A. 1975. "Social Objects." *Proceedings of the Aristotelian Society* 76:1–27.

Rawls, J. 1971. *A Theory of Justice.* Oxford: Oxford University Press.

———. 1993. *Political Liberalism.* New York: Columbia University Press.

Rousseau, J.-J. [1750, 1755, 1762] 1973. *The Social Contract and Discourses.* London: J. M. Dent.

Rovane, C. 1997. *The Bounds of Agency: An Essay in Revisionary Metaphysics.* Princeton: Princeton University Press.

Rubenfeld, J. 2001. *Freedom and Time: A Theory of Constitutional Self-government*. New Haven: Yale University Press.

Sunstein, C. 1993. "Democracy and Shifting Preferences." In *The Idea of Democracy*, edited by D. Copp, J. Hampton, and J. E. Roemer, 196–230. Cambridge: Cambridge University Press.

Waldron, J. 1999. *Law and Disagreement*. Oxford: Oxford University Press.

Deliberative Democracy, Subordination, and the Welfare State

John Medearis

The American debate about the welfare state has often been both harsh and misleading. Generally, it is only the programs serving the most vulnerable recipients that are designated as "welfare." And when such programs are discussed, poor people are frequently deplored, but the condition of poverty, as a rule, is not. Advocates made extravagant promises a decade ago to justify welfare "reform," but neither the press nor elected officials have shown much interest since then in whether the poor benefited from the changes. Meanwhile, the debate about Social Security, Medicare, and health insurance regulation—all welfare schemes, if rightly understood—follows a different course. Many Americans want such programs to be humane, universalistic, and efficient. But their failure to acknowledge the meaning of their expectations makes them prey to privatization rhetoric and other arguments from welfare's most implacable domestic enemies. Such distortions in the public discourse on welfare ought to prompt doubts about how public decisions are reached, and thus about how public power is deployed, in American democracy. It therefore might seem that deliberative democracy—the family of contemporary theories that put public discourse at the center of democratic philosophy—would be a strong candidate to guide thinking about the nexus between democracy and welfare. This essay argues, however, that two central strategies of deliberative democrats for analyzing welfare issues are inadequate because they fail to scrutinize the subordination and the limits to self-governance that confront clients of contemporary welfare states. Subordination, a critical concept in Carole Pateman's analyses of participatory democracy, must be central to democratic thinking about welfare.

One of the deliberative approaches to welfare I discuss, the *deliberative norms* approach, focuses on the content of deliberation about welfare and holds that programs ought to be the outcome of an appropriately themed deliberative process. The other, the *deliberative prerequisites* approach, claims that welfare programs ought to provide recipients with the necessary material resources, and help develop the individual capacities, for participating in public discourse. These approaches to welfare, I contend, do not adequately address a typical recipient's democratic problems. First, questions of how welfare is deliberated ("deliberative norms") and what sort of material resources and educational services a welfare state provides ("deliberative prerequisites") are distinct from other important issues concerning the character of the social relations in which welfare provision is enmeshed. Welfare state activities have often buttressed subordinating social relations in the workplace and family, and welfare programs themselves constitute power structures in their own right. Second, philosophical attention to the way in which welfare is deliberated, or to the way welfare provision could facilitate deliberation, cannot provide the requisite conceptual tools for considering the kind of social-structural issues I highlight in this essay—problems like the welfare state's contribution to subordination in the family, its role in labor commodification, and its capacity both to alter and to reinforce the structure of race relations.

A typical recipient spends a significant amount of time in a welfare bureaucracy, answering the demands of caseworkers, providing information about her life, and filling out forms. She—overwhelmingly the recipients are women—has likely held the sort of hierarchical, low-wage, high-turnover jobs the U.S. economy now produces in abundance. The welfare reform that produced the Temporary Aid to Needy Families program was designed, in part, to place her back in another. She is disdained by a broad swath of the American public, who stereotype her as undeserving—probably on racial grounds—and who thus consider it essential that her time on the welfare rolls be cheap, short, and unpleasantly regimented. If an unmarried mother, she is reviled by a smaller but well-organized group who consider her morally suspect and insist that welfare programs support their vision of a traditional family. Although these may appear to be entirely contemporary problems, in fact, any successful analysis of them must view them in light of the momentous economic, racial, and gender conflicts that have shaped the American welfare state for at least a century.

I begin my essay by briefly examining of the role of subordination in Carole Pateman's participatory democratic theory. Subordination is a conceptual key for my understanding of how welfare and democracy are related. Next, I look at the ways that deliberative theory can and does approach welfare. I then review literature about the U.S. welfare state, especially concerning its development in relation to the capitalist economy and to conflicts over gender and race. I draw out the democratic implications of this development and elucidate the conceptual limits that make it difficult for "deliberative norms" and "deliberative prerequisites" to respond adequately to these matters. I conclude by arguing that analysis of subordination must be a central part of any democratic theory about welfare.

Participatory Democratic Theory and Subordination

Theorists today too often characterize participatory democracy as little more than a demanding ideal of active citizenship linked to dismay about low levels of political knowledge and anemic voter turnout. Some even wrongly claim that participatory theorists promote participation at the expense of "personal freedom" (Gutmann 1993, 415–16). But participatory theory has usually entailed something more than an idealistic standard of citizen involvement. Carole Pateman's approach, in works from *Participation and Democratic Theory* (1970), through *The Sexual Contract* (1988), to recent writings on basic income, has been particularly characterized by a focus on problems of subordination. In her hands, democratic theory has stressed subordination because of a concern for people's ability to be self-governing in all the major social relations in which they take part. *Participation and Democratic Theory* responded to a narrow postwar consensus that derogated participation and assumed that most people's democratic capacities were naturally limited. The book was also motivated positively by the argument that democratic participation was required as a matter of principle in many, if not all, "political systems" and "authority structures" and, concomitantly, by a critique of any institution characterized by a division between those who decided and their "permanent subordinates" (Pateman 1970, 35, 43, 70). By refining and elaborating a critique of subordinating social relations, and linking it—in *The Problem of Political Obligation* (1979) and *The Sexual Contract*—to skepticism about venerable conceptions of contract and property in the person, Pateman demonstrated the potential breadth and radicalness of democratic theory. For subordination—the loss or yielding of capacities for personal or common self-governance—is implicated in a range of enduring social relations or institutions, and the power created and distributed by them.

The most troubling aspect of subordination, for Pateman, arises when parties permanently forfeit some aspect of their person—especially aspects implicated in their ability to govern themselves—as a condition of entering or re-creating some social relation. And Pateman has pursued this problem through investigations of three fundamental and interrelated sets of institutions: citizenship and the state, marriage and the family, and employment and the economy (Pateman 2004). The focus on subordination is clear in the link Pateman makes between democratic theory and welfare. Both in her essay "The Patriarchal Welfare State" (Pateman 1988a) and more recently in essays on basic income, Pateman has been especially concerned to analyze how actual welfare programs reinforce or undermine subordinating social relations, and to investigate the relations welfare recipients enter into with the state and others when they receive state aid. Tellingly, she writes that her advocacy of a basic income responds to "the mutually reinforcing structures of marriage, employment and citizenship, and . . . the possibility that these institutions could be re-made in a new, more democratic form" (Pateman 2004, 97). This is precisely the set of problems that I argue ought to be central when democratic theory turns to welfare.

Deliberative Norms, Deliberative Prerequisites, and Welfare

Since the early 1990s, the deliberative strand has become the most prominent one in Anglo-American democratic theory. Although deliberative democrats are divided into Rawlsian and Habermasian camps, and they disagree about a number of issues, they are united in the view that it is only deliberation—a special form of public discourse—that can legitimate democracy. What characterizes true deliberation, they argue, is persuasion, or an uncoerced exchange of reasons. The precise portrayal of such an uncoerced exchange varies, especially between those who derive their understanding of it from John Rawls's theory of public reason, and those who are more influenced by Jürgen Habermas's conceptions of ideal speech and communicative rationality. The former attempts to find a possible common political language for people who share few, if any, religious, metaphysical, or basic ontological commitments. The latter tries to construct an intersubjective, discursive rationality that would be free from the pathologies of narrow instrumental reason.[1]

---

1. It is also possible to share such a general aim, and yet not fit comfortably within the category of deliberative democrats. This, I think, is the case with Iris Marion Young, who has articulated a communicative theory of democracy, while expressing strong misgivings about the exclusivity of "deliberation" and the applicability of the paradigm under conditions of structural inequality (Young 1996; Young 2000, chaps. 1–3; Young 2001).

Neither of the democratic theories so closely wedded to these philosophical projects has been entirely successful in addressing welfare.

A regulating ideal—one of fully open, nondeceptive, uncoerced deliberation—lies at the heart of deliberative democracy. This ideal is intended to be more than an imaginary counterfactual. Deliberative theorists have applied it in various ways to actual politics. Since ideals stand as abstractions in relation to almost infinitely complex social situations, there are myriad ways any ideal can be applied to such situations. In this case, one obvious possibility is to apply the deliberative standard to the conduct or the speech of parties to public discourse—to construct and apply deliberative norms. Variations notwithstanding, it is clear that this approach indeed suffuses many works on deliberative democracy, which contain guidelines for engagement in a particular kind of public discourse, as well as claims that certain parties or processes have or have not adhered to deliberative norms (Dryzek 1990, chap. 2; Bohman 1996, chap. 1; Gutmann and Thompson 1996; Rawls 1996, lecture 6). Since it would be futile—perhaps incoherent—to propose reforming discourse, in general, the tendency of the deliberative norms approach is toward the establishment of deliberative domains, bounded and characterized by the application of these norms, especially in or coterminous with the public sphere. Insofar as the deliberative ambition is successful and such domains exist, they would have to be relatively transparent with respect to their extent and the rules operative in them.

Another approach, sometimes arising in response to criticisms that deliberative democracy is insufficiently responsive to disadvantaged persons, is to consider what resources and capacities a person must have to engage effectively in deliberation, and to argue that deliberative democracy demands access to such resources and the means of developing such capacities (Bohman 1996, chap. 3; Gutmann and Thompson 1996, chap. 8; Knight and Johnson 1997; Laden 2001, chap. 6).

Each of these alternatives for applying the deliberative ideal to concrete situations can be linked to an approach to welfare. The first—the *deliberative norms* approach—shapes a prominent discussion of welfare in the deliberative literature, leading to the consideration of the substantive values that ought to infuse deliberation about the state's response to poverty. The second approach—what I will term the *deliberative prerequisites* approach—has naturally turned to the subject of welfare as a mechanism for providing the services and resources needed to enable people to be effective participants in public discourse.

The exemplar of the deliberative norms approach to welfare is chapter 8 of

Gutmann and Thompson's influential *Democracy and Disagreement* (1996). One way that deliberative norms could be related to some particular subject would be strictly formal or procedural—to argue that the programmatic outcome of appropriate deliberation would necessarily be legitimate, regardless of its substance. But such an advance endorsement would not really constitute a unique deliberative approach to any concrete problem. Gutmann and Thompson devote a whole chapter to welfare in part because they contend that deliberative democracy must provide guidance for the principled content, and not just the form, of deliberation.[2] Thus with respect to welfare, Gutmann and Thompson advance a guiding principle, "basic opportunity," which holds that government is obligated "to ensure that all citizens may secure the resources they need to live a decent life and enjoy other (nonbasic) opportunities in our society" (Gutmann and Thompson 1996, 217). "Basic opportunity," they say, should serve as a kind of "constitutional" principle constraining deliberation; but its precise meaning should also be filled in by deliberation (199). Policies that are simply inconsistent with "basic opportunity" are to be excluded as unjustifiable. (The check on such policies is internal; deliberators themselves are called on to "invoke" the principle.) And yet the full "content" of "basic opportunity" is also to be shaped by deliberation—or "moral discussion in the political process" (223).

In Gutmann and Thompson's account, the deliberative elaboration of "basic opportunity" is accomplished chiefly by application of the principle of "reciprocity." Citizens are called on to recognize that this principle, which ought to govern their deliberation, ought also to govern a domain of practical life. This deliberative principle is introduced as one that "asks us to appeal to reasons that are shared or could come to be shared by our fellow citizens" (Gutmann and Thompson 1996, 14). But, crucially, "reciprocity" has to be translated from the domain of public deliberation to the domain of the institutions and social relations of welfare. In this latter domain, Gutmann and Thompson give "reciprocity" a meaning that is at once less specifically deliberative and less determinate. Reciprocity in welfare policy comes to involve the recognition of "mutual dependence" and the acceptance of "mutual" obligations by citizens (276). Thus, according to Gutmann and Thompson, citizens

2. One of the controversies among proponents of deliberative democracy is whether the theory should prioritize the procedure for making laws or the substance of the laws made. For an overview, see Gutmann and Thompson 2004, 23–26. Gutmann and Thompson themselves argue that neither procedure nor substance should take priority. Their particular approach—specifying principles that should structure the content of deliberation, not just its form—is more nuanced than simply asserting that deliberative democracy encompasses both procedure and legislative substance.

are morally constrained to propose welfare arrangements that embody this mutuality. With that in mind, Gutmann and Thompson themselves ultimately propose a welfare policy of what they term "fair workfare"—welfare with sometimes-stringent work requirements—because they say it upholds the idea that "each" person is "obligated to contribute his or her share in a fair scheme of social cooperation" (292).

It is worth reemphasizing that I am concerned with deliberative norms as a means by which deliberative democrats can reach concrete conclusions about welfare policy and the welfare state. It is possible, of course, to agree with Gutmann and Thompson that public discourse about welfare ought to be consistent with certain democratic or communicative norms, but disagree that such norms could provide substantive guidance to welfare policy. Iris Marion Young takes such a position, criticizing the 1996 welfare reform debate as noninclusive but arguing that democratic theory "in itself should have little to say about the substance of welfare policy" (Young 1999, 156).[3]

An essay by Knight and Johnson (1997) provides perhaps the clearest demonstration of how a deliberative prerequisites approach could link a concern for deliberative equality, or "equal opportunity of political influence" to the concrete problem of welfare provision. Knight and Johnson note that "[a]symmetries in material resources can affect democratic deliberation in a number of ways," especially "the promises and the threats that this material advantage affords [some parties]" (Knight and Johnson 1997, 294). Commenting favorably on work by Bohman (Bohman 1996, chap. 3), they argue that deliberation also requires some measure of equality with respect to capacities that allow citizens to persuade each other. Indeed, they consider these two things inextricably linked. Thus, noting the multiple ways that poverty can hamper the development of such capacities, they argue that government support for education is necessary, but not sufficient, and end up favoring "government expenditures to guarantee the social and economic prerequisites of effective participation" (Knight and Johnson 1997, 306). Here, then, the approach is to say that welfare programs must provide the material resources as well as the capacities to engage in public discourse. Anthony Simon Laden makes a similar case. Noting that "economic inequality" can mean that some deliberators are not in a position "meaningfully" to refuse claims that are

---

3. Young's position is premised on the argument that democratic theorists should not "specify a particular conception of social justice as a condition of democratic legitimacy" (Young 1999, 153). In contrast to Young, I argue below that there are a number of very significant *democratic* problems associated with the substantive policies of the welfare state.

made in deliberation, he offers several "remedies" (Laden 2001, 133, 139, 143). These consist essentially of classic welfare state activities, especially "purely economic programs to ensure that all have adequate material resources to participate" and "programs to provide all citizens with the nonmaterial resources, such as education and time, necessary to participate effectively in political deliberation" (143).[4]

Interestingly, Gutmann and Thompson agree that political empowerment should be an aim of welfare policy—a position they endorse "because, in the United States, the poor are politically weak" (Gutmann and Thompson 1996, 303). On this point a considerable body of research on the American welfare state backs them up.

The Welfare State, Enduring Social Relations, and Subordination

The welfare state and welfare programs are proper subjects for democratic theorists because they exist in a close and reciprocal relationship with social relations of various kinds, some of which are subordinating and all of which generate and allocate power. Welfare states themselves can also be dominating forces in the lives of recipients, ones that regulate and subordinate them. In regimenting and making distinctions among recipients, welfare states do not simply rectify unearned disadvantages or meet human needs; they actively order and stratify society in various ways. Three relatively distinct literatures—relating welfare states to the capitalist political economy, and to race and gender relations—make clear the nature of these democratic problems.

The first of these literatures is the varied and contentious one on capitalism and the origins of welfare states. One of the most important claims in this literature is that the state should not be identified with government or political life per se, but must be seen as something distinctive, arising out of historically produced relations among political, social, and economic realms. What is crucial is the bifurcation of state and civil society, citizen from consumer and worker—or to put it differently, the protection of market and workplace as spheres of private interest in which common political action finds little or no purchase (Marx 1967; Thomas 1994, 1–82; Marx 2000). From this perspective, even when the state regulates the economy—when it acts as a welfare state—it does so from without, as an intruder, and bound by real constraints.

---

4. In arguing that welfare programs should aim at fostering democratic participation, Timothy J. Gaffaney makes an argument that is broader than "deliberative prerequisites," since he does not limit participation to deliberation (Gaffaney 2000, 145–47).

As far back as Joseph Schumpeter ([1918] 1991), scholars have noted that this bifurcation makes the state dependent on the capitalist economy. One of the most prominent claims of many theorists of the state, then, is that it tends to act in the interest of capitalists because of structural dependence on them for investment and tax revenues (Block 1977; Lindblom 1977, 170–88; Offe 1984). One implication for the welfare state is the possibility that many state actions that ordinary people view as serving human needs may in fact be undertaken to protect capitalism or business interests. Different scholars maintain that the true functions of the welfare state include the promotion of labor discipline (Piven and Cloward 1971), the socialization of production costs (Habermas 1975, 35), and compensation for the tendency of businesses to underinvest in human capital (Pierson 1994, 3). Such functionalist claims, of course, have to be balanced by consideration of the actual consciousness, capacities, and intentions of actors (Barrow 1993, 71–72, 74). Notably, it is possible for capitalists and those who staff the state to be wrong, to disagree, or even be unaware of the precise nature of the actions the state "must" or "must not" take to aid capitalism or avoid punishment by capitalists. And taken by themselves, such broad functional arguments have difficulty explaining the variation among welfare states and programs. Many of the important differences between "liberal" and "social-democratic" welfare states, for example, may be attributed to the relative strength of working class movements (Esping-Andersen 1990; Noble 1997). Or, more precisely, the shape of welfare states can be explained, in part, with reference to the strength of working class mobilization and the way other groups, including business, must respond to labor's strength and tactics (Goldfield 1989).

The commodification of both human needs and labor—the treatment of both of these as things that can be bought and sold unproblematically like sugar and oil—is also an important theme in this literature, demonstrating crucial links between state and citizenship, on one hand, and workplace and employment, on the other. A number of contributors to the literature, including Offe and Esping-Andersen, make it clear that (in the latter's words) the commodification of labor power, which challenges people's "rights to survive outside the market" constitutes "one of the most conflictual issues in social policy" (Offe 1984, 139–40; Esping-Andersen 1990, 35). Contemporary Anglo-American political thought seems to take little interest in the paradoxes and concrete problems associated with selling one's labor power, or what Pateman calls the employment contract (Pateman 2002). Offe, however, views labor power as a fictional commodity because it cannot be sold separately from the mind and body that are constantly engaged in producing it. Barring legal limits, making good on the sale of one's labor power entails subordinating one's body and mind to the discipline of another. In the United States, like much of the developing world, the practical consequences of this subordination can be seen in the regularity and impunity with which employers squelch their workers' exercise of rights to engage in free speech and free association (Bronfenbrenner and Juravich 1994).

Various social groups may demand welfare measures that have the effect of partly decommodifying labor and human needs—making it possible to survive for some period of time or, in some respect, autonomously from the market. Although it seems contrary to the logic of capitalism, this may frequently benefit businesses (Pierson 2001, 422)—for example, when it relieves businesses of costs, such as those of employee health care.[5] Yet at other times, more predictably, business sectors may benefit from policies that force people into labor markets. A key result of U.S. "welfare reform" was further to undermine the position of low-wage workers in general, and ensure a supply of cheap labor in a service economy that increasingly requires it (Solow 1998; Pierson 2001, 435). In this case, welfare state policy reinforces the subordinating relationship between workers and managers, especially in the low-wage sector where job security is minimal and union representation relatively rare.

Racial and gender subordination have also structured and in turn been structured by the welfare state in ways that are equally important. Feminist scholars have shown that welfare states have been organized from the start around gendered conceptions of recipients and with an eye toward the structure of the family. The degree to which the welfare state reinforces or undermines women's autonomy from traditional family structures, these scholars show, is a distinct issue from commodification and decommodification (Bussemaker and Kersbergen 1994). An important branch of the literature has been devoted to demonstrating the significance of gendered concepts in the historical development of welfare states—concepts dealing with who can be autonomous, who can be a citizen, and therefore who ought to receive autonomy-enhancing state aid. Nancy Fraser and Linda Gordon show, for example, that conceptualizations of dependency changed with industrialization in England and the United States (Fraser and Gordon 1994). While in the preindustrial world, many categories of people were thought of as dependents of various feudal masters, the industrial revolution dissolved many such ties, leaving only a few residual categories of supposedly natural dependents, in-

---

5. Indeed, in Offe's view, decommodification in one area may support commodification of labor over all.

cluding women. In the wake of this change, women were quite broadly seen to be uniquely incapable of autonomous republican citizenship but naturally suited to caregiving within the family (Mink 1990). Pateman points out, for example, that Hegel's analysis makes women social exiles by nature (Hegel [1821] 1952, 110–16; Pateman 1988a).

Conceptualizations of women as naturally dependent and the attempt to reproduce them as social realities contributed to the creation of what is now widely termed a two-channel welfare system, characterized by different sorts of welfare programs for women and men (Nelson 1990). In the United States, for Northern white industrial working men, the key early welfare program was workmen's compensation, which provided benefits routinely and as a matter of right, thus arguably enhancing autonomy. For the widows of such workers, the central early program was mothers' aid, in which women were subject to discretionary denial and nonroutine administrative scrutiny. With the advent of such programs, conceptualization and institution came mutually to condition each other, so that by the late twentieth century, only non-wage-earning women who received government benefits were stigmatized as dependent, having been both ideally and programmatically separated off from others (Fraser and Gordon 1994). Even after Aid to Families with Dependent Children (AFDC) began to push women into the labor market—rather than keep them at home—the program continued to include provisions for the surveillance and manipulation of women's lives that male-targeted programs did not have. As Young has pointed out, the welfare reform debate in the 1990s was *about* poor single mothers, but rarely, if ever, *included* them.[6] This exclusion made possible a singular preoccupation with controlling the sex lives and fertility of recipients. Moreover, under AFDC's successor program, Temporary Aid to Needy Families (TANF), so-called "personal responsibility agreements" and expanded work requirements "provide a steady stream of opportunities for sanctions—failure to keep appointments for screening, assessments, counseling, medical exams, job search, [and] task assignments" (Handler 2000).

The American welfare state has also reflected hierarchy and perpetuated subordination due to race. As Robert C. Lieberman has pointed out, the conflictive structure of race relations in the New Deal era crucially shaped the American welfare state, and this, in turn, guaranteed that race and welfare issues would be closely associated in American public life (Lieberman 1998,

---

6. Young uses the example insightfully to link grammatical usage to social position. She notes that when "a public debate across mass society refers to persons or social segments only in the third person" this can be taken as an indication that the person or group suffers exclusion (Young 2000, 62). And see Young 1999, 157.

6). Until the Civil Rights movement, the racial political-economy of the American South rested, on the one hand, on overt political and civic exclusion, and, on the other, on an agricultural labor system that isolated African Americans in rural captivity, kept them economically dependent on white landowners and lenders, and subjected them to comprehensive social control (McAdam 1982, 65–116). Generous, universalistic welfare programs providing even a temporary alternative to agricultural and domestic labor might have acted as a solvent to this system, had they been passed as part of the New Deal. But Southern Democrats, aware of the danger, insisted that each of the programmatic components of the Social Security Act be riddled with exclusions or decentralized (Noble 1997, 59–61). Thus, originally Old Age Insurance (now popularly "Social Security"), which was always intended to be an efficient, automatic, nonstigmatizing, national program, simply excluded the vast majority of African Americans by excluding agricultural and domestic employees (Lieberman 1998, 39–43). Aid to Dependent Children (ADC), a program more likely to have African American recipients (since employment categories could not be used to exclude them en masse), was relegated to local control and often administered in discretionary, demeaning, and regulated ways, making the program a tool of social control (Lieberman 1998, 48–55, 118–70). The structure of the U.S. welfare state—its general failure to decommodify labor and human needs, the prominence of stigmatizing means-tested programs, the reliance of many people on both private and public social insurance schemes that stratify people institutionally and ideologically—reflects the nation's historical struggles over race.

Over time, the Social Security and ADC programs were made inclusive and formally race-neutral. But attempts to use welfare programs to undermine local, racially inscribed power structures still met massive resistance in the 1960s (Quadagno 1994, chap. 2). And in the same decade, just at the time that African Americans began to receive AFDC payments in proportion to their numbers among the poor, media attention began to exaggerate the predominance of African Americans among recipients—and to associate negative stories about poverty with African Americans, while focusing sympathetic ones on whites (Gilens 1999, chap. 5). In the early twenty-first century, many white Americans have come to "hate" welfare, and continue to support stigmatizing, intrusive welfare programs, because they believe that welfare recipients are lazy. Martin Gilens has shown that this view is premised on age-old racial stereotypes and a false belief that welfare programs overwhelmingly have served African Americans (Gilens 1999, chaps.1–4). In this sense, racially coded views underwrite policies that demean and intrude deeply in the lives of recipients.

The Democratic Problems of the Welfare State

The historical development of the U.S. welfare state in reciprocal relation with race, gender, and the capitalist economy demonstrates that democratic theorists should not view welfare policy abstractly or in isolation. Welfare states are shaped by and help shape a variety of institutions and social relations that distribute power and can subordinate some people. For this reason, it is possible to derive from the previous section a list of "democratic problems" connected to welfare states. These problems are distinct from those addressed by *deliberative norms* (whether public discourse on welfare adheres to certain content guidelines) or *deliberative prerequisites* (whether individuals are provided with material resources and education necessary to enable their participation in deliberation). I enumerate and expand on these democratic problems below.

States and democratic abnegation. States are not universal political institutions but particular ones, characterized by specific interrelations between politics and other notionally depoliticized realms of life. Too often, deliberative theory has taken the state for granted.[7] The deliberative norms approach and the deliberative prerequisites approach both reinforce this tendency. They ask what benefits the welfare state should provide or how such policy should be deliberated, but not what that state itself represents from the standpoint of democratic theory: a limit, an unacknowledged settlement about the extent of democratic practices, which are all but excluded from vast realms of society and the economy.

Welfare states as buttresses of other social relations. Just as welfare states are not institutions unto themselves, they cannot be adequately theorized if they are considered only in relation to ideal social agreements or abstractly conceived human needs and capacities. Welfare states instead stand in con-

---

7. One scholar, for example, simply asserts that the state "in a democracy is our collective power" (Laden 2001, 104). John Dryzek (2000, chap. 4) constitutes a notable exception to this neglect of the state by deliberative democrats. But his work is not characterized by the "deliberative norms" or the "deliberative prerequisites" approaches to the welfare state. Moreover, in precisely those passages in which Dryzek discusses the state most incisively, he adopts a language that in my view is foreign to deliberative democracy—one acknowledging coercion, fear, interests, the threat of political instability, state imperatives, and cooptation (87, 94, 96, 101).

crete relationships to other social institutions—the family, racial hierarchies, the market, and the workplace. The structure of these institutions, their distribution of power, and the degree to which they subordinate some parties or undermine their autonomy must be of great concern to democratic theory. But this subordination is obscured if welfare is understood mainly as a way of providing benefits that may prepare a person to deliberate or if welfare is considered simply as one topic among many that must be deliberated properly by citizens. To put this somewhat differently, democratic theory has to take a stand with respect to these social relations separate from how they affect and are affected by public deliberation.

Welfare states as mechanisms of stratification. The welfare state's social-constructive capacity is not limited to reinforcing preexisting social relations. It can also actively reform or change the character and meaning of such relations. In particular, liberal and conservative welfare states treat different groups differently, according them not just different levels but different types of benefits and placing them in programs that are structured differently. Frequently, the result of this power of the welfare state has been to place the most vulnerable people in society in the most stigmatized, regulated and punitive programs, characterizing and constructing them as uniquely dependent, while placing others in efficient programs that grant benefits as a matter of right and that carry no stigma. This aspect of the welfare state cannot be reduced to or derived from the nature of actual or imagined deliberative agreements about mutual obligations among citizens, because it is a feature of the actual, existing welfare state, whether known and agreed to by deliberators or not. It cannot be reduced to the prerequisites—material resources or developed capacities—needed to enter into political deliberation, because it is about the structures and social relations formed in the process of providing such resources and developing such capacities.

The significance of the problem of *subordination* becomes clear from the considerations above. Subordination for our purposes refers to a social relation in which one or more parties cede their individual or collective capacity for self-governance. Thus subordination intrinsically is a problem of social relations and power. Pateman has focused on the way that the marriage contract creates (and claims to legitimate) a subordinating familial relationship, and the way in which the employment contract does the same for a subordinating economic relationship. Certain kinds of programs might provide people with alternatives to entering or staying in such subordinating relationships. Frequently, however, welfare programs have been used to ensure the opposite: to make women more dependent upon other family members, especially husbands, for economic support, and to push workers into precisely those low wage job markets with the most insecure and hierarchical employment.

Welfare states as networks of social relations. In accepting aid, recipients enter into definite relations with welfare states. Even the most routinized and tenuous of such relations are relations nevertheless—not just sums of cash or other resources appearing mysteriously to fulfill needs. For example, the awarding of tax breaks for those who invest in private retirement accounts is a (highly market-friendly) welfare program serving upper income people. It is, however, one that comes with no stigma and can be claimed easily without much question and as a matter of right. Thus the social relation in question is a nonintrusive one between an autonomous rights-bearing individual and a fairly efficient and distant bureaucracy. Of course, such a welfare program also stratifies welfare clients, separating recipients of tax breaks from those who do not receive them, and (because of its reliance on markets) treating people differently based on their ability to purchase retirement benefits.

The existence of a social relation between state and recipients is even clearer, however, when we examine *the welfare state as a system of personal regulation*. In contrast to beneficiaries of tax breaks for private retirement accounts, recipients in the most stigmatizing and regulated programs enter into relations with caseworkers and an extensive welfare bureaucracy, empowered to interrogate, search, demand appointments, and so on. One of the main effects of American "welfare reform" in the 1990s was to enhance the powers and intrusiveness of such bureaucracies. Such programs, then, undermine autonomy and self-governance in as direct and personal a way as possible. Historically, women and African Americans, especially, have been subject to probing questions and inspections, as well as encounters with bureaucracies and caseworkers who retain considerable discretionary powers over them.

The *subordination* of welfare recipients is thus actually two-fold. As a condition of receiving state aid, recipients of some welfare programs give up not only aspects of self-governance, down to control over key aspects of personal life, but also important claims to privacy. In this sense, they enter subordinating social relations with the welfare state itself.

Welfare states as authority structures. Welfare states raise even more questions of democratic interest that are not reducible to problems related to deliberation. One of the key arguments of Pateman's *Participation and Democratic Theory* was that people's sense of political efficacy—their belief that they can intervene and make a difference in politics—is crucially conditioned by the authority structures they encounter in their daily lives. Pateman's prime example was the workplace. Joe Soss has found, analogously, that because AFDC recipients extrapolated from their experiences with welfare agencies, they were less confident than other similarly situated people that government in general would be responsive to them (Soss 1999, 368–71). AFDC clients were particularly likely to describe government as autonomous from popular control (370–71). One client told Soss: "There's nothing I can do because the government is going to do what they want to do regardless of what the people say" (370). Comparisons to clients of Social Security Disability Income (SSDI), a less stigmatizing program, were particularly striking. While 60 percent of SSDI clients thought that "government officials listened to people like them," only 8 percent of AFDC clients thought so (370).

Welfare states and alien agendas. From yet another democratic perspective, many welfare recipients become subject in crucial ways to social forces and powers over which they have little or no control and which are expressions of the interests or agendas of social groups quite separate from recipients themselves. When the United States and other countries have passed "welfare reforms" in the last decade, recipients have been made unwitting instruments of efforts to restructure the economy, reduce labor costs, increase labor flexibility, and generally pave the way for corporations that operate on the business model of Wal-Mart. Women in "conservative" welfare regimes, similarly, become instruments of religiously inspired programs to preserve a particular model of the family (Esping-Andersen 1990, 27; Borchorst 1994).

Insofar as these agendas are not fully recognized or understood by many people upon whom they exert important effects—and insofar as they acquire their strength from social formations that deliberative bodies cannot readily alter or master—we arrive at the intersection of *welfare states, democracy, unintended consequences, and incomplete consciousness*. Deliberative democrats frequently say that they are concerned with "collective decisions" (Dryzek 2000, 1). But power and social structures, crucial problematics with which democratic theory must concern itself, are not reducible to decisions (or even nondecisions) (Bachrach and Baratz 1970; Isaac 1987). Similarly, deliberative democracy seeks the establishment of a domain of deliberation, governed and given boundaries by particular norms. But the power relations and social forces that must concern democratic theory are not necessarily manifest in such deliberative domains. For example, democrats ought to be concerned if the structure of labor markets undermines the autonomy and democratic capacities of some people, even if no collective decision or deliberation has intentionally brought this about. Deliberative democracy can take a position in favor of deliberation that is open to any "reason" but it has difficulty with "reasons" that are largely unexpressed or unacknowledged.

Welfare states as products of social stratification and conflict. Esping-Andersen and others stress that the welfare state stratifies people by ordering them into differently structured and administered programs. But we have also already seen that the shape of the welfare state results in large measure from social structure and conflict at key moments in its history. Thus, race relations in the United States in the 1930s have much to do with the relative weakness of the nation's welfare state. By contrast, social-democratic welfare states arose in countries where working-class movements were strong and capable. Good deliberation did not lead to the establishment of welfare programs that may help foster political participation. Rather, it is the relative power of working class movements—and their willingness and ability to use this power against opposition—that typically had this effect. The coercive use of such power not only transcends the deliberative paradigm, but probably violates some of its core principles.[8]

A Closer Look at Deliberative Norms, Deliberative Prerequisites, and the Democratic Problems of Welfare States

This enumeration of the democratic problems of the welfare state is not yet the whole story. For it is not just that these problems are distinct from those issues highlighted by "deliberative norms" and "deliberative prerequisites." In addition, the conceptual tools that constitute these two approaches are also inadequate for locating and exploring such democratic problems. These conceptual limitations make it unlikely that a person attempting to apply appropriate deliberative norms or consider the prerequisites for deliberation—however earnestly—would address the U.S. welfare state's reinforcement of subordinating gender, race, and economic relations.

The deliberative norms approach derives its intuitive appeal from envisioning ideal, equally situated participants in public discourse and the kind of norms that would govern them in a deliberative domain. It then attempts to turn these deliberative norms into substantive guides for discussing the problems surrounding welfare. But this is fraught with difficulty, because the problems of the welfare state—like the problems of any domain of social relations—are not fully accessible from or reducible to the way the subject is or

---

8. For a more complete discussion of this argument, see Medearis (2005).

ought to be addressed in any discursive realm. The institutions and social relations of welfare are not, after all, created uniquely by decisions made in public discourse. They are created and re-created—in part intentionally and in part unintentionally—by the actions of a variety of different social agents, with different purposes guiding them. Moreover, while these social relations and institutions enable various parties to act, they also express limits both of their agency and of their understanding, especially insofar as they are the product of unintended consequences. In other words, in the limiting case, it is quite possible for public deliberators to be both ignorant and impotent with respect to these crucial democratic problems. Parties could fully embody appropriate deliberative norms without reaching or resolving the social-relational problems of the domain under discussion. Power and subordination in the social relations surrounding the welfare state need not arise from or even manifest themselves in relations or discussions between deliberators in order to be problematic.

Given all this, the norms designed to govern ideal public discourse—reciprocity, for example, or nondeception—may appear rather indeterminate and one-sided when directly applied to the context of the real social world of welfare. This should be no surprise. As I have pointed out, the deliberative norms approach must begin by imagining ideal, equally situated deliberators and the kind of norms that would govern them. What must necessarily be suppressed in envisioning this domain is precisely those aspects of many social arenas that are problematic from the standpoint of democratic theory: the conflict between different social agents and their interests, the unintended consequences of their actions, the structures that exist in reciprocal relation with these agents, and the resulting issues of power and subordination. A norm that may have a sufficiently clear meaning in the domain constituted by deliberation has to be translated for application to a given conflictive social domain. Yet deliberative theory itself can provide little guidance for the translation. Take reciprocity, for example, and the various social worlds to which it might be applied. In the deliberative realm, it means "appeal[ing] to reasons that are shared or could come to be shared by our fellow citizens" (Gutmann and Thompson 1996, 14). Here the concreteness results not merely from an act of definition but from the fact that this kind of reciprocity has obvious referents and correlates in the deliberative domain, which, insofar as it exists or can be imagined, is created by common communicative purpose and a set of norms known to those who are actually deliberating. In other domains, matters are quite different. There we find multiple agents, multiple interests and intentions, and so on. Of course, since all social institutions are created and re-created by the actions of multiple parties, all such institutions—even the most subordinating and oppressive ones—can potentially (but not very adequately) be described as involving some sort of reciprocity. There is, after all, a feudal theory of reciprocity between serf and master, and a patriarchal theory of reciprocity between wife and husband. But this just goes to show that reciprocity alone cannot provide an adequate guide to what is democratically defective about these domains. What is needed to give a term such as "reciprocity" a democratic sense is an additional vocabulary appropriate for characterizing and critiquing such a domain: a vocabulary of power, unintended consequences, purposeful action, conflicting agendas, interests, competition, and incomplete consciousness. Such a vocabulary, however, is not intrinsically a part of the effort to construct a deliberative domain. It is, in fact, a vocabulary that is frequently disdained by deliberative democrats.

This translation gap is likely behind Gutmann and Thompson's failure to ask difficult democratic questions about crucial economic institutions. The neglect has its origins in their defining democracy in terms of the deliberative domain, which in their account is intended to promote moral discussion. In the deliberative domain, the moral discussion of welfare should emphasize mutual obligations between individual members of society, as well as the allotting of goods and "life chances" to individuals according to criteria of moral desert (Gutmann and Thompson 1996, 209). Moral (and hence democratic) discussion, then, comes to hinge on a distinction between that which is morally deserved and that which is morally "arbitrary" (209). Although plausible enough analytically, such a distinction can be deleterious to critical democratic theory, especially when it undergoes a slippage from *morally deserved versus morally arbitrary* to *morally deserved versus natural*, as it indeed does with Gutmann and Thompson. For after such a slippage, one may conclude that that which is not morally deserved is essentially natural and not subject to democratic criticism. It is likely because of such a slippage that Gutmann and Thompson liken the existing allotment of resources and economic power, quite inaptly, to a "natural lottery" or a "natural disaster" (209, 284). But while one may not in fact deserve one's place in the economy, the economy is not for that reason a "natural" lottery. Here the "moral" distinctions structuring ideal deliberation are simply inadequate to the task of critical social analysis. If one makes such an illicit equation of "morally arbitrary" and "natural," much of the economy—its mechanisms and structure—is naturalized and left out of critical democratic reflection.

Gutmann and Thompson go on to treat a historically distinct contemporary economic institution—the market sale of labor power—as if it were natural, universal, and transhistorical—simply identical, as they say, with "contributing [one's] own labor to society," "productive work," "carrying [one's] share of the social burden," and being a "free remunerated worker" (Gutmann and Thompson 1996, 280, 281, 293, 302). For Gutmann and Thompson's democratic theory, what matters is that citizens be willing mutually to contribute their labor to society. But their paradigm obscures from them the fact that various ways of actually doing this are not natural and universal and immune to criticism, but socially and historically differentiated. The market sale of labor power may indeed be widely equated in our society with "productive work," but to fail to notice what is distinctive and problematic about this labor institution obscures questions that are highly relevant to democratic thought and action. The seriousness of this mistake is clearest when Gutmann and Thompson claim that refusal to sell one's labor power constitutes refusal "to participate in a scheme of fair social cooperation" (279, 292, 303). Here their democratic theory simply assumes the fairness of a system it ought to question and analyze.

Like the "norms" approach, the "prerequisites" approach also begins with a deliberative ideal. But instead of seeking to implant that ideal in the content of deliberation about welfare, the "prerequisites" approach proposes to use "government expenditures to guarantee the social and economic prerequisites of effective participation" by "individual citizens" (Knight and Johnson 1997, 306). In this sense, the deliberative prerequisites approach recognizes from one standpoint that welfare policy is crucially implicated in social conditions that are democratically significant, such as poverty. But, as we have seen, there are a number of democratic welfare state problems that are distinct from the provision of material resources and the development of deliberative capacities by the state—problems such as the democratic limits inscribed in the state itself, the socially stratifying effects of welfare programs, and the subordinating features of client-bureaucracy relations.

There are good reasons to think that the conceptualizing of welfare in terms of the provision of material resources and the development of deliberative capacities is not a promising standpoint from which to explore these distinct issues. The material resources approach to welfare postulates a person in relation to money or to essentials like food and shelter that are required to enter into deliberation. The addition of "capacities" to this picture is intended to account for the fact that a deliberator must be able to use material resources effectively, to reflect on her needs, and to make decisions. But the problems I have outlined above are not ones concerning only the relationship of a person (or persons) to things or cognitive capacities. They have to do primarily with the character of complex relations between persons. Almost all forms of society have in some way made provision for children, the sick, the elderly, and even those who for one reason or another remained outside the dominant productive relations. None of these social forms—least of all the various welfare state regimes—has ever been reducible simply to the material goods or even the education provided. Of course, it would be unfair to imply that the deliberative prerequisites approach in general neglects social relations. Deliberative theory, especially in its Habermasian version, is very much about social relations and intersubjectivity. But the deliberative prerequisites approach does not look at the welfare state as a problem of social relations, power, and subordination in its own right. Instead, it deals with welfare provision essentially as a prelude to the interpersonal, deliberative interactions that are the focus of attention.

Conclusion: The Place of "Subordination" in Democratic Theory and Inquiry

A critical democratic theory should give a high priority to criticizing social relations of subordination and be responsive to the sort of democratic problems mentioned above, such as state pressure to work in insecure and hierarchical workplaces, and the social stratification of welfare recipients in ways that reinforce longstanding racial and gender divides.

A strong a priori case can be made for the centrality of antisubordination for democratic theory. Here I am discussing subordination in the sense of the alienation of capacities or rights that are deeply implicated in self-governance (Pateman 2002, 33, 47, 49). Pateman criticizes as undemocratic any social relation that is based on selling or yielding the direction of such capacities or the right to control one's person. Many arguments for democracy, even in the most narrow sense, are premised on a right to self-government, however that right may be conceived. Conversely, undemocratic social relations have frequently been justified by the claim that it is legitimate to yield up self-governing capacities on entering marriage or employment.

Accepting antisubordination as central to democratic theory, however, does not simply mean subjecting the definition of "democracy" to (another) philosophical analysis. Nor is the point to replace "agonistic democracy" or "deliberative democracy" or even "liberal democracy" with "antisubordination democracy." Rather, what is important is relating democratic thought to the network of concepts within which subordination can be understood and analyzed. Subordination produces and reproduces enduring social relations that give some people the capacity to direct others—that is, relations that generate and distribute power. And when enduring social relations and power—in a variety of social, economic, and political contexts—are recognized as democratically significant, then not just subordination but also domination comes to the foreground. Many social relations simultaneously entail subordination and domination. But whereas the term "subordination" calls attention to the alienation of a person's capacities, "domination" highlights the use of socially constituted power over other people, often against their wishes or interests.

I argue for a democratic theory that takes the character of a wide variety of enduring social, political, and economic relations as a primary object of critical interest and concrete study. There are many ways such social relations can be explored. The democratic situation of a low-wage worker who has received TANF can be illuminated by studies of several different institutions and practices—government programs, capitalist firms, labor markets, families, and welfare rights movements, to name a few—and from a variety of perspectives, such as structural, historical-developmental, and discursive. Few political theorists now would object to the claim that every act and every institution has an interpretive, discursive dimension. The language of the welfare reform debate and of the welfare office certainly shed light on the subordinate position of recipients. But so do studies of the properties of low-wage labor markets, structural analyses of the staffing and institutional capacities of government bureaucracies, and historical narratives of attempts by welfare recipients to organize politically. A form of critical democratic inquiry concerned with subordination and domination could not be content to approach these subjects only from the standpoint of public discourse about welfare. Indeed, my arguments about "deliberative norms" and "deliberative prerequisites" both point to the intrinsic limits of these forms of discursive analysis, viewed as ways of casting light on welfare and democracy. Since the social relations of welfare states are not products solely of decisions made in public discourse—nor are they fully transparent results of conscious decisions—norms designed to govern public discourse are inadequate to judging those social relations. Similarly, guidelines for the types of material benefits and education an individual needs in order to take part in deliberation do not provide sufficient tools for characterizing the complex relations that arise among persons as a result of government attempts to meet basic needs.

An approach to democratic theory sensitive to the democratic problems faced by welfare recipients—problems such as the intrusive nature of bureaucratic questioning and regulation, and the tendency of market-oriented welfare programs to push people into hierarchical workplaces—would have to be, more generally, attentive to concrete groups of people and the social relations, forces, and structures that most affect their lives. It would examine the character of those social relations, especially their distribution of power and their implication in subordination or domination. Such democratic inquiry would take an interest in the attempts of such groups to organize and oppose the subordinating relations they face. And it would explore the possibilities of transforming such relations and institutions in the name of democracy and self-governance.

References

Bachrach, Peter, and Morton S. Baratz. 1970. *Power and Poverty: Theory and Practice.* Oxford: Oxford University Press.

Barrow, Clyde W. 1993. *Critical Theories of the State: Marxist, Neo-Marxist, Post-Marxist.* Madison: University of Wisconsin Press.

Block, Fred. 1977. "The Ruling Class Does Not Rule: Notes on the Marxist Theory of the State." *Socialist Revolution* 7, no. 3:6–28.

Bohman, James. 1996. *Public Deliberation: Pluralism, Complexity, and Democracy.* Cambridge, Mass.: MIT Press.

Borchorst, Annette. 1994. "Welfare State Regimes, Women's Interests, and the EC." In *Gendering Welfare States*, edited by D. Sainsbury, 26–44. London: SAGE Publications.

Bronfenbrenner, Kate, and Tom Juravich. 1994. *The Impact of Employer Opposition on Union Certification Win Rates: A Private/Public Sector Comparison.* Washington, D.C.: Economic Policy Institute.

Bussemaker, Jet, and Kees van Kersbergen. 1994. "Gender and Welfare States: Some Theoretical Reflections." In *Gendering Welfare States*, edited by D. Sainsbury, 8–25. London: SAGE Publications.

Dryzek, John S. 1990. *Discursive Democracy: Politics, Policy, and Political Science.* Cambridge: Cambridge University Press.

———. 2000. *Deliberative Democracy and Beyond: Liberals, Critics, Contestations.* Oxford: Oxford University Press.

Esping-Andersen, Gosta. 1990. *The Three Worlds of Welfare Capitalism.* Princeton: Princeton University Press.

Fraser, Nancy, and Linda Gordon. 1994. "A Genealogy of Dependency: Tracing a Keyword of the U.S. Welfare State." *Signs* 19, no. 21:309–36.

Gaffaney, Timothy J. 2000. *Freedom for the Poor: Welfare and the Foundations of Democratic Citizenship.* Boulder, Colo.: Westview Press.

Gilens, Martin. 1999. *Why Americans Hate Welfare*. Chicago: University of Chicago Press.

Goldfield, Michael. 1989. "Worker Insurgency, Radical Organization, and New Deal Labor Legislation." *American Political Science Review* 83, no. 4:1259–82.

Gutmann, Amy. 1993. "Democracy." In *A Companion to Contemporary Political Philosophy*, edited by R. E. Goodin and P. Pettit, 411–21. Oxford: Blackwell.

Gutmann, Amy, and Dennis Thompson. 1996. *Democracy and Disagreement*. Cambridge, Mass.: Harvard University Press.

———. 2004. *Why Deliberative Democracy?* Princeton: Princeton University Press.

Habermas, Jürgen. 1975. *Legitimation Crisis*. Boston: Beacon Press.

Handler, Joel. 2000. "Winding Down Welfare." *New Left Review*, 2nd ser., 4:114–36.

Hegel, G. W. F. [1821]. 1952. *Hegel's Philosophy of Right*. Translated by T. M. Knox. London: Oxford University Press.

Isaac, Jeffrey C. 1987. *Power and Marxist Theory: A Realist View*. Ithaca: Cornell University Press.

Knight, Jack, and James Johnson. 1997. "What Sort of Equality Does Deliberative Democracy Require?" In *Deliberative Democracy: Essays on Reason and Politics*, edited by J. Bohman and W. Rehg, 279–319. Cambridge, Mass.: MIT Press.

Laden, Anthony Simon. 2001. *Reasonably Radical: Deliberative Liberalism and the Politics of Identity*. Ithaca: Cornell University Press.

Lieberman, Robert C. 1998. *Shifting the Color Line: Race and the American Welfare State*. Cambridge, Mass.: Harvard University Press.

Lindblom, Charles E. 1977. *Politics and Markets: The World's Political-Economic Systems*. New York: Basic Books.

Marx, Karl. [1843–44]. 1967. *Critique of Hegel's "Philosophy of Right."* Edited by M. Cowling, G. R. Elton, E. Kedourie, J. G. A. Pocock, J. R. Pole, and W. Ullman. Cambridge Studies in the History and Theory of Politics. Cambridge: Cambridge University Press.

———. [1844]. 2000. "On the Jewish Question." In *Karl Marx, Selected Writings*, edited by D. McLellan, 46–70. Oxford: Oxford University Press.

McAdam, Doug. 1982. *Political Process and the Development of Black Insurgency, 1930–1970*. Chicago: University of Chicago Press.

Medearis, John. 2005. "Social Movements and Deliberative Democratic Theory." *British Journal of Political Science* 35, no. 1:53–75.

Mink, Gwendolyn. 1990. "The Lady and the Tramp: Gender, Race, and the Origins of the American Welfare State." In *Women, the State, and Welfare*, edited by L. Gordon, 92–122. Madison: University of Wisconsin Press.

Nelson, Barbara. 1990. "The Origins of the Two-Channel Welfare State: Workmen's Compensation and Mothers' Aid." In *Women, the State, and Welfare*, edited by L. Gordon, 123–51. Madison: University of Wisconsin Press.

Noble, Charles. 1997. *Welfare as We Knew It: A Political History of the American Welfare State*. New York: Oxford University Press.

Offe, Claus. 1984. *Contradictions of the Welfare State*. Cambridge, Mass.: MIT Press.

Pateman, Carole. 1970. *Participation and Democratic Theory*. Cambridge: Cambridge University Press.

———. 1979. *The Problem of Political Obligation: A Critical Analysis of Liberal Theory*. New York: John Wiley and Sons.

———. 1988a. "The Patriarchal Welfare State." In *Democracy and the Welfare State*, edited by A. Gutmann, 231–60. Princeton: Princeton University Press.

———. 1988b. *The Sexual Contract*. Stanford: Stanford University Press.

———. 2002. "Self-Ownership and Property in the Person: A Tale of Two Concepts." *Journal of Political Philosophy* 10, no. 1:20–53.

———. 2004. "Democratizing Citizenship: Some Advantages of a Basic Income." *Politics and Society* 32, no. 1:89–105.

Pierson, Paul. 1994. *Dismantling the Welfare State? Reagan, Thatcher, and the Politics of Retrenchment*. Cambridge: Cambridge University Press.

———. 2001. "Coping with Permanent Austerity: Welfare Restructuring in Affluent Democracies." In *The New Politics of the Welfare State*, edited by P. Pierson, 410–56. New York: Oxford University Press.

Piven, Frances Fox, and Richard A. Cloward. 1971. *Regulating the Poor: The Functions of Public Welfare*. New York: Vintage.

Quadagno, Jill. 1994. *The Color of Welfare: How Racism Undermined the War on Poverty*. New York: Oxford University Press.

Rawls, John. 1996. *Political Liberalism, with a New Introduction and the "Reply to Habermas."* New York: Columbia University Press.

Schumpeter, Joseph. [1918] 1991. "The Crisis of the Tax State." In *Joseph Schumpeter: The Economics and Sociology of Capitalism*, edited by R. Swedberg, 99–140. Princeton: Princeton University Press.

Solow, Robert M. 1998. "Guess Who Pays for Workfare?" *New York Review of Books* 45, no. 17. Available at http://www.nybooks.com/articles/694.

Soss, Joe. 1999. "Lessons of Welfare: Policy Design, Political Learning, and Political Action." *American Political Science Review* 93 (June): 363–80.

Thomas, Paul. 1994. *Alien Politics: Marxist State Theory Retrieved*. London: Routledge.

Young, Iris Marion. 1996. "Communication and the Other: Beyond Deliberative Democracy." In *Democracy and Difference,* edited by S. Benhabib, 120–35. Princeton: Princeton University Press.

———. 1999. "Justice, Inclusion, and Deliberative Democracy." In *Deliberative Politics: Essays on Democracy and Disagreement,* edited by S. Macedo, 151–58. New York: Oxford University Press.

———. 2000. *Inclusion and Democracy.* New York: Oxford University Press.

———. 2001. "Activist Challenges to Deliberative Democracy." *Political Theory* 29, no. 5:670–90.

Afterword
Carole Pateman

First, I want to express my gratitude and appreciation to the editors and contributors for their generosity in producing this volume of essays. But, very sadly, none of us can take quite the same pleasure in the book now that it is overshadowed by the untimely death of Iris Young. I could not have been more delighted when I learned that she was one of the editors—indeed, I subsequently discovered that this volume was her idea, which makes the loss even more poignant—and it is very hard to believe that she will not be here to celebrate the publication. Her unwavering commitment to social justice and lack of pretension will remain an inspiration.

Reading the essays has also prompted reflections about how many years have vanished since the day I opened the letter (naturally, it feels as if it were yesterday) telling me, to my astonishment, that *Participation and Democratic Theory* (1970) was to be published. When I finally plucked up enough courage to go and see my book on display in Blackwell's in Oxford I was so overwhelmed at the sight that I fled from the store.[1] I had little or no appreciation then that printed words gain a life of their own, but various lives of my arguments appear in these rich essays. They provide me with a great deal to think about, but much of that has to be for the future; here I want to make some comments around the broad themes of democracy, autonomy, consent, and contract.

---

1. Being an author was so remote from my experience that it had no reality until I saw the material object. I had followed Brian Barry's instruction to send the manuscript to Cambridge University Press; just to put the record straight, *Participation and Democratic Theory* was not my D. Phil thesis but was written, but never submitted, for a B. Phil. degree.

It might seem that it is a much better time today to be writing about democratic theory than when I was working on my first book. We are now surrounded by democracy-talk from all quarters, and for the first time in history democratic elections are seen around the world as the only acceptable means to produce a legitimate government. In contrast, in the late 1960s relatively few countries had minimally democratic electoral institutions, universal suffrage, and the associated civil liberties. This was true of some countries in Europe; women did not have the vote in Switzerland, for example, although I do not recall being aware of it at the time. Despite or perhaps because of this, it was a period of vigorous demands for wider participation and greater democracy. This meant that the meaning of "democracy" was questioned and challenged both inside and outside universities.

Notwithstanding all the democracy-talk, the early twenty-first century is not an easy time to think about democracy. At what might be called the official level, where democracy is being promoted globally, a narrow Schumpeterian view is hegemonic. "Democracy" is identified with "free and fair" elections plus a market economy organized on the lines of the Washington consensus. In academic work, the official conception is also alive and well and discussion of democracy is often conducted within a narrow theoretical framework. Within political theory, "democracy" is now qualified by democratic theorists with a variety of adjectives, such as agonistic, cosmopolitan, deliberative, or republican, and although this has opened up new avenues of debate, particularly about globalization and rights, some important questions remain neglected.

When I began my work, I took the minimal basic requisites for electoral democracy for granted; this is no longer possible. In Britain and the United States, there has been a very marked strengthening of executive power, a steep decline in effective opposition, and an erosion of the rule of law and civil liberties as "the war on terror" is prosecuted. A gulf has been opening up between citizens and official democracy. As many commentators have noted, in Western countries voters are disaffected and popular confidence in old-established political institutions is fading. Inequalities are growing, the political influence of the rich increasing—indeed, Alan Ryan bluntly states that Britain and the United States are not democracies but are governed by the rich, albeit that they compete for votes—and gigantic corporations wield more and more power globally (democratic theorists have neglected corporations). And cynicism about democracy-talk is hard to avoid, not least when the destruction and occupation of Iraq has been justified in its name, and the duly elected government in Palestine was boycotted by the European Union and the United States after elections in January 2006 declared by international observers to be free and fair.

My remarks about civil liberties and executive power might be viewed as typically liberal. Jane Mansbridge stresses that the meaning of liberalism depends on what is understood by liberty or autonomy. But do liberals have a monopoly on freedom, civil liberties, rights, or consent? Democracy depends on the revolutionary premise of individual freedom and equality, again a premise often seen as "liberal." But there is, as Michael Goodhart argues, a democratic emancipatory tradition that has not been given its due. It has been obscured until very recently in standard histories of political theory that were focused on theorists all too willing to transmute the premise of individual freedom into subordination or to exclude sections of the population from freedom altogether.

When I wrote *The Problem of Political Obligation* in the 1970s I thought I knew what "liberal" meant. For some time, however, it has seemed to me that the ubiquitous terms "liberal" and "liberalism" (which also function as terms of political abuse in the United States) are used to refer to such a wide array of thinkers and arguments that, unless their meaning is carefully specified, they are more of a hindrance than a help. Thus even though I used to argue in terms of liberalism versus democracy I cannot now get very exercised about an unqualified "liberalism." In *The Sexual Contract* (1988) my argument about civil subordination depends on a context of individual, juridical freedom and equality, usually taken to be one of the hallmarks of "liberalism," but my book was not about liberalism. It was about contract theory, a distinct line of argument.

The sentence from the latter book that has perhaps been most quoted, usually by critics, is "A free social order cannot be a contractual order." Both the editors and Moira Gatens ask how it should be read. Let me reproduce what follows: "There are other forms of free agreement through which women and men can constitute political relations, although in a period when socialists are busy stealing the clothes of contract little political creativity is directed towards developing the necessary new forms" (1988, 232). The first of two points encapsulated in these sentences is that contract theory has been swallowing up other ways of thinking about freedom and voluntary agreement. We hear a great deal about freedom from proponents of the official view of democracy but for too long the market has been cornered by a contractual conception. An alternative discourse of freedom is badly needed in the strange circumstances of the early twenty-first century.

Charles Mills argues that I should be able to accept contract theory once it is modified to expose racial and sexual domination. While I am very appreciative of his work and while I believe that the more theoretical weapons turned against domination the better, we remain at odds over contract theory.[2] Contract is an important and admirable commercial device—but one that must be kept in its place. The second point of my claim about a free noncontractual order is that contract and markets cannot be the model for an entire social order. When that path is taken, contract soon begins to undercut the conditions of its own existence, which is hardly an original point. The noncontractual bases of contract—that contract presuppose the existence of (noncontractual) practices and social relations—were emphasized by a number of famous theorists; it is a lesson that Hobbes teaches and can be found, for example, in Durkheim, Parsons, and Polanyi.

By refusing to accept contract as the emblem of freedom and as the primary theoretical lens for political theorists I am swimming against the strong tide of Rawlsianism. Arguments about the Rawlsian ideal of society as a voluntary, cooperative scheme—a democracy—can be made directly, without recourse to hypothetical agreements by abstract parties about principles suited to ideal theory. Democratic theory needs to begin from where we are at present and in light of how we got here to circumstances that are very far from ideal. Moreover, contemporary argument deriving from the classic theorists of an original contract embodies the sexual and racial contracts—the social contract is only one dimension of the original contract—and the embarrassing baggage cannot merely be jettisoned to reveal a neutral contract; it is built into the structure of the argument.

Contemporary contract theory nods toward classic theories but takes for granted the general justification of government in the modern state, which its predecessors saw as a problem and, I argued in *The Problem of Political Obligation*, remains so. By not acknowledging the problem, contemporary contract theorists tacitly accept all the dimensions of that "original" justification and so fail to recognize how the sexual and racial contracts still shape social structures. Rawlsian contract theory is largely concerned with moral reasoning and moral principles, and, as many of its practitioners admit, contract does no real work in their analyses, another reason why the political problem of sexual and racial hierarchies is ignored. That is to say, contemporary contract theory neglects democratization, the creation of a more demo-

---

2. We explore our differences over contract theory in more detail in "Contract and Social Change: A Dialogue between Carole Pateman and Charles W. Mills," chapter 1 of Pateman and Mills 2007.

cratic social and political order, and fails to question the meaning of "democracy."

These are subjects in which I have always been interested, notwithstanding that academic preoccupations tend to vary as the political climate alters and political movements wax and wane. I noted at the beginning of *Participation and Democratic Theory* that demands for more participation were widespread; some years later, I could not have written about the sexual contract without the revival of the women's movement; and basic income is now on the popular agenda in a number of countries. It is not surprising that participatory democracy is no longer fashionable among democratic theorists and that the minimal, official view of democracy seems eminently sensible when neoliberal economic doctrines have achieved global power. However, I began my work by criticizing the "realism" of Schumpeter's conception of democracy and I remain unwilling to accept the hegemony of its successor.

Participatory democracy is now commonly referred to under the heading of deliberative democracy. "Participatory" and "deliberative" democracy are often assumed to be synonyms but, while vigorous deliberation would be part of any participatory democracy, I do not share this assumption. I agree, as Philip Pettit suggests that I would, with his argument that deliberation is about the formation of judgments, that it differs from the bare aggregation of preferences, and that to avoid repeating some of the aggregative problems participants must see themselves as members of a cooperative endeavor. However, I am doubtful about the terminology of "we-thinking," which can too easily gloss over the epistemological problems discussed by Brooke Ackerly, problems raised by the appeal to intuitions in Rawlsian contract theory (whose intuitions are authoritative?) and the long-standing problems about who is a full member of the citizenry and how "we" are connected to others.

Lack of interest in participatory democracy on the part of democratic theorists does not mean that it is dead. It is alive, most notably in Brazil. The exciting development of participatory budgets demonstrates that a great deal more participation, even by poor citizens who have taken part in large numbers, is feasible. Moreover, in participatory budgets they are participating about the allocation of public resources, a matter usually regarded as too difficult and complex for anyone but experts or elected representatives to deal with. Mansbridge notes that the diffuse educative effects of participation are not easy to measure. A new source of valuable empirical evidence is available from the participatory budget process.[3] And, from the other direction, lack of

3. There is a growing literature on the subject, especially about Porto Alegre. One of the earliest studies (which looks at my hypotheses about participation) is

opportunities for participation can provide evidence; John Medearis refers to a study that finds that efficacy levels are lower in citizens in the United States who extrapolate from their experiences with welfare agencies.

Much discussion of deliberative democracy is very abstract, but the interest in deliberation has an empirical side, especially in citizens' juries and deliberative polls. Attention has mostly been focused on the extent to which deliberation leads citizens to change their views and judgments on given topics, and the polls and the juries remain either a social science experiment (the polls) or advisory bodies (the juries).[4] It is telling that there is little discussion of a potential democratic development of such bodies, an innovation or, rather, its wider application, in the spirit of Ryan's invocation of representatives chosen by lot. In 2004, 160 randomly chosen citizens presented the conclusion of the Citizens' Assembly on Electoral Reform in British Columbia, and their proposal was voted on by the electorate in a referendum the following year. This example could be extended and decision-making bodies, at the local level in the first instance, could be established composed of a random sample of citizens to examine and decide on possible remedies for selected problems. Such bodies would supplement elections and would provide a wide cross-section of citizens with the experience of meaningful participation about subjects in which they would probably have a keen interest. Evidence suggests that individuals enjoy being part of the deliberative polls and citizens' juries and take their duties seriously, so they may well feel the same way about service on bodies that have a modicum of power in their communities.

That such a possibility has not been seized upon is indicative of the distance of deliberative democracy from participatory democracy. For the most part, theorists of deliberative democracy have focused on the quality of reasoning in deliberation, and there has been much discussion of what counts as proper reasoned deliberation. While improvements in deliberation are certainly needed—leaders might set an example by not lying about economic matters or about such important matters as decisions to go to war—the problem is that the preoccupation with deliberation presupposes a background of democracy, and the meaning of "democracy" is taken for granted. Too much is pushed into an unexamined area and shielded from critical scrutiny. Medearis shows, for example, how deliberative democratic theory looks past structures

---

Abers 2000. One of the newest is a systematic empirical investigation of variations in the outcome of participatory budgeting in eight Brazilian cities: Wampler 2007.

4. I am using the term "citizens' juries" to cover a variety of bodies of this kind. For a discussion of the political impact of these bodies, see Goodin and Dryzek 2006.

and practices that undermine and negate citizens' autonomy in the welfare state in the United States.

The tacit acceptance of existing power structures is a major reason why I do not see deliberative and participatory as synonymous or deliberative democracy as the direct successor to participatory democracy. Participatory democracy has a much broader scope. It is about changing the common sense meaning of "democracy" and the hegemony of the official view; in short, it is about democratization. Structural change, refashioning undemocratic institutions, and undermining subordination and domination are the heart of participatory democracy. Consider consent, for example. Many advocates of deliberative democracy see deliberation as the way of creating legitimacy for decisions. Consent is central to democratic legitimacy, and deliberation could be seen as a way of obtaining consent, but discussion of consent has been scarce in deliberative democracy.

Nearly thirty years ago, I discussed some of the problems with consent and elections, usually seen as the major vehicle of consent, in *The Problem of Political Obligation*. These problems remain and have been exacerbated by, among other things, the ever-increasing use of very sophisticated marketing and advertising techniques (Schumpeter was ahead of his time in seeing their importance) and leaders who ignore the consent of the governed in favor of belief in their own incorrigible moral rectitude. I also published an article that raised some questions about women and consent, questions that Anne Phillips now addresses in a new context. The reason that many people seem to find it hard to appreciate that there is a distinction between an "arranged" and a "forced" marriage, between consent and nonconsent, is that, as I highlighted all those years ago in the case of rape (Pateman [1980] 1989), they assume that women's words, in this case the words of young women from certain cultural backgrounds, cannot be taken at face value and so they are reinterpreted. In arranged marriage it is the women's "yes" that is rejected and in rape their "no" ("everyone knows" that in sex when women say "no" they really don't mean it). A similar process can be observed in controversies in Europe over young women who wear the *hijab* and other items of Islamic women's clothing.

If the practice of consent is to be meaningful it must be possible for individuals both to give and refuse consent. Therefore, when an individual says "yes" or "no," no matter who utters the words, the presumption must always be that the individual means what he or she says. Adjudicating particular cases can, of course, be very tricky, but the problem is not one of specific cases. Rather, it is a general problem about the practice of consent. Consent in a meaningful sense is jeopardized when the words of a certain category of citizens, or half the citizen body, are always open to invalidation. If women's "yes" and "no" cannot be accepted, how can they take part in political life—or in deliberation—as equal citizens? And if women's equal participation is in doubt, then so are deliberative claims about legitimacy.

When a young woman consents (or refuses) to enter into an arranged marriage she is consenting (refusing) to participate in this form of the institution of marriage. Entry into the marriage contract creates a new marital relationship. This is an example of the distinction between contract and consent that I first used in my study of political obligation. I have written more about contract than about consent. When consent is given, the object of consent already exists; consent is given to something. Contract brings new relationships into being (and thus reflects the original contract that brings—is said to bring—the modern state and its institutions into being), and contract about property in the person is the vehicle through which relations of subordination are reproduced in central institutions of modern society.

In the United States and Britain, husbands have lost their legal powers, but the institution of employment is much as it was when I was writing *Participation and Democratic Theory*. My argument about the employment contract in *The Sexual Contract* has often been interpreted as a familiar claim about involuntary entry and coercion. But unless entry into the contract is a voluntary act there can be no engagement with the assumption, which runs through much political philosophy as well as much current public policy, that contract can be identified with freedom. My argument was about the consequences of that free act. When individuals decide voluntarily to enter into a contract they have exercised their freedom, but the consequence in the case of workers and the employment contract is their incorporation as subordinates. To focus on entry at the expense of consequences allows wage labor to be unambiguously separated from unfree labor and the institution of employment to fit comfortably into democracy.

Perhaps it might be objected that individuals consent to an undemocratic arrangement when they enter into the employment contract. The contract entered into by a particular worker creates a new relationship that takes its place as part of the wider structure of power and subordination in the workplace. Continued participation within this structure of authority and acceptance of the commands of the employer might be said to indicate consent to the arrangement. But then well-known problems about consent are hard to avoid. For instance, how is consent refused; where is consent when workers are unilaterally "downsized"? It might be argued that, rather than giving consent, the individual assents or acquiesces to the power structure, but this raises other equally familiar difficulties about tacit consent.

Democratic theorists seldom criticize the institution of employment despite its undemocratic character. Indeed, participation in paid employment is now widely seen to be necessary for democratic citizenship, not least by some leading theorists of deliberative democracy. A free market of a deregulated and privatized form is part of the official view of "democracy," and the labor market is central to this conception. Employment is being established around the world, and welfare reform, in particular, is being driven by the belief that all able-bodied adults must be employed—that is, employment should be universal.[5]

The failure of democratic theorists to recognize the significance of employment is a large obstacle to thinking about democratization, not least where questions of sexual difference and women's unpaid work are concerned. Acceptance of employment as a necessary part of "democracy" relies on the political fiction of property in the person, an abstraction that can take no account of human embodiment. Yet embodiment, and the human fact that women but not men can become pregnant and give birth, is at the heart of sexual difference. To make this point is not, let me emphasize, to suggest that varying conceptions of the different social place of men and women follow directly from biology. On the contrary, they derive from the meanings given to this human fact by cultures and institutional structures of power, including male power. Nonetheless, the fact remains that it is women who give birth.

Bob Goodin uses the assumptions of neoclassical economics to show why women's unpaid domestic work is distinctive and why it has no close market substitutes. Women's work as mothers is fundamental to its distinctiveness, and motherhood has also been at the center of the welfare state. The United States stands apart from other rich countries in the assumption that mothers (parents) need little public provision to care for children and that it is primarily a private matter that mothers themselves must find the time and resources to undertake. But the idea of universal employment, the insistence on privatization and the demands of structural adjustment also work to deny any distinctiveness to motherhood or its social and political contribution. Or, to put this another way, Wollstonecraft's dilemma is being accentuated as markets extend their reach and more and more of human life is commodified. Burdens on mothers around the world have been increased by international economic policies. Production and profit making have been speeded up, but the time

---

5. I have discussed the 1996 reform of welfare in the United States in Pateman 2005.

and resources necessary for human and social reproduction stand in the way; they must therefore be reduced (Brennan 2003).

The increase in commodification and the idea of universal employment both imply a proprietary, contractual view of rights. In everyday speech it is hard to avoid referring to individuals "having" rights, which suggests that rights are owned and implicitly conjures up the notion of the individual as owner of property in the person. In my most recent analysis of property in the person I discussed three logical possibilities: that all rights are alienable, only some rights are alienable, and all rights are inalienable (Pateman 2002). I also emphasized that the right of self-government is treated as alienable in employment but as inalienable in democracy; voters are prohibited from selling their votes, but they are encouraged or required to sell their labor power. The terminology of "alienable" and "inalienable" rights was part of the literature I was discussing and helped highlight the points I wanted to make. But the notion of total alienability that allows voluntary submission to absolutism or slavery (the master as absolute proprietor or sovereign) is the other side of the coin from total inalienability (the individual as sovereign proprietor), and both are part of the development of a contractual conception of rights.

It does not follow from my analysis that, as Gatens suggests, I am advocating inalienable rights in the form of legal prohibition of contracts about property in the person. There is a very good pragmatic reason for not adopting the latter course. Blanket legal prohibitions on alienability are virtually guaranteed to be ineffective, not least when profits from what is being traded are often huge and so many people are destitute. However, there is a major practical problem about commodification that needs to be addressed. An extremely powerful body of opinion is that all limitations on alienability should be swept away and everything treated as potential (private) property, open to patenting and rent or sale as a commodity in a market. Provided the capital is to hand, it is now possible to rent or buy, sometimes illicitly, anything from human wombs to bits of humankind's heritage of plant life, a municipal water supply, human organs and genetic material, and animals genetically engineered to order. A good deal more discussion is urgently required about the implications for democracy of this rapid expansion of commodities and about appropriate democratic responses. The debate is hindered in democratic theory by the reluctance to subject the trade in labor power to critical scrutiny (the right to sell labor power is universal) and to explore alternatives to employment as a way of organizing the production of goods and services.

In her criticism of the epistemological limitations of conventional accounts of rights, Ackerly links a proprietary view of rights to rights seen as entitlements. I am not sure that they are so tightly linked. My references to the right to a basic income as an entitlement were to underline that it is not a privilege, not contingent and subject to conditions, but is indeed a *right*. As an alternative to a contractual understanding of rights I have been thinking of rights as relationships that help constitute institutional structures and help maintain and strengthen individual autonomy. The question then is what rights are required to minimize subordination and maximize individual freedom, and what mechanisms are needed to maintain their effectiveness. Democratic theorists have typically focused on self-government in the sense of collective government in the state, and individual self-government has been neglected. The terminology of alienability and inalienability encapsulates a specific view of individual autonomy or self-government, but other conceptions are available or can be developed. I have recently been writing of "democratic rights" in the hope (probably overoptimistically) that it might help provide a way to an alternative to the proprietary view and help cut through some of the unhelpful standard debates about human rights, such as the endless wrangling over the status of "economic" rights and whether they are properly rights like their civil and political counterparts.

A basic income is crucial to establishing and maintaining individual autonomy because it provides the material basis necessary for social participation and for secure standing as a citizen, and it is a symbolic affirmation of that standing. A right to a basic income is analogous to the right to vote—a democratic right of all citizens. The very long duration and bitterness of the struggle to achieve universal suffrage is typically glossed over now that voting is promoted globally. Government *by* the people, as Ryan notes, is the sticking point in Lincoln's formula. There is an unwillingness to create the conditions that would make government by the people more of a reality; that is, there is an unwillingness to democratize. Citizens virtually everywhere are now encouraged to go to the polls, and what was once a privilege of the few has become a universal right. But subsistence is not regarded as a universal right: it is still a privilege or a matter of charity. The official view of democracy, tied to the institution of employment, remains heavily laden with the outlook of the nineteenth-century Poor Law, the basis of the construction of a national labor market in Britain. The relief of poverty is perpetually on the political agenda, but poor people have to prove that they "deserve" to live at a decent level by meeting conditions imposed on public benefits.

Universal basic income is not just another scheme to ameliorate poverty but (potentially) part of a democratic transformation to create citizenship of equal worth for everyone. A basic income is the simplest way to help create the conditions for all citizens to enjoy individual autonomy. In one sense, the introduction of a basic income is a logical next step in the European countries that already have a variety of generous income replacement measures in place. The biggest transformation would come globally (I support arguments, such as Goodhart's, for a global basic income but have not yet had the opportunity to discuss it), in the countries where two and half billion people—30 percent of the world's population—still live on less than $2 a day and command only 5 percent of global income, while the richest 10 percent monopolize 54 percent of global income. The transformation would be most striking for women, the poorest of the poor, whose autonomy is still fiercely contested. In another sense, a basic income is much more radical precisely because it imposes no conditions on recipients. Even some supporters of the policy draw back at this point, apprehensive that without an "incentive" too many individuals would cease to make a social contribution and, in particular, that they would turn away from employment, but I have seen no convincing evidence that this would be the consequence.

The demand that either conditions must be imposed on public grants or that individuals must (voluntarily) submit to an undemocratic authority structure to obtain their subsistence are at odds with democratic citizenship and have no place in a very wealthy world. Despite the wealth, inequality and insecurity have increased over the past quarter century and public provision for citizens (but not militarization and warfare) has been under attack. The road to democratization is still very long and hard, but if it is to be followed the meaning of "democracy" has to be put back on the political agenda, and governments and economies have to be brought into the service of citizens.

References

Abers, Rebecca Neaera. 2000. *Inventing Local Democracy: Grassroots Politics in Brazil*. Boulder, Colo.: Lynne Rienner Publishers.

Brennan, Teresa. 2003. *Globalization and Its Terrors: Daily Life in the West*. London: Routledge.

Goodin, Robert, and John Dryzek. 2006. "Deliberative Impacts: The Macropolitical Uptake of Mini-publics." *Politics and Society* 34, no. 2:1–26.

Pateman, Carole. 1970. *Participation and Democratic Theory*. Cambridge: Cambridge University Press.

———. [1979]. 1985. *The Problem of Political Obligation: A Critique of Liberal*

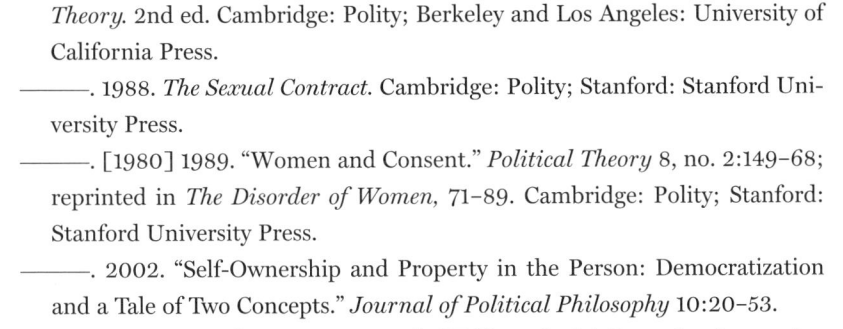

Theory. 2nd ed. Cambridge: Polity; Berkeley and Los Angeles: University of California Press.

———. 1988. *The Sexual Contract.* Cambridge: Polity; Stanford: Stanford University Press.

———. [1980] 1989. "Women and Consent." *Political Theory* 8, no. 2:149–68; reprinted in *The Disorder of Women*, 71–89. Cambridge: Polity; Stanford: Stanford University Press.

———. 2002. "Self-Ownership and Property in the Person: Democratization and a Tale of Two Concepts." *Journal of Political Philosophy* 10:20–53.

———. 2005. "Another Way Forward: Welfare, Social Reproduction, and a Basic Income." In *Welfare Reform and Political Theory*, edited by Lawrence Mead and Christopher Beem. New York: Russell Sage Foundation.

Pateman, Carole, and Charles Mills. 2007. *Contract and Domination.* Cambridge: Polity.

Wampler, Brian. 2007. *Contestation and Cooperation: Constructing Participatory Budgeting in Brazil.* University Park: Pennsylvania State University Press, 2007.

List of Contributors

Brooke Ackerly is Associate Professor, Department of Political Science, Vanderbilt University. Her research interests include democratic theory, feminist methodologies, human rights, and social and environmental justice. She integrates into her theoretical work empirical research on activism. Her publications include *Political Theory and Feminist Social Criticism* (Cambridge: Cambridge University Press, 2000); "Women's Human Rights Activists as Cross-Cultural Theorists," *International Journal of Feminist Politics* (2001); "Is Liberal Democracy the Only Way? Confucianism and Democracy," *Political Theory* (2005); and *Universal Human Rights in a World of Difference* (Cambridge: Cambridge University Press, 2008).

Moira Gatens is Professor of Philosophy at the University of Sydney. She is author of *Feminism and Philosophy* (Bloomington: Indiana University Press, 1991); *Imaginary Bodies* (New York: Routledge, 1996); with Alison Mackinnon, *Gender and Institutions: Welfare, Work and Citizenship* (Cambridge: Cambridge University Press, 1998); and with Genevieve Lloyd, *Collective Imaginings: Spinoza, Past and Present* (New York: Routledge, 1999). Her present research centers on Spinoza, Feuerbach, and George Eliot.

Michael Goodhart is Associate Professor of Political Science and Women's Studies at the University of Pittsburgh. His research focuses on democratic theory and human rights, especially in the context of globalization. Recent publications include "Civil Society and the Problem of Global Democracy" in *Democratization* (2005), and "Origins and Universality in the Human Rights Debates: Cultural Essentialism and the Challenge of Globalization" in *Human Rights Quarterly* (2003). Goodhart's first book, *Democracy as Human Rights: Freedom and Equality in the Age of Globalization,* was published by Routledge in 2005.

Robert Goodin is Distinguished Professor of Social and Political Theory and Philosophy in the Research School of Social Sciences, Australian National University. He is founding editor of *The Journal of Political Philosophy*, general editor of the ten-volume series of *Oxford Handbooks of Political Science*, and author, most recently, of "What's Wrong with Terrorism?" *Polity* (2006). Currently he is extending comparative welfare state studies to incorporate time use, the major product of which will be a book called *Discretionary Time: A New Measure of Freedom*, to be published by Cambridge University Press.

Jane Mansbridge is the Adams Professor at the Kennedy School of Government, Harvard University. She is the author of *Beyond Adversary Democracy* (Chicago: University of Chicago Press, 1983) and *Why We Lost the ERA* (Chicago: University of Chicago Press, 1986); editor of *Beyond Self-Interest* (Chicago: University of Chicago Press, 1990); co-editor, with Susan Moller Okin, of *Feminism* (Aldershot: Edward Elgar Publishing, 1994); and co-editor, with Aldon Morris, of *Oppositional Consciousness: The Subjective Roots of Social Protest* (Chicago: University of Chicago Press, 2001). Her work combines normative democratic theory with the empirical study of how democracies work. She has never given up her commitment to a more participatory democracy.

John Medearis is Associate Professor of Political Science at the University of California, Riverside. He is author of *Joseph Schumpeter's Two Theories of Democracy* (Cambridge, Mass.: Harvard University Press, 2001). His articles have appeared in the *American Political Science Review, American Journal of Political Science, British Journal of Political Science,* and *Polity*. In his recent writings he views democratic theory from the standpoint of complex, conflict-ridden phenomena, such as social movements and the development of welfare states.

Charles W. Mills is John Evans Professor of Moral and Intellectual Philosophy at Northwestern University. He works in the general area of oppositional political theory and is the author of four books: *The Racial Contract* (Ithaca: Cornell University Press, 1997), *Blackness Visible: Essays on Philosophy and Race* (Ithaca: Cornell University Press, 1998), *From Class to Race: Essays in White Marxism and Black Radicalism* (New York: Rowman and Littlefield, 2003), and, with Carole Pateman, *Contract and Domination* (Malden, Mass.: Polity Press, 2007).

Daniel I. O'Neill is Assistant Professor of Political Science at the University of Florida. His research centers on the history of political thought, particularly as that history intersects with and illuminates a broad array of contemporary theoretical issues, ranging from the meaning of conservatism, feminism, and democracy, to the relationship between liberalism and multiculturalism. He is the author of *The Burke-Wollstonecraft Debate: Savagery, Civilization, and Democracy* (University Park: Pennsylvania State University Press, 2007). His work has also appeared in *Political Theory, History of Political Thought, Journal of the History of Ideas, Polity,* and *The Review of Politics.*

Carole Pateman is Distinguished Professor of Political Science at the University of California, Los Angeles, and currently Research Professor at the School of European Studies, Cardiff University. She is the author of *Participation and Democratic Theory* (Cambridge: Cambridge University Press, 1970); *The Problem of Political Obligation: A Critique of Liberal Theory* (2nd ed., Cambridge: Polity and Berkeley and Los Angeles: University of California Press, 1985); and *The Disorder of Women: Democracy, Feminism, and Political Theory* (Cambridge: Polity Press, and Stanford: Stanford University Press, 1989). In 2005 her third book, *The Sexual Contract* (Stanford: Stanford University Press, 1988) received the Benjamin E. Lippincott Award from the American Political Science Association for "a work of exceptional quality by a living political theorist that is still considered significant after a time span of at least 15 years since the original publication." In 2004, Professor Pateman received the Lifetime Achievement Award from the U.K. Political Studies Association. Her most recent book, co-authored with Charles Mills, is *Contract and Domination* (Cambridge: Polity, 2007).

Philip Pettit is L. S. Rockefeller University Professor of Politics and Human Values, and Affiliate Professor of Philosophy, at Princeton University. He works in moral and political theory and on background issues in philosophical psychology and social theory. His recent single-authored books include *The Common Mind* (Oxford: Oxford University Press, 1996), *Republicanism* (Oxford: Oxford University Press, 1997), *A Theory of Freedom* (Oxford: Oxford University Press, 2001), *Rules, Reasons and Norms* (Oxford: Oxford University Press, 2002), *Penser en Societe* (Paris: PUF 2004), and *Made with Words: Hobbes on Language, Mind and Politics* (Princeton University Press, 2007). He is the co-author of *Economy of Esteem* (Oxford: Oxford University Press, 2004), with Geoffrey Brennan; and *Mind, Morality and Explanation* (Oxford: Oxford University Press, 2004), a selection of papers with Frank Jackson and Michael Smith. He is currently working on a book on group agents with Christian List.

Anne Phillips is Professor of Political and Gender Theory at the London School of Economics, where she holds a joint appointment between the Gender Institute and Government Department. Most of her work deals with issues of equality and democracy, and is informed by feminist theory. Her publications include *Multiculturalism without Culture* (Princeton: Princeton University Press, 2007), *Which Equalities Matter?* (Cambridge: Polity Press, 1999), *The Politics of Presence* (Oxford: Clarendon Press, 1995), *Democracy and Difference* (University Park: Pennsylvania State University Press, 1993), and *Engendering Democracy* (University Park: Pennsylvania State University Press, 1991). She is co-editor, with John Dryzek and Bonnie Honig, of the *Oxford Handbook of Political Theory* (Oxford: Oxford University Press, 2007).

Alan Ryan is Warden of New College, Oxford, and was formerly Professor of Politics at Princeton University. He is the author of a dozen books on numerous thinkers and topics, including *John Dewey and the High Tide of American Liberalism* (New York: Norton, 1995); *Bertrand Russell: A Political Life* (New York: Allen Lane/Hill and Wang, 1988; New York: Oxford University Press, 1993); *The Philosophy of John Stuart Mill* (Basingstoke: Macmillan, 1970); *The Philosophy of the Social Sciences* (London: Macmillan, 1970); *Liberal Anxieties and Liberal Education* (New York: Hill and Wang, 1998); and *Property and Political Theory* (Oxford: Blackwell, 1984). He has written extensively in non-academic journals such as *The New York Review of Books* and *The Times Literary Supplement*.

Mary Lyndon (Molly) Shanley is Professor of Political Science on the Margaret Stiles Halleck Chair at Vassar College. She is author of *Feminism, Marriage and the Law in Victorian England* (Princeton: Princeton University Press, 1989), *Making Babies, Making Families: What Matters Most in an Age of Reproductive Technologies, Surrogacy, Adoption, and Same-Sex and Unwed Parents* (Boston: Beacon, 2001), and *Just Marriage,* ed. Deborah Chasman and Joshua Cohen (Oxford: Oxford University Press, 2004). She is editor, with Carole Pateman, of *Feminist Interpretations and Political Theory* (University Park: Pennsylvania State University Press, 1990), and with Uma Narayan, of *Reconstructing Political Theory: Feminist Essays* (University Park: Pennsylvania State University Press, 1997). Her current work is on feminist perspectives on social justice issues in family formation, and on bioethics and human reproduction.

Iris Marion Young (1949–2006) was Professor of Political Science at the University of Chicago. She authored *Justice and the Politics of Difference* (Princeton: Princeton University Press, 1990), *Intersecting Voices: Dilemmas of Gender, Political Philosophy and Policy* (Princeton: Princeton University Press,

1997), *Inclusion and Democracy* (Oxford: Oxford University Press, 2000), and *On Female Body Experience* (Oxford: Oxford University Press, 2004). With Patrice DiQuinzio she edited *Feminist Ethics and Social Policy* (Bloomington: Indiana University Press, 1997), and with Stephen Macedo, *Child, Family and State:* Nomos XLIV (New York: New York University Press, 2003). At the time of her death she was working on the question of how to conceive of responsibility for large-scale structural injustices that can't easily be traced back to the doings of any single person or group. Throughout her life, she engaged in grassroots political activity for affordable housing, workers' rights, women's human rights, and racial justice.

Index

abortion, 110
Ackerly, Brooke, 235, 240–41
ADC (Aid to Dependent Children), 216
AFDC (Aid to Families with Dependent Children), 215, 220
Affluent Worker, The (Goldthorpe), 177
After the Revolution? (Dahl), 177
Aid to Dependent Children (ADC), 216
Aid to Families with Dependent Children (AFDC), 215, 220
Alcibiades, 181
Aliens Act (Denmark), 109
Ancient Law (Maine), 31
Aristotle, 84, 168–69
Austin, John, 198–99
autonomy, 27, 44–45, 89–90, 99, 241–42

Barber's Paradox, 43
basic income, 5–6, 135, 139–41, 150–57, 241–42
Beauvoir, Simone de, 99–100
Bentham, Jeremy, 18, 19
body-contracts, 112–13
Bohman, James, 211
Boucher, David, 51, 52
Brown, Wendy, 7, 40–42

Cambridge Companion to Rawls, 65
Cambridge Companion to Rousseau, 52
Capital (Marx), 111–12
capitalism, 133, 134, 179, 212–13
Capitalism, Socialism and Democracy (Schumpeter), 181, 182
caring labor, 129–30, 135
CEDAW (The Convention for the Elimination of all forms of Discrimination against Women), 85–87

Chicago economics, 120
Cicero, Marcus Tullius, 167
Citizens' Assembly on Electoral Reform in British Columbia, 236
civil subordination, 34, 40, 112, 233
Coase, Ronald H., 128
Cole, George Douglas Howard, 2, 18, 20, 21, 168
consent
    equality and, 23–24
    illusion of, 44–45
    Patemen on, 22, 108, 237–39
    in *The Problem of Political Obligation* (Pateman), 21–22, 237
    women and, 35–37, 38, 108
contractarianism, 45, 52–60, 62, 66–68, 70–71
contracts
    employment of, 50–51
    Pateman on, 5, 7–8, 25, 40, 44, 51, 52, 77, 102
    in *The Problem of Political Obligation* (Pateman), 25
    property in the person and, 37, 45–47
    Rawls on, 56, 64–65, 70
    relationships of power and, 111
    Rousseau on, 51–52, 71
    subordination and, 25–26, 32
contracts: types of
    body-contracts, 112–13
    descriptive contracts, 60, 62–63, 67, 70
    domination contracts (*see* domination contracts)
    employment contracts, 33–34, 213, 238
    epistemological contracts, 76–79, 84, 90, 91
    liberal contracts, 23

contracts: types of (*continued*)
  mainstream contracts, 56, 60, 62–70, 71–72
  marriage contracts, 5, 35–36, 113–14, 218
  normative contracts, 60, 62, 67, 69
  racial contracts, 57, 70, 76–77, 234
  radical contracts, 68, 70
  sexual contracts (*see* sexual contracts)
  slave contracts, 5
  social contracts (*see* social contracts)
contract theory, 4, 7–8, 25, 53–54, 233–35
Convention for the Elimination of all forms of Discrimination against Women, The (CEDAW), 85–87

Dahl, Robert, 170–71, 177
Darwall, Stephen, 53
Declaration of the Rights of Man and of the Citizen (French document), 142
deliberation, 198, 208–12, 235–37
deliberative democracy, 208–12, 220, 235
deliberative norms approach (to welfare), 206, 209–12, 217, 221–24
deliberative prerequisites approach (to welfare), 206, 209–12, 217, 224–25
democracy
  Dahl on, 170–71
  definition of, 169–70
  freedom and, 141–42
  in Great Britain, 167, 232
  human rights and, 141–42, 144–50, 153–57
  in *Participation and Democratic Theory* (Pateman), 235
  Pateman on, 166, 168
  representation and, 171–74
  Rousseau on, 168, 186–88
  Schumpeter on, 18, 166, 168, 179, 180–82
  subordination and, 157
  in the United States, 167, 232
democracy: types of
  deliberative democracy, 208–12, 220, 235
  industrial democracy, 188
  liberal democracy, 21–22, 27, 142
  participatory democracy (*see* participatory democracy)
  workplace democracy, 168
Democracy and Disagreement (Guttmann & Thompson), 210
democratic theory
  participatory democracy and, 17–21, 143

  renewal of, 2
  subordination and, 207–8, 225–27
  welfare and, 208
  Young on, 92
descriptive contracts, 60, 62–63, 67, 70
Discourse on Inequality (Rousseau), 51–52
discrimination, human rights and, 84–87
Disorder of Women, The (Pateman), 3–4
domination contracts
  descriptive contracts and, 62, 67
  egalitarianism and, 60
  epistemological contracts and, 90
  equality and, 8
  historical uses of, 65–67
  mainstream contracts and, 62–65, 68–70
  majority and, 71
  Mills on, 51, 52
  sexual contracts and, 54, 90–91
  social contracts and, 54
  subordination and, 8
Donnelly, Jack, 88
Dryzek, John, 217n7
Durkheim, Émile, 234

East India Company, 169
education, 18–19
egalitarianism, 58, 60, 71
emancipation, 27, 144–47, 149, 152, 154
embodiment (women's), 3–4, 239
employment, universal, 239–40
employment contracts, 33–34, 213, 238
entitlements, 87–90, 240–41
epistemological contracts, 76–79, 84, 90, 91
equality
  consent and, 23–24
  domination contracts and, 8
  Hobbes on, 58
  nondiscrimination and, 84–87
  in *Participation and Democratic Theory* (Pateman), 23
  Pateman on, 23–24, 58, 90, 142
  in *The Problem of Political Obligation* (Pateman), 23
  Rousseau on, 68
  in *The Sexual Contract* (Pateman), 90
  women and, 58, 68, 85–87
Esping-Andersen, Gøsta, 213, 221
exploitation, 69, 102, 132–36

Fabre, Cécile, 154
factionalism, 172
feminism, 7, 39–40, 99
feminist agency, 39–40

Fishkin, James, 180
Forced Marriage Unit, United Kingdom's, 114
Fraser, Nancy, 214
freedom, 44, 101, 141–42

Gaffaney, Timothy J., 212n4
Gatens, Moira, 233
Gauthier, David, 53
Gilbert, Margaret, 199
Gilens, Martin, 216
Gladstone, William, 171
globalization, 153, 156–57
Goldthorpe, John H., 177
Gompers, Samuel, 178
Goodhart, Michael, 233
Goodin, Robert, 239
Gordon, Linda, 214
Gouges, Olympe de, 38–39
governance, 149, 153. *See also* self-governance
Great Britain (democracy in), 167, 232
Guttmann, Amy, 210–11, 223–24

Habermas, Jürgen, 208
Hampton, Jean, 53, 54–55, 59–60, 62
Hawthorne experiments, 176
Hirani v Hirani, 106
Hobbes, Thomas
  contract theory and, 234
  on equality, 58
  on participatory democracy, 186–87, 194
  on property in the person, 54n2
  social contracts and, 4, 55–56
  on women, 58
housework
  accounting of, 121–24
  caring labor and, 129–30
  division of labor and, 131–32
  exploitation and, 132–36
  internalizing, 128–29
  Pateman on, 125
  in *The Sexual Contract* (Pateman), 120–21
  unpaid, 120–21
  value of, 129
  women's preference for, 124–28
human rights
  consensus arguments about, 79–83
  democracy and, 141–42, 144–50, 153–57
  entitlement-centric arguments about, 87–90
  fundamental, 145–50, 153

nondiscrimination arguments about, 84–87
practice of, 78
social conditions of, 89–90
theory of, 78–79, 90–93
Hume, David, 170, 172

"Idea of Public Reason Revisited, The" (Rawls), 81
IGOs (international governance organizations), 153
illusion of consent, 44–45
immigration control, 109
income, basic, 5–6, 135, 139–41, 150–57, 241–42
industrial democracy, 188
international governance organizations (IGOs), 153

Johnson, James, 211

Kant, Immanuel, 27, 56, 60n3
Kaufman, Arnold
  on autonomy, 27
  death of, 18n2
  on participatory democracy, 18
  on radical liberalism, 17, 23
Kelly, Paul, 51, 52
Knight, Jack, 211
Kukathas, Chandran, 101n1, 107
Kymlicka, Will, 51, 53, 70

labor, caring, 129–30, 135
labor power, 213–14, 224
Laden, Anthony Simon, 211–12
Law of Peoples (Rawls), 81
LeFort, Claude, 148
Levellers, 142
Lever, Annabelle, 42
liberal contracts, 23
liberal democracy, 21–22, 27, 142
liberalism, 23, 40, 52, 66, 233. *See also* radical liberalism
liberal theory, 2–3
libertarianism, 27, 33, 40, 45, 154
libertarians, 5, 143
liberty, 23–24, 27–28, 145, 169n2
Lieberman, Robert C., 215
Locke, John, 4, 5, 32–33, 54n2, 142
Lukes, Steven, 79–80

MacKinnon, Catharine, 84
Macpherson, C. B., 45
Madison, James, 170, 172
Mahmood v Mahmood, 106, 107

Maine, Henry, 31
Mansbridge, Jane, 233, 235
Maritain, Jacques, 81
marriage bars, 131
marriage contracts, 5, 35–36, 113–14, 218
marriages, arranged, 9, 102–11, 113
Marx, Karl
    contractarianism and, 67–68
    emancipation and, 27
    liberalism and, 52, 66
Marx, Karl: Works
    Capital, 111–12
    On the Jewish Question, 42
Mayo, Elton, 176
Medearis, John, 236
Mill, John Stuart
    East India Company and, 169
    freedom and, 142
    participatory democracy and, 2, 18, 19, 168
Mills, Charles, 51, 52, 76, 90–91, 233–34
Morals by Agreement (Gauthier), 53
Morris, Christopher, 52, 58–59

nondiscrimination, 84–87
Nozick, Robert, 5
Nussbaum, Martha, 65, 100, 112

OECD (Organization for Economic Cooperation and Development), 121
Offe, Claus, 213
Okin, Susan Moller, 54, 61–63, 65
Old Age Insurance (Social Security), 216
Only Paradoxes to Offer (Scott), 38–39
On the Jewish Question (Marx), 42
Organization for Economic Cooperation and Development (OECD), 121
Ortega y Gasset, José, 174
ownership, self-, 45

Paine, Thomas, 142
paradoxes (rights as), 40–42, 43, 46
parental decisions and involvement (in marriage), 105
Parijs, Philippe Van, 125n9
Parsons, Talcott, 234
Participation and Democratic Theory (Pateman)
    authority structures in, 219–20
    democracy in, 235
    equality in, 23
    participatory democracy in, 2, 235
    Rousseau in, 24
    subordination in, 27, 207

participatory democracy
    aggregating preference orderings of, 190–93
    applications of, 188–89
    common goals and, 202
    decision-making processes of, 186–88, 190–93
    deliberation and, 198
    deliberative democracy and, 235
    democratic theory and, 17–21, 143
    Hobbes on, 186–87, 194
    judgments in, 190–97, 202
    Kaufman on, 18
    Mill and, 2, 18, 19, 168
    nonpolitical, 177–80
    in *Participation and Democratic Theory*, 2, 235
    Pateman on, 17–20, 23, 168, 202, 235
    popularity of, 174–77
    Rousseau and, 2, 18, 186–87
    subordination and, 207–8
    voting members of, 187
Pateman, Carole
    on autonomy, 44–45
    on basic income, 5–6, 135, 140, 152, 157, 241–42
    on caring labor, 135
    on consent, 22, 35–37, 38, 108, 237–39
    on contractarianism, 45
    on contracts, 5, 7–8, 25, 40, 44, 51, 52, 77, 102
    on contract theory, 53–54, 233–35
    on democracy, 166, 168
    on employment contracts, 238
    on equality, 23–24, 58, 90, 142
    on feminism, 7
    on freedom, 44, 101, 142
    on housework, 125
    on liberal democracy, 21–22
    on marriages, 9, 218
    model of industrial democracy and, 188
    on paradoxes, 46
    on participatory democracy, 17–20, 23, 168, 202, 235
    on patriarchy, 66, 108
    on political obligation, 21–23
    on property in the person, 33, 35, 40–41, 46, 53, 111–15, 240
    on radical liberalism, 6–8, 23, 27–28
    on rights, 5–6, 45
    on Rousseau, 22
    on Schumpeter, 235
    on self-ownership, 45
    on sexual contracts, 4–5, 25–26, 40, 54, 59–60, 62, 71, 235

on social contracts, 4, 22, 35n2, 84, 90–91
on subordination, 3, 25–26, 32, 42, 45, 101, 157, 207–8, 218, 225
Pateman, Carole: Works
The Disorder of Women, 3–4
Participation and Democratic Theory (see *Participation and Democratic Theory* (Pateman))
"The Patriarchal Welfare State," 4, 119, 208
The Problem of Political Obligation (see *Problem of Political Obligation, The* (Pateman))
The Sexual Contract (see *Sexual Contract, The* (Pateman))
"Women and Consent," 3
"Patriarchal Welfare State, The" (Pateman), 4, 119, 208
patriarchy, 66, 108
Peloponnesian War, 181–82
Pericles, 181
Persian Wars, 181
Pettit, Philip, 23, 235
Polanyi, Karl, 234
Political Liberalism (Rawls), 80–81
political obligation, 21–23
polyarchy, 170
Polybius, 167
Preface to Democratic Theory (Dahl), 170
Problem of Political Obligation, The (Pateman)
consent in, 21–22, 237
contracts in, 25
contract theory in, 234
equality in, 23
liberalism in, 233
liberal theory in, 2–3
subordination in, 27
property in the person
contracts and, 37, 45–47
Hobbes on, 54n2
Locke on, 32–33, 54n2
Pateman on, 33, 35, 40–41, 46, 53, 111–15, 240
in *The Sexual Contract* (Pateman), 46, 111–13

Quinton, Anthony, 199

racial contracts, 57, 70, 76–77, 234
radical contracts, 68, 70
radical liberalism, 17, 23, 27–28
rape, 3, 237
Rawls, John

contractarianism and, 62
on contracts, 56, 64–65, 70
on exploitation, 69
on judgment, 191
on overlapping consensus, 81
on reflective equilibrium, 196
theory of public reason, 208
Rawls, John: Works
"The Idea of Public Reason Revisited," 81
Law of Peoples, 81
Political Liberalism, 80–81
A Theory of Justice, 49, 53, 61
"Rawls and Feminism" (Nussbaum), 102
Real Freedom for All (Van Parijs), 125n9
reciprocity (in welfare), 210–11, 222–23
representation, 171–74
rights
alienable rights, 45
citizen's rights, 5–6
discrimination and, 84–87
human rights, 141–42, 144–50, 153–57
paradoxes and, 40–42, 43, 46
in *The Sexual Contract* (Pateman), 35
Roemer, John, 120, 132
Rousseau, Jean-Jacques
on contracts, 51–52, 71
on democracy, 168, 186–88
on emancipation, 27
on equality, 68
freedom and, 142
in *Participation and Democratic Theory* (Pateman), 24
participatory democracy and, 2, 18, 186–87
Pateman on, 22
sexual contracts and, 51–52, 70–71
social contracts and, 69
Rousseau, Jean-Jacques: Works
Discourse on Inequality, 51–52
Social Contract, 51–52
Ryan, Alan, 232, 236, 241

Saharso, Sawitri, 109–10
Scanlon, T. M., 53
Schumpeter, Joseph
on capitalism and the state, 213
on democracy, 18, 166, 168, 179, 180–82
Pateman on, 235
Schumpeter, Joseph: Works
Capitalism, Socialism and Democracy, 181, 182
Scott, Joan W., 7, 38, 39–40
Second Treatise (Locke), 32–33

self-governance, 205, 206, 225
self-ownership, 45
Sen, Amartya K., 23
Sexual Contract, The (Pateman)
  body-contracts in, 112–13
  contractarianism in, 54
  contract theory in, 4, 7–8, 25
  equality in, 90
  exploitation in, 135
  freedom in, 101
  housework in, 120–21
  impact of, 49
  liberalism in, 40
  liberty in, 27
  Okin on, 61
  property in the person in, 46, 111–13
  rights in, 35
  subordination in, 25, 42, 101, 207–8, 233
sexual contracts
  civil and political rights and, 35
  domination contracts and, 54, 90–91
  Okin on, 62–63
  Pateman on, 4–5, 25–26, 40, 54, 59–60, 62, 71, 235
  Rousseau and, 51–52, 70–71
  social contracts and, 35, 234
  subordination and, 57
Shapiro, Ian, 144–45
Shue, Henry, 88, 145–50
slave, wage, 34
slave contracts, 5
Smith, Rogers, 65
Social Contract (Rousseau), 51–52
social contracts
  critiques of, 90–91
  domination contracts and, 54
  epistemological contracts and, 76–79
  Hobbes and, 4, 55–56
  Pateman on, 4, 22, 35n2, 84, 90–91
  Rousseau and, 69
  sexual contracts and, 35, 234
  women and, 86
Social Security Act, 216
Social Security Disability Income (SSDI), 220
Sohrab v Khan, 106
Soss, Joe, 220
SSDI (Social Security Disability Income), 220
Stammers, Neil, 76
Stanton, Elizabeth Cady, 142
States of Injury (Brown), 40–41
Stiehm, Judith, 84

subordination
  civil subordination, 34, 40, 112, 233
  contracts and, 25–26, 32
  democracy and, 157
  democratic theory and, 207–8, 225–27
  domination contracts and, 8
  gender and, 49, 62, 214–15
  labor power and, 214
  in *Participation and Democratic Theory* (Pateman), 27, 207
  participatory democracy and, 207–8
  Pateman on, 3, 25–26, 32, 42, 45, 101, 157, 207–8, 218, 225
  in *The Problem of Political Obligation* (Pateman), 27
  racial, 49, 57, 58, 66, 214, 215–17
  in *The Sexual Contract* (Pateman), 25, 42, 101, 207–8, 233
  sexual contracts and, 57
  welfare states and, 214–17, 218–19
  of women, 57, 66
systematicity, 193–97
Szechter v Szechter, 105–6

Talbott, William J., 90
TANF (Temporary Aid to Needy Families), 206, 215, 226
Taylor, Charles, 79, 80–83, 147
Temporary Aid to Needy Families (TANF), 206, 215, 226
Theory of Justice, A (Rawls), 49, 53, 61
Thompson, Dennis, 210–11, 223–24
TNCs (transnational corporations), 153
Tocqueville, Alexis de, 183
trade union bans, 131
transnational corporations (TNCs), 153
Tully, James, 45

United Kingdom's Forced Marriage Unit, 114
United States, democracy in, 167, 232
universal employment, 239–40

wage slave, 34
Wagner Act, 178
Walzer, Michael, 21, 55–56
Weber, Max, 171, 179
welfare
  deliberative norms approach, 206, 209–12, 221–24
  deliberative prerequisites approach, 206, 209–12, 224–25
  democratic theory and, 208
  material resources approach to, 224

reciprocity in, 210–11, 222–23
reform, 219
welfare states
   capitalism and, 212–13
   democratic problems of, 217–21
   subordination and, 214–17, 218–19
we-thinking, 198–202, 235
White, Stuart, 152
white supremacy, 65, 66
Will, George, 169
Wolfe, Tom, 176
Wollstonecraft, Mary, 35, 142
Wollstonecraft's Dilemma, 4, 239
women. *See also* housework
   Beauvoir on, 99–100
   consent and, 35–37, 38, 108
   equality and, 58, 68, 85–87
   Hobbes on, 58
   Pateman on consent and, 35–37, 38, 108
   as property, 38
   social contracts and, 86
   subordination of, 57, 66
   women's embodiment, 3–4, 239
"Women and Consent" (Pateman), 3
workplace democracy, 168

Young, Iris Marion, 89, 91–92, 208n1, 211, 215

WITHDRAWN